Preface

This book is addressed to all students of industrial relations. By 'students' we mean not only those who study for the purpose of passing examinations. Though the book does have specific relevance for those in universities, polytechnics, and technical colleges or seeking membership of professional associations, we have avoided a narrowly academic approach so as to appeal to the largest possible readership.

And that is for a number of reasons. Industrial relations is a subject of such vital importance for the economic well-being of this country that a purely academic treatment would be tantamount to irresponsibility. The 'student' population we have in mind includes those managers and supervisors and trade unionists who are confronting each other every day on the shop floor and wishing they better understood the process in which they are engaged.

The book could also be read with advantage by members of the general public, who sometimes suffer more in times of acute industrial conflict than the actual participants themselves. Their irritation might be tempered if they were able to take an informed and analytical look at the events which led to the dispute in question.

It is well-nigh impossible to pick up a newspaper nowadays without finding some reference to industrial relations. More often than not the report will have to do with a situation of conflict. Some wishful thinkers foresee a future in which the conflict will disappear as both parties come to appreciate the interests they have in common. Such an appraisal seems to us naïve. It implies that conflict is by its nature harmful.

We take the view that conflict between managers and managed is an inherent part of the industrial relations scene. What does seem worth exploring is the nature of that conflict. Is it constant? Does it vary from country to country? Does it have harmful and avoidable results? What does it owe to history and to technology? What can governments do to influence it one way or the other? Is the conflict structural or behavioural?

What we can say, as a consequence of observation and study, is that the sources of conflict are complex and imperfectly understood.

vii

Conflict is frequently more bitter than it need be and the parties to it are frequently not fully aware of the issues that divide them. For example, a dispute may appear to be about the application of an incentive scheme, but deeper and more potent forces may be at work, influencing the behaviour of the participants. The real issue may be power, personal adequacy, educational deprivation, or managerial prerogative, questions which seem to have little to do with the immediate problem. Or underlying the conflict there may be fundamental differences about values or about the nature of the work contract. These issues, though they may play a significant part in the behaviour of both parties, are seldom openly discussed by them.

One of the purposes of this book is to open up such matters to analysis and debate. The early chapters describe the present complex system of collective bargaining and the way it evolved. We look at the curious part the law has played and why, in contrast to other countries, British trade unionists have always opposed the regulation of IR by statute. We trace the influence of the growth of 'white-collar' unions and the effects of increased state intervention.

Later chapters discuss the nature of management's response to the demands of organized labour, and two developments in particular. Were Productivity Agreements merely a device for overcoming government wage restrictions or were they, as we would argue, tentative steps towards a new relationship? And do proposals for worker participation hold out a better hope? Is it right to assume that workers want to exercise greater control over company decision-making? If so, at what level?

Drawing upon both our own experience in running joint management/union workshops and upon research and work in the wider field of conflict analysis, we attempt to analyse the dynamics of industrial relations conflict situations and to evaluate a number of strategies which have been used by parties in dispute to make more explicit the nature of their differences.

The final chapters examine the paradox whereby each side, management and union, deems power to reside with the other. They also deal with the role of industrial relations training.

In writing this book we have been influenced by a number of forces: firstly, by our personal experience in industry; secondly, by close contact with managers and shop stewards, particularly in the context of industrial relations training; and lastly by the writings of

Contents

those distinguished authors to whom acknowledgement is made in the text.

We would like to acknowledge here our indebtedness to two people who have particularly influenced our thinking, Professor R. W. Revans and Jock Haston, formerly Education Officer for the E.E.T.U./P.T.U. and now for the General and Municipal Workers' Union.

We are also grateful to our colleague Richard Mapstone for his valuable suggestions, particularly on state intervention.

Lastly, we would like to thank our wives who have endured our silence with admirable patience.

BMC
AFB

PART I

1

The Burden of the Past

Industrial relations in Britain to this day reflects the haphazard manner in which the system came into being. Things could so easily have been different. We could have had, for example, industrial unionism on a widespread scale, a stronger Trades Union Congress and Confederation of British Industry, and a rational collective bargaining system. Instead the contrary is, by and large, the rule. Trade unions are usually organized on an occupational basis. The T.U.C. and C.B.I. have no direct authority over their members. And the collective bargaining system is fraught with conflicting circumstances. This situation owes more to history and expedience than to logic and planning. Such piece-meal, *ad hoc* developments as this country has witnessed, have given rise to certain expectations and aspirations on the part of those affected, leading to patterns of behaviour and attitudes which cannot simply be swept out of existence.

THE TRADE UNION MOVEMENT

Workmen's organizations existed before the Industrial Revolution but the vast majority of them were of a temporary nature. Most businesses were small and employed small work forces. Often businesses would collapse overnight and with them such workmen's combinations as they embodied. Wages were low and workers had little surplus money to keep a combination in being. Near the end of the seventeenth century there began to operate certain combinations of workmen for purposes of mutual insurance against sickness, old age and death. They became known as Friendly Societies and spread rapidly during the eighteenth century. They held regular meetings, usually in public houses, at which dues were collected in a box. The members present checked and accounted for the contents – such gatherings therefore became known as 'Box Meetings'. These organizations received legal protection under the Friendly Societies Act, 1793.

Tradesmen gathered sometimes for more radical purposes in Trade Clubs. These would agree to:

> . . . use their collective power to decide who should and who should not be allowed to work at their trade, how many apprentices and how many journeymen a master should employ, and went as far as paying their members not to work for masters who would not agree to these conditions.[1]

Many small organizations did not survive the Combination Acts; those which did were to be found largely amongst the craftsmen. They managed to keep their organizations intact for several reasons. A craftsman, with earnings normally half as large again as a labourer's, could afford union dues more easily. He had the necessary learning to keep books, hold meetings, write minutes and so forth:

> Whether for mutual benefit or trade unionism, he was bound to his brothers of the craft by the strong sense of kinship that arises not from any calculation of advantage but from the spontaneous identification of oneself with those who have been through the same school and are practising the same art.[2]

Many public houses to this day indicate by their names that they were used as meeting places for trade clubs – The Bricklayers' Arms, The Carpenters' Rest, and so on.

A craftsman had another distinct advantage over his less fortunate labouring brethren – he had a definite and identifiable job which was easy to protect. He might move from place to place and employer to employer but always in the same craft. Having been through the same 'school', with all its attendant hardships and doing the same type of work as his brother craftsman, he tended to side with him rather than a man from another trade. In addition he had to ensure that 'illegal men' were not permitted to work with him, nor apprenticeships ratios increased, in order to restrict entry to the trade and thus maintain the scarcity (and price) of his labour.

Trade Clubs grew rapidly and on a local basis. The determinants of this growth must be kept in perspective – they took place under a cloak of criminality and at a time when communications were poor.

In the absence of these determinants it might have been possible for trade unions to be organized nationally and on an industrial basis:

> The direction of this development is so familiar that it may seem inevitable, but it is not the only one that unionism has followed, and even in Britain the unions might have taken another path if they had come later – have grouped by industry, for example, rather than by occupation, or have been organized from the centre instead of having the springs of their energies in their branches.[3]

GENERAL UNIONS

As workers in Britain had nowhere else to look to for lessons in union organization and discipline they were left to their own devices to a very large extent. There were some who tried to point the way forward but their message rarely had appeal for the masses of workmen or, where there was such appeal, it was only of a temporary nature. The attempt of an Irishman called John Doherty to establish a 'general union' clearly illustrates this point. Having worked among cotton spinners in the Manchester area (with little organizing success) he summoned a conference at the Isle of Man in December, 1829. The result was the establishment of a 'Grand General Union of the Operative Spinners of Great Britain and Ireland'. Given this impetus Doherty sought to establish a general union known as the 'National Association for the Protection of Labour' (N.A.P.L.). This became an organization of local unions based on trade clubs which were affiliated to a Council which met once a month in Manchester. Regular contributions were made to a central fund for use in strikes against wage cuts.[4] Its influence spread widely in 1830, but a trial of strength at the end of that year imposed severe strains. This was a strike of the Lancashire spinners against wages cuts; they attempted to spread the strike by calling out other workers throughout the land who received wages below a certain level.

The reaction was instructive. The Scottish and Irish spinners did not come out, and in England there was but a partial response. The strike was broken by March, 1831, and the Grand General Union of Operative Spinners had disbanded. The N.A.P.L. never recovered from this blow and it 'seems to have disappeared in 1832'.[5] There might have been a different result had this attempt been made later in the century. National communications were still largely undeveloped in 1832. The railway system was just getting under way; the Stockton and Darlington line was opened in 1825 and the Liverpool and Manchester line in 1830. Rowland Hill's penny postage was not to be until 1840. It was not until 1837 that Wheatstone made the earliest practical telegraph for use in this country and the system only came into popular use in 1851, when the first electric cable was laid from Dover to Calais. With poor communications and a working population, the vast majority of whom were illiterate, failure was virtually certain. In addition, the unions which sought to form such general organizations had not been in existence long enough to develop the administrative and disciplinary skills which effective organizations of this kind required.

These lessons were brought home in 1834 when Robert Owen formed the 'Grand National Consolidated Trades Union'. Owen felt that the competitive striving for wealth among manufacturers led them to ignore the human needs of their workers. He hoped to eliminate such evils by basing production upon 'National Companies' as opposed to private ownership. In his opinion workmen of all kinds – not just craftsmen – had more interests in common than they had differences. The Grand National was to be a general union with the long-term aims of co-ordinating working class actions such as strikes, providing financial support for workers in dispute, rationalizing the structures of combinations and laying the basis of co-operative production among the unemployed. In the London building trades the employers counter-attacked by insisting that their workmen sign 'the document' – an undertaking not to join a union.[6] 1834 was also the year in which the trial of the Tolpuddle Martyrs took place. These and other attacks underlined the weaknesses of the Grand National and it fell rapidly into decline. It was unable to provide financial support for strikers, to halt sectional struggles and to maintain a stable membership: 'The Webbs claimed that it recruited half a million workers within a few weeks but subsequent research has revealed a *paying* membership of little more than 16,000'.[7]

The failure of general unionism in this period meant that the motive force of trade union growth came from the Trade Clubs. Their members shared not only the same craft but also the same benefits. The main benefit was known as a 'tramping grant'. This was paid to members who were unemployed and sought to gain a job in another town or region. The member would obtain a card from his branch secretary which indicated the amount of benefit he was entitled to draw. He would furnish this card at each local club he visited, whereupon he would receive money to obtain food and board while he searched for work. Sometimes other benefits were available such as sickness pay and superannuation. This system of benefits ensured a corresponding system of rules and discipline. A member who abused the benefits, for example, would have them withdrawn, and could in some circumstances be expelled from the Club.

THE NEW MODEL UNIONS

As Trade Clubs had so much in common it was natural for them to seek amalgamation with one another. At first these amalgamations were of a local or regional nature but they gradually grew in importance and extent in the years following the collapse of the general unions, culminating in the 'New Model' unions of the 1850s. This term was meant to imply that they established a pattern to which other emergent unions should conform. One such union was the Amalgamated Society of Engineers – the forerunner of the modern A.U.E.W. – which was formed in 1851. This was the result of the desire of a number of different unions, comprising skilled workers in the metal trades, for amalgamation in order to meet the challenges of the factory system. In 1815, the cotton industry was the only area in which the factory system was firmly established, but by the 1850s it had become much more widespread. The New Model unions were not the only form of trade union organization at this time:

> Trade unionism everywhere underwent great changes corresponding to the new economic and social conditions; but the new Unions assumed many different forms, and followed to a large extent different policies . . . the new 'Amalgamated Societies' were by far the most characteristic Trade Union products of the Victorian age; but the new organizations of the miners and cotton operatives are of no less interest, and represent, in some degree, a different attitude and policy based on their different economic circumstances.[8]

The main feature of the Amalgamated Societies, however, was the hitherto unprecedented professionalism which was brought to bear upon the task of union organization. A businesslike and centralized control of funds, a centralized national administration, a uniform system of rules under which branch secretaries were to pay benefits, and control by the executive over strikes and strike pay were the distinguishing characteristics of the New Model unions. The reduction of local or branch autonomy was more apparent than real as there was no attempt to control local custom and practice – such matters were left to the branches. They provided a wide range of benefits including strike pay, superannuation, sickness payments and unemployment benefit. It can be readily appreciated that, for example, the Amalgamated Society of Engineers could not have survived had they repeated two basic mistakes of the earlier general unions, viz. an unstable membership and infrequent financial contributions. In fact they had a 'permanent paying membership of 11,000 and a regular income of £500 a week – a financial stability without precedent'.[9] Subscriptions were high – to such an extent as to exclude all but skilled artisans – but the benefits and services were considerable.

The largest Amalgamated Societies had as their leaders such influential and respected men as William Allen (Engineers), Edwin Coulson (London Brickmakers), Robert Applegarth (Carpenters), Daniel Guile (Ironfounders) and George Odger (Secretary of the London Trades Council). The Webbs, in their history of the trade unions, referred to them as the 'Junta'.

They were instrumental, among other things, in presenting a new perspective to the role of trade unions in society, in their evidence to the Royal Commission of 1867 on Trade Unions. Employers had expressed alarm at a series of disturbances in the cutlery trades in Sheffield – termed the 'Sheffield Outrages'. These were a series of acts of violence directed chiefly against blacklegs and non-unionists. The employers wanted an enquiry into the outrages but the unions sought, and obtained, an enquiry into the entire subject of trade unionism. The Junta, wishing to dissociate themselves from the Sheffield outrages, set up the Conference of Amalgamated Trades with the purpose of conducting the trade unions' case. The disturbances at Sheffield involved only a small number of unions but in 1867 the Court of Queen's Bench gave a decision which threatened the very basis of the Amalgamated Societies themselves – their Friendly Society benefits. These benefits gave the movement a cohesion that it had lacked in earlier years but the Court held – in the case of *Hornby* v. *Close*[10] – that a trade union official who had embezzled union funds could not be prosecuted, and that a trade union did not come under the Friendly Societies Acts. In addition, unions were illegal at common law as their objects were in 'restraint of trade'. Thus Courts could not give protection to union funds – a protection which the unions had taken for granted for many years.

The Conference wanted to be certain that their side of the case was fully examined, as public opinion had swung away from the unions because of the incidents at Sheffield. To this end they sought to have at least two trade unionists on the Royal Commission, but their demand was refused. They were, however, allowed to nominate one member. The Christian Socialist Hughues was placed and so was another ally of the Amalgamated Societies, Frederick Harrison. The unions were permitted to have representatives present during the examination of witnesses; the Conference appointed Applegarth.[11] He and his colleagues did a remarkable job of public relations. They took every opportunity to emphasize the peaceful and constructive aspects of trade unionsim; they presented and consolidated a new 'respectable' image of union activity:

> That Applegarth, Harrison and Hughues conducted their case with extraordinary skill is evident. . . . From a wholesale attack on Trade Unions, the Royal Commission began to turn into a justification of them, where they were really as respectable as Applegarth and his friends made out.[12]

The Majority Report recommended measures to legalize trade unions and to permit them to register as Friendly Societies – but with certain qualifications. The Minority Report, on the other hand, recommended the removal of legal restraints aimed specifically at trade unions and workmen.

The craftsmens' organizations had arrived. They were strong and cohesive bodies with secure finances. There were also significant political pressures which worked to their advantage. The Reform Act of 1867 gave the vote to skilled artisans in the towns. These new members of the electorate gave their weight largely to members of the Liberal party who were sympathetic to their aims. The result was that the Liberals adopted the Report of the 1867 Royal Commission in passing the Trade Union Act, 1871. Political pressure, while important, did not solve all union problems – the same government passed the anti-union Criminal Law Amendment Act, 1871. Some measure of balance was restored by the Conspiracy and Protection

9

of Property Act, 1875, but the point was brought home that there was no such thing as a trade union government but that governments were susceptible to political, as well as industrial, pressures.

The craftsmen were grouped by *occupation*, not by industry. They were able to survive periods of trade depression and sometimes defeat at the hands of employers, because they had a large degree of control over entrants to their occupations. As noted earlier, they secured this by restriction of apprentices, the restriction of 'illegal men' and a readily identifiable job – one which they could call their own to the extent that they had a virtual 'property' right. Industrial unionism did not fare so well. One clear example is that of the coal-miners. Having little effective control over entrants to the industry, they found their attempts at forming strong organizations often smashed either by the attacks of the owners or the pressures of trade slumps. When trade was strong, so were the miners' unions, but when it was weak and there was little demand for coal, their unions, particularly in the 1840s, were almost swept out of existence: 'No industry had registered more clearly than coal-mining the ebb and flow of the tides of trade unionism, or the difficulty with which the union was becoming part of the recognized industrial organization of the country.'[13]

Miners built their organizations initially on a local or regional basis. Poor communications, to some extent, contributed to this tendency but even when they improved in the 1850s the miners still had not built effective national organizations. Even the Miners' Federation of Great Britain in 1889 might have been divided easily had it not happened at a time of economic upsurge: 'It was fortunate for the Federation that it came into being during an economic recovery, and that none of the owners' associations chose to test the miners' solidarity before the new organization had been able to build up its strength.'[14] Another and very important factor, besides the owners' ferocity, gave the miners the distinct nature of their attitude not only to employers but the outside world as well – their marked sense of community. This saw them through the worst times of dispute and trade depression, making them the industrial union they are today:

> All over the world these communities are marked by special characteristics. . . . Usually . . . they were also isolated geographically, and many mining towns and villages were worlds of their own.

10

Consequently, they developed unusually powerful loyalties and strong social sanctions against those who flouted them . . . once the union had established itself in the community, it could rely on the community to maintain its membership.[15]

THE NEW UNIONISM

The last quarter of the nineteenth century witnessed the rise of the general unions. Their members had no skills or jobs capable of being defended in the manner that the craftsmen had employed, nor had they the strong communal solidarity of the miners. Thus they were sensitive to both trade booms and recessions, and their membership fluctuated rapidly – expanding in times of economic upsurge and contracting in time of depression. Towards the end of the 1880s, however, there came an upsurge of trade union activity which became known as the 'New Unionism'. Some of the unions formed were not new but simply old wine in new bottles. They were perhaps considered new in that they represented an aggressive and militant outlook, as opposed to the 'respectability' of the Amalgamated Societies. The movement was new, however, in that it took trade unionism and applied it to previously untouched areas of the working class.

The successful strike of Mrs Besant's match-girls in London in 1888 against their squalid and onerous conditions heralded the wave of agitation which started in 1889. This was the year of the London Dock Strike, regarded by many as a turning point in labour history. It had a great deal of public support, but even so the strike might have failed (strike money was getting low) but for the intervention of dock workers in Australia who donated £300,000 to the struggle. Thus the strikers were victorious in gaining the 'dockers' tanner'. This victory, together with the success of Tom Mann, Ben Tillet and John Burns in establishing the Gasworkers' and General Labourers' Union in 1889 (which quickly won concessions from the London gas employers), ensured the spread of unionism among the general workers in the population. Lacking enough funds to sustain Friendly Society benefits, these unions relied on the strike weapon in order to gain quick successes.

New Unionism was aided by both the development of trade union political representation and the spread of socialist thinking. The Radical element in the Liberal party had learnt the value of the working-class vote but, as noted earlier, they were limited in their

11

ability to pursue trade union political objects. Nonetheless, they provided an important dimension to working-class endeavour, until eventually an alliance of a number of trade unions and socialist bodies produced the Labour Representation Committee in 1900, which became the Labour Party in 1906. Support from this group and the Liberals brought the reversal of the Taff Vale decision in the shape of the 1906 Trade Disputes Act. Even the political arm of the unions was not immune from attack by the courts as evidenced by the Osborne case in 1909. In that case[16] the Law Lords held that the Trade Union Acts of 1871 and 1876 were framed in terms which precluded the expenditure of trade union funds for political objects, and that it was therefore beyond the powers of unions to impose a levy upon its membership for the pursuit of such objects. This decision might ultimately have meant the end of the new Labour Party, as it relied heavily upon financial support from the unions. Political and industrial agitation, however, brought about the Trade Union Act, 1913, by which the definition of a trade union was amended to enable a union to include political aims among the objects it might lawfully pursue.

There were – and still are – various brands of thinking termed 'socialist'. Marx and Engels considered socialism to be the first stage of communism in which the working-class, led by a revolutionary party, would take over the means of production, distribution and exchange and build the foundation for the new communist society under which classes would be abolished. Other forms of socialist thought did not encompass the revolutionary view, but insisted rather on measures to re-distribute the wealth of the nation in a just and equitable manner; these may be loosely termed 'social-democratic'. Differing emphasis was placed upon the role of trade unions in achieving the desired social order. The Marxists did not preclude the struggle for better wages, conditions and hours from their view of the struggle for socialism. The Social Democratic Federation, on the other hand, which was founded by H. M. Hyndman in the 1880s, felt that trade union endeavour, by way of strikes and other forms of industrial action, was counter-productive as it detracted from what they considered the correct role of the unions, viz. the acquisition of political power: 'It was Hyndman's view that as allies of Liberalism the unions had consistently "acted as bulwarks of capitalism".'[17] John Burns and Tom Mann had been early members of the S.D.F. but left it because of the prevalence of this attitude. However, these men and others who were influenced by socialist thinking were key figures in the building of the New Unionism. Socialist theory had contributed to some extent because, whatever the brand favoured, they had some common aims: 'Although their political views differed considerably, they were agreed on two things: that the *whole* of the working-class should be organized; and that it should as an *independant* factor play a decisive part in industry and politics.'[18]

INDUSTRIAL TRUCE

From the end of the 1880s until the outbreak of the First World War trade unionism progressed steadily onwards into new areas, e.g. women workers, teachers and office (white-collar) workers. The majority of unions agreed to an 'industrial truce' with the employers to facilitate the conduct of the war. However, as trade union officials and managers were to discover the hard way, the truce was not always effective at shop-floor level. For example, union officials could agree in general terms that because of the manpower shortage, created by conscription, it was necessary to admit men with brief periods of training to do skilled men's work – these were known as 'dilutees'. Unfortunately it was the men on the shop-floor who had to work with them, and quite often dilutees would not submit to union discipline in matters such as output restrictions – to give but one example. In addition, officials could not be expected to envisage all the situations on each shop-floor in different engineering or munitions factories up and down the country. Even if they had been able to they had nonetheless specifically abdicated such responsibility (in the interests of the war effort) by virtue of the Treasury Agreement and the Munitions Act of 1915. Thus the unions' leadership had committed themselves to abide by the following: no strike or lock-out unless twenty-one days notice was given, compulsory arbitration, controls on the movement of labour, the introduction of dilutees and the suspension of restrictive practices[19] for the duration of the war.

This situation left open the field of shop-floor representation to shop stewards. Their numbers grew apace with the high incidence of plant and local grievances. They did not feel committed to an industrial truce and often pursued their objectives against union policy and advice. In many cases this led to a split between shop stewards and full-time officials and even after the war, when some of the differences had been apparently resolved, there still remained a certain amount of distrust between the rank-and-file member and his official. Stewards readily took to the political doctrine known as syndicalism, which had as its main objective the transfer of the means of production, distribution and exchange from owners to unions of workers. Some union leaders were adherents of this doctrine and, along with other forms of socialist thinking, it had a marked effect on the unions' attitude to political struggle. Previously the main political strategy for unions had been to back certain parliamentary candidates with a view to gaining specific reforms considered advantageous to trade unionism, e.g. the Trade Disputes Act, 1906.

Syndicalism went much further. Why be content with mere reforms; why not expend the unions' efforts on changing the entire system? The socialism of Marx and Engels envisaged the revolution being secured by the working-class; syndicalism considered that only the organized (unionized) elements of the working-class could develop the consciousness required to seize power. One of the factors which gave this theory its popularity had been the rapid growth of trade unionism – and general unionism in particular – in the periods before, during and after the First World War. Owing to manpower shortages during the war, it became easier to organize the dilutees in general unions. In 1914 the 'Triple Alliance' between the National Union of Railwaymen, the Miners' Federation, and the Transport Workers' Federation was established, its purpose being to co-ordinate industrial sanctions such as strikes and to encourage further amalgamations in the movement. The 1920s also witnessed the establishment of powerful new unions such as the Transport and General Workers' Union and the National Union of General and Municipal Workers.

This new-found strength made many trade unionists feel that such a powerful force should play a decisive political role. In practice, however, attractive political theories such as syndicalism or workers' control played only a small part in day-to-day industrial relations; shop stewards and some union leaders could have interesting discussions on such topics, but they were never effective as guides to action in matters of industrial conflict. What they did though was to inject a militancy into industrial relations, giving the processing of grievances and disputes a wider (and thus more interesting) political perspective – a 'cause'. These political aspirations were more apparent than real, and any illusions to the contrary were rudely shattered by the defeat of the miners and the T.U.C. in the 1926 General Strike. The massed might of the unions had been set in motion but had failed to change the situation. Thereafter unions set about renewing and protecting once more their individual organizations. Political interests they often still had in common but this did not lead to any major action. Each organization guarded its own autonomy – each had been established in response to particular situations. Also, different unions were affected in different ways by the depression between the two world wars:

> Whether their growth was on the craft, the industrial, the general or some other principle, they scarcely ever stopped to consider. The defence and improvement of the wages and working conditions of their members was their law of development; beside it theoretical structural arguments were largely irrelevant.[20]

The Second World War witnessed another period of growth in the power of the shop-floor and the shop stewards. The previous shop stewards' movement, developed after the first war, had collapsed during the 1920s. During the period 1939–45, however, there occurred a significant resurgence of shop-floor activity. Stewards were consulted by management to a larger extent by way of works committees, joint production committees and so forth. Management became accustomed to dealing with the stewards – a habit which persisted after 1945. While the war was in progress, strikes and lock-outs were prohibited and resort to arbitration was compulsory. There was also an element of protection for shop stewards in the exercise of their duties. The Essential Work Order of 1941 stipulated that certain workers could not leave their jobs without the consent of the Ministry of Labour. Conversely, this meant that employers could not simply dismiss workers at will, a situation which 'gave stewards some protection in their efforts to gain recognition'.[21]

The fact that the country was at war engendered a spirit of self-sacrifice which in collective bargaining terms meant that workers generally did not press for what might, in peacetime, have been considered just claims. This attitude obtained for a brief period after the war because of the post-war electoral triumph of Labour, a period which ushered in the foundations of our modern welfare state. Thus the support of the unions was gained for the pay freeze of 1948–50. Another significant aspect of the immediate post-war period was the emergence of the state as a major employer through Labour's nationalization measures. This sometimes meant that the government could not maintain the position of a concerned spectator while industrial disputes were in progress because major disputes often occurred in the nationalized industries. The late 1960s and recent years have witnessed a major escalation of strikes and other forms of industrial action in the railways, steel and coal-mining. This increased state involvement has its direct corollary in the increased political power of the T.U.C.

THE TRADES UNION CONGRESS

In 1868 the Manchester and Salford Trades Council summoned thirty-four delegates from interested trade societies and associations to a congress in Manchester. This was the beginning of the T.U.C. Its early ambitions were relatively modest. Trade unionists had painfully built up their respective organizations over different periods of time to meet specific circumstances. They were unwilling to attempt the construction of yet another central body with wide powers because of the manifest ineffectiveness of such ventures in earlier times. The 1868 Congress was content to build a political pressure group with a related propaganda function which was 'to redress "the profound ignorance which prevails in the public mind" regarding trade union activity'.[22] Since then the T.U.C. has held its Congress every year, except in 1870 and 1919. Its traditional role has been that of furthering and progressing legislation and seeking to influence government in matters relating to the interest of trade unionists.

Its membership has fluctuated widely since its inception. Failure to maintain the struggles in the 1926 General Strike – and in the depression years – took its toll in terms of membership. It did not meet with the unqualified approval of all trade unionists then and to some extent this is true today. Its embryonic years witnessed struggles between right-wing, left-wing and moderates for power and even today such political tendencies can still be observed in its General Council. The layman might be forgiven for thinking that the T.U.C. has authority over its member unions analogous to that of Parliament over the country. Every year the week-long session of Annual Congress is covered by the mass media in the same manner as it would be in the case of a major political party. Calls are often made to the T.U.C. to bring its membership in line with declared policy. Political sloganeers sometimes compound the mistake by asking such questions as who is to rule the country – Parliament or the T.U.C.? This gives currency to the belief that the United Kingdom has 'two Parliaments'.

However, the analogy breaks down when the actual role and powers of the T.U.C. are examined. It does not possess direct authority over its constituents. Unions become affiliated to Congress on a voluntary basis and on their own initiative – their membership is not sought by canvassing or advertizing. Having obtained affiliation each union is under only a moral obligation to heed the decision of Congress. The authority of the T.U.C. over affiliates is therefore persuasive in nature although – as unions have joined of their own free will – the moral pressure to comply is strong. There are limits, however, to the extent to which an affiliate can digress from Congress policy. Should a digression be of a very serious nature the General Council may suspend a union from membership until the case is heard by Annual Congress; whereupon the errant union may be expelled. This was the fate suffered by the National Union of Seamen, for example, because they registered under the Industrial Relations Act, 1971, in order to obtain an approved closed shop in their industry – registration being contrary to T.U.C. policy.

Two major tasks, among others, are undertaken at Annual Congress. Policy for the coming year is determined and the General Council is elected to carry out policy between Congresses. Unions may send delegates on the basis of one for every 5000 members or 'fractional part thereof'. Each union may submit two motions for the agenda – the General Council may submit three. Because of the pressure of time (Congress lasts five days) many of these motions are consolidated into Composite Motions on the Saturday before Congress. They must be approved by the General Purposes Committee before submission on the Agenda. Over the five days the delegates discuss and take decisions on these motions. They also discuss the work done by the General Council – as shown on its report – for the previous year.

Decisions are normally taken either by voice or a show of hands. Sometimes a card vote is called for by delegates. Each delegation is issued with a card giving it one vote for every 1000 members or 'fractional part thereof'. Although this means that large unions may dominate discussion, it must be borne in mind that the phrase

17

'fractional part thereof' also permits, for example, the 260 members of the Sheffield Sawmakers' Protection Society to have one vote as if it had 1000 members. Again the same tiny union may send a delegate to Congress even though it has not got 5000 members but merely a 'fractional part thereof'. It would be virtually impossible for many large unions to send delegations of the size to which they are entitled as the Annual Congress would have to provide for almost twice the actual number of delegates. This makes the card vote necessary: 'The real importance of this procedure is that it allows the large bodies full representation without the trouble and expense of sending delegations up to the full strength allowed by Congress rules.'[23]

Unions are divided into eighteen trade groups and another group of 'unions organizing women workers' for the purpose of nominating members for the General Council – which consists of thirty-seven members. Each group may nominate for a number of seats depending upon its size; for example Railways have two seats, Agriculture, one, General Workers, three and Women Workers, one. Each nomination must be submitted to Congress for election. Those elected have to undertake a dual role. They must represent not only the movement but also their own union. Sometimes this leads to a conflict of loyalties. It is not uncommon to find General Council members advising affiliated unions to do one thing and, when speaking in their capacity as leaders of individual unions, doing quite the opposite.

A great deal of the day-to-day work of the T.U.C. is done through committees. Central policy is implemented through a series of Regional Councils and Committees. Scotland and Wales have their own T.U.C.s. The Committees are made up of local full-time officials and their meetings are normally chaired by a member of the General Council. Members of the General Council also represent the T.U.C. on a number of bodies concerned with national and international matters. In this way, the voice of the trade union movement is heard at many levels and on a wide variety of subjects.

Contrary to another popular fallacy, the T.U.C. has no authority to call strikes and it cannot order the lifting of strike action once this has been undertaken. What it can, and often does, attempt is to use its considerable influence to bring about settlements. Affiliated unions are required to notify the General Council of any differences arising between them and employers, or between one union and another, where large numbers of workers are likely to be directly or indirectly involved. Until 1955 the Council could not intervene in a dispute until negotiations had actually broken down, but at the Southport Congress of that year the Council sought, and obtained, a new power. This was that, although there would normally be no intervention until negotiating machinery had been exhausted (unless requested by the parties), the General Council could intervene where negotiations appeared on the point of breakdown and the wages and employment of a large number of workers would be directly or indirectly affected. Intervention involves calling representatives of the unions involved before the General Council for consultation and advice; but the union or unions involved are free to ignore or reject such advice if they wish. The caution with which unions treat any apparent encroachment on their autonomy was illustrated by the amount of opposition to this extension of T.U.C. power at Southport.

Another important aspect of the T.U.C.'s function lies in the field of inter-union disputes. These may take several forms but the most important from the General Council's point of view are 'poaching' disputes and differences over the transfer of members between unions. Poaching occurs where one union seeks to organize in an area in which another union has a majority of workers in its membership and has customarily negotiated wages and conditions with the employer concerned. These jurisdictional disputes have been on the increase in recent years and the expansion of white-collar unionism would seem likely to create even more. Disputes also arise where workers are transferred from one union to another without enquiry into their relationship with their former union. The transferred member may have been behind with subscriptions, or involved in a trade dispute; he may even have been under discipline. In order to help resolve such matters the Annual Congress at Bridlington in 1939 constructed a set of rules known as the Bridlington Agreement.

In regard to poaching, the rules state that a union should not undertake organizational activity at any establishment where another union has in its membership a majority of the workers employed and negotiates wages and conditions for such workers – unless by arrangement with that union. To this end, unions are requested to draw up working arrangements among themselves to deal with matters which include spheres of influence, conditions under which members may be transferred and machinery for reconciling other differences. Where a transfer of members is concerned, each union which receives an application for membership should ascertain whether the prospective entrant is or was a member of another affiliated union. Where prior membership is established the union should send a form of inquiry to the previous union. If the reply indicates that the applicant is in arrears, under penalty or discipline, or the previous union is engaged in a trade dispute, the application should be rejected.

Where there is an alleged breach of the Agreement, and the parties cannot resolve the issue through their own machinery, the General Council may, under Rule 12 of the T.U.C. constitution, refer the matter to its Disputes Committee. In order to discourage frivolous or unwarranted claims, Rule 12 states that where a complainant union fails to make its case it will have to bear the full cost of investigation, which may include the expenses of the defendant union. An additional power is given to the General Council under Rule 13 to investigate the conduct of any affiliated union thought to be acting in a manner 'detrimental to the interests of the Trade Union Movement or contrary to the declared principles and policy of the Congress'. The union so charged must send representatives to appear before the General Council; if it fails to do so the case will be investigated in their absence. If the union is found to be acting in the manner charged, the General Council will direct it to discontinue such activity and require an undertaking not to repeat the offence. Non-compliance with this direction or failure to give such an undertaking will result in suspension until Annual Congress where the ultimate result could be expulsion from the T.U.C.

The T.U.C. has a range of international political involvements, its main one being support for the non-communist International Confederation of Free Trade Unions in its efforts to build trade unionism in developing countries. Its international commitments will no doubt grow as a consequence of the employers' international creations, the multi-national corporations. The T.U.C. is best known, however, for its political activity at home. Without its support for, or acquiescence in, incomes policy, government attempts to regulate prices and incomes in order to beat inflation are doomed to failure. The Conservative Government which resigned in January, 1974, discovered this to its cost. The 'social contract' of 1974, concluded with the minority Labour Government, is a clear example of the political impact of the T.U.C. It also threw its weight successfully behind the £6 a week anti-inflation legislation introduced by the Labour Government in 1975. With the shift in emphasis from industry-level negotiations to plant bargaining in post-war years, the T.U.C.'s influence on the realities of collective bargaining is decreasing, while its political influence is growing stronger with each passing year. Speaking of both the T.U.C. and C.B.I., Professor Clegg observes:

> Since their constituents allow them only a peripheral part in the process of collective bargaining, their importance lies mainly in their dealing with the government. . . . The severe limitation of their powers is in large measure due to the date of their creation. Each was established at a time when many of its constituents were already developed and mature. They wished to guard against any encroachment on their own autonomy and they had the strength to do so.[24]

Trade union structure and organization was one of the areas examined between 1965 and 1968 by the Royal Commission on Trades Unions and Employers' Associations under the chairmanship of Lord Donovan. The Commission was established to examine the system of industrial relations and the possible reform and extension of collective bargaining. Its report is examined in Chapter 5. The Commission summarized the bewildering position which existed by the late 1960s. There were 574 unions, of which only 170 were affiliated to the T.U.C., but this latter group had a membership of 9 million employees. The T.U.C.'s position was put in perspective by the size of the unionized work force in 1966 – 10,111,000. One-half of all trade unionists were in the nine largest unions and four-fifths were in the thirty-eight largest. On the other hand, of the total of 574 unions there were 245 with fewer than 5000 members.[25] All of this in a total work force of 23¾ million employees! The part played by the structure of industry itself must be kept in mind. The companies normally in the news are large ones with big work forces and therefore one important fact is continually overlooked by casual observers – the number of small companies with tiny work forces. The Donovan Commission reported that there were some 200,000 different establishments in manufacturing alone, three-quarters of which had only ten or less employees.[26]

Certain groups of unions have joined forces to act together for purposes of joint negotiation. The biggest of these is the Confederation of Shipbuilding and Engineering Unions, which consists of some thirty-five separate organizations in the engineering and allied industries. Sometimes Confederation objectives run counter to T.U.C.

21

policy – a position made all the more complex because often Confederation officials are also members of the General Council. For example, the T.U.C. in its 'social contract' with the Labour Government of 1974 decided to advise unions to moderate wage claims, yet Hugh Scanlon, President of the A.U.E.W., concurrently tabled a wage claim with the Engineering Employers' Federation which could be termed anything but moderate. In the course of the same negotiation, tensions have appeared between Confederation members themselves. Jack Jones, General Secretary of the Transport and General Workers, stated that he was willing to rely on plant negotiations for his members rather than national bargaining: 'This would be the kiss of death to the . . . Confederation. . . . The T.G.W.U. would happily replace the "Confed" with a T.U.C. engineering committee which could provide much better facilities and also negotiate on non-wage matters. For the A.U.E.W. this is heresy.'[27]

MULTI-UNIONISM

The development and growth of British trade unionism on a largely occupational basis has given rise to the phenomenon of multi-unionism. In a typical plant or establishment, different unions organize among different sections of the work force. Different unions often exist in the same department and among the same grade of workers. This leads to a confusing situation for both plant managers and full-time union officials. Annual negotiations must be conducted not with one union but with several; or different unions may negotiate at different times of the year. Resolving grievances or disputes with one union may be inhibited as management must have regard to the consequences for workers in the other unions in the plant. A wage claim pursued and won by one group of workers often leads to claims being pressed by other groups on the basis of relativity. This makes control by management over payment or remuneration systems very difficult and, in some cases, impossible.

Multi-unionism can also lead to inter-union rivalry, where different unions are trying to establish or extend membership in the same plant or among the same sections of the work force. The Bridlington Agreement goes some way to alleviating this problem, but in many cases rivalry never reaches open conflict and thus it is not brought to the attention of the Disputes Committee of the T.U.C. It may then become manifest in other ways. Rival unions in the same workplace may, for example, refuse to co-operate in working an otherwise acceptable payment or incentive system, or their stewards may obstruct joint arrangements such as consultative committees, for mostly superficial reasons – the real one being their unwillingness to sit down together.

Another aspect of multi-unionism is the weakening of trade union authority at the workplace. Shop stewards from different unions often have to work together on matters which affect them all in the same plant. To call in the full-time officials of their various unions every time an issue cropped up which required them to work together would be completely unrealistic; so stewards tend to sit on joint committees which they have set up solely on their own initiative. Such joint endeavours may conclude working arrangements or terms and conditions of employment over which union officials have no control; agreements arrived at in this way may even be contrary to union policy.

One possible answer to the problem of multi-unionism is industrial unionism, whereby one union organizes for all grades of workers in a particular industry – there are sixteen such unions affiliated to the West German equivalent of the T.U.C. But unionism of this kind would involve a massive re-structuring of British unions, and the T.U.C. is ill-equipped to undertake such a venture, even if the General Council had a radical change of attitude and tried to do so. The issue has been put to the T.U.C. on several occasions – the last in 1962 – and each time it has been specifically rejected by the General Council.

The T.U.C. has sought instead to promote amalgamations between unions and, although it has no formal power to do so, it has used its influence to persuade union leaders to consider the advantages of more mergers and the feasibility of joint working arrangements. It was aided by the passing of the Trade Union (Amalgamations, etc.) Act, 1964, which helped with the technicalities of mergers. Since 1964 there have been over fifty such mergers. The Foundry Workers Union and the Amalgamated Engineering Union joined to form the present Amalgamated Union of Engineering Workers (A.U.E.W.), whose ranks were later augmented by the addition of T.A.S.S. (formerly D.A.T.A.). The Association of Scientific Workers and the Association of Supervisory Staffs, Executives and Technicians united to form the modern and sophisticated Association of Scientific, Technical and Managerial Staffs (A.S.T.M.S.). These are but two examples of a tendency towards amalgamation and federation. These movements are not taking place at a fast rate, but gradually over a period of time, in keeping with the origins of British trade unionism where major advances did not take place overnight.

EMPLOYERS' ASSOCIATIONS

As with trade unions, employers' associations were formed in response to specific circumstances. In many instances they took the form of tacit understandings – about matters such as price or wage levels – rather than formal arrangements. This was the case during the period of the Combinations Acts which, as noted earlier, were not used against employers. Sometimes they were formed for the purpose of combating strikes – in many cases lasting no longer than the strike itself.

Often employers united for purposes of commercial and industrial advantage, e.g. in trade associations, and concerned themselves only marginally with concerted industrial relations actions. Where they did so concern themselves, they initially provided a greater impetus to the collective regulation of pay and other conditions of work than did the unions. In coal-mining, for example, employers adjusted wages to the price of coal and often imposed cuts in pay before stable trade unions were formed in the industry. This is not a criticism of trade unions. Employers had greater resources – both in terms of finance and facilities – than unions. From the 1860s until the onset of the First World War, employers' associations were innovators to an even greater degree. In certain industries, e.g. iron and hosiery, they took the initiative in developing collective bargaining with the unions. This was not always a peaceful path, sometimes pressure was exerted:

> ... in several of our most important industries, including engineering and building, the employers' associations forced the unions, in some instances through prolonged lock-outs, to accept the first principle of industry-wide bargaining – that local disputes should be submitted to a central conference before a strike or lock-out is begun.[28]

State intervention during the 1914–18 war, however, took the initiative from employers' associations, and since that time virtually every major innovation or advance in industrial relations has come from the government, the unions or, in more cases, individual firms pioneering new forms of working relationships.

Employers' associations originated and developed on a local and industrial basis but eventually they formed industry-wide associations or federations, until a central body – the British Employers' Confederation – was established in 1919. After the 1926 General Strike, they missed a golden opportunity to take the initiative once again. In 1927 the T.U.C. expressed the wish to discuss joint consultative machinery and negotiating arrangements with representatives of employers. Sir Alfred Mond and a group of leading industrialists then entered into a dialogue with the chairman of the T.U.C. General Council, Ben Turner. Their discussions became known as the Mond–Turner talks.

Their proposals were submitted to both the Federation of British Industry (a body formed for commercial and trade purposes) and the Confederation. They were welcomed by the Federation and received cautiously by the Confederation. The latter body was strongly (and adversely) influenced by the Engineering Employers' Federation who still vividly recalled the strife in their industry during the First World War – although the year was now 1928. Their opposition carried the day and in April, 1929, the employers submitted to the T.U.C. a weak version of the machinery originally proposed as a result of the Mond–Turner talks. The employers' bodies thus found themselves in the same position in regard to their constituent members as the T.U.C. had in relation to its affiliated unions – viz. they could persuade but not compel. The machinery proposed was cumbersome and unwieldy, falling quickly into disuse. Professor Clegg notes the importance of this stage in the history of employers' associations:

> On this occasion Britain missed an opportunity to reconstruct its system of industrial relations to meet the requirements of the future . . . the Confederation had clearly indicated to individual employers that the path to reform in industrial relations did not lie through employers' associations. If they wanted reform they must pursue it in their own companies through their own personnel policies.[29]

Another central employers' body, whose principal work lay outside the industrial relations field, the National Association of British Manufacturers, joined with the Federation of British Industry and the British Employers' Confederation in 1965 to form the Confederation of British Industry. The C.B.I.'s membership includes individual companies (unlike the B.E.C.), employers' associations, the boards which administer the nationalized industries, and trade associations. It also includes as 'commercial associates' such undertakings as banks and insurance companies. The C.B.I.'s member associations cover some eighty per cent of the total work force in private industry and transport.

The C.B.I. has no authority to compel its members to take or refrain from taking any course of action they might choose. Its powers are merely persuasive in nature. Unlike the T.U.C. it cannot intervene in disputes where substantial numbers may be affected – it can only offer advice, which may be either taken or ignored. Its main industrial relations function is to represent the employers' view in dealings with the Government, the T.U.C., and the public. Individual companies and associations could easily leave the Confederation and suffer little or no repercussions.

Employers' associations can also find themselves in this position. Esso and Alcan, for example, both withdrew from their respective associations in order to conclude productivity agreements, because the constraints imposed by industry-wide agreements were felt to be unworkable at plant level. Industry-wide bargaining requires the continued existence of employers' associations, but increasingly collective bargaining is becoming a matter best dealt with in individual plants and undertakings. Industry-level agreements cannot cover many of the situations which arise at the level of the plant or shop-floor and therefore: 'The central responsibility of employers' associations in the reconstruction of industrial relations is to promote and support effective and comprehensive agreements in the company and in the factory.'[30]

Employers, by and large, have stayed in their respective associations for a number of reasons. From the industrial relations viewpoint, these include the establishment of industry-wide minimum rates of pay and other conditions of employment – e.g. overtime premiums and holiday periods, access to a disputes procedure, training and advisory services on matters such as work-study and incentive schemes and advice on the application of legislative enactments and regulations in their particular industries. There is also the prospect of support from other employers – sometimes material, more often moral – in times of dispute with unions or workers.[31]

A SOCIOLOGICAL PERSPECTIVE

The uneven development of the British industrial relations system has left its mark on the behaviour of those involved. This is clearly illustrated in the case of trade unions. Their behaviour seems strange at times, and often contradictory, to people outside the system – not to mention many within it. Individual workers and shop stewards may criticize their union leadership one moment, then swing solidly behind them when disputes loom. Rank-and-file members may not support – they may even oppose – the political views of their leaders, yet they permit them to remain in office. The movement may be united over one issue but certain unions in the very same movement can be found engaged in bitter jurisdictional disputes with one another. Unions and work-groups have sometimes been involved in prolonged disputes with employers where little or no actual increase in wages is anticipated but rather some elusive point of principle.

The work of Alan Fox[32] provides some interesting insights into these and related problems. His sociological analysis of the workings of collectivities in general, and employee collectivities in particular, can only be roughly summarized here but they are extremely useful in highlighting the constraints imposed upon individuals and leaders by both the collectivity itself and the environment in which it has to operate. When a collectivity, such as a union, is formed, its main purpose is to combine the isolated efforts of individuals into an agency for mobilizing collective power. The organization so formed might at first reflect accurately the aspirations of all the individuals who gave it initial legitimacy; but differing circumstances may in the course of time require the organization to pursue goals which particular individuals or groups may not desire. The individual's continued membership of the organization will then depend on the extent to which it pursues the minimum objectives which he supports. Provided minimum requirements are met, the collectivity will command the individual's loyalty.

This constitutes a continual strain on the relationship between union and member. If enough members become disillusioned with the union's objectives they will transfer their loyalty to the workplace representatives; they may even change unions. The divergence or 'gap' between individual and organizational interests may become

27

greater or less with different situations and circumstances. When the entire collectivity is under attack, whether apparent or real, the members will tend to forget what separates them and concentrate on what unites them – even major differences between members and leaders are dropped at such times, but they may reappear when danger passes. Shop stewards and work-groups may act in defiance of union officials and yet join ranks solidly on questions such as union recognition or the pressing of a wage claim. Once recognition is achieved or the wage claim met, the old dichotomies may recur.

When a worker joins a union he is contributing to the creation of a social structure which can at times frustrate his original intention. When workers participate in concerted action it is reasonable to assume a certain degree of consensus. The union's main efforts will be devoted to the maintenance of this because without it the exercise of collective power would be impossible. To this end the social structure created originally by consensus will lay down rules and regulations, establish norms, elect officers and invest them with power and authority. Should an individual member experience a change of heart on certain organizational objectives, he is in fact seeking to withdraw from the 'pool' of consensus. In that case, the social structure he helped create will use its powers against him. In the case of a union he may be visited with sanctions such as fines, removal of benefit, expulsion and perhaps, where a 'closed shop' exists, loss of employment. Provided a union can maintain a working consensus by pursuing appropriate goals, it will have the necessary independence and authority to employ disciplinary measures.

The maintenance of a working consensus requires not only coercive sanctions but also the propagation of an ideology which stresses the necessity for the continued existence of the organization. This involves the principle of solidarity. Workers who would normally be disturbed at widening relative pay levels in a plant may be hostile to the ambitions of other groups of workers in regard to wages. Yet the same workers can be called upon to commence forms of industrial action which do not benefit them directly at all but involve the collective interests of their union. They may, for example, strike in sympathy to help members elsewhere to obtain recognition for their union. They may not have given any consideration to the question of solidarity when joining the union, but in adopting collective norms and patterns of behaviour they come to realize that it is expected of them – thus they will accord this solidarity even when certain of them disagree with the particular objectives being sought. When pursuing matters of principle they are often acting in accordance with uniform behavioural patterns which the collectivity has designated as vital for its survival.

Different collectivities seek to impose constraints on the individual. A worker is required to conform to the norms of the work-group, factory rules, union rules and T.U.C. policies. Such conformity is by no means always forthcoming; where it is present it will be found in varying degrees, depending on the nature of the collectivity involved.

The T.U.C. comes last on the list. It is further removed from individual employees than are work-groups, unions and factory management. Much depends on the policies that it pursues from time to time. If lay members do not agree with particular policies they will act in defiance of them, even where the unions follow the T.U.C. line. An important factor in the social 'distance' between the lay member and the T.U.C. is the question of immediacy, both physically and in terms of objectives. The work-group is daily in contact with the member, and its goals are based on shop-floor situations, which cannot be the case at T.U.C. gatherings. The individual will be fortunate indeed if he meets the leading T.U.C. figures other than through the mass media. Another important factor is that work-group and union representatives are elected by the members and they have some say in determining goals.

The range of sanctions available to work-groups and unions in regard to their members is greater than those of the T.U.C. in relation to its affiliate unions. This makes the T.U.C. more vulnerable to deviants which threaten its cohesion, and lays severe limitations on its possible courses of action. Lacking direct authority over its membership, it is susceptible to pressures from below. As long as it meets the minimum aspirations of its constituents, however, they will continue to permit it to make representations on their behalf. When it appears to exceed the limits of its authority, the affiliates are by no means chary of calling attention to the transgression. In its social contract or 'compact' with the Labour Government elected in 1974, the T.U.C. agreed to request its unions to seek moderate wage claims and not to quote the miners' settlement of the same period as a precedent. There were signs of dissent, however, which do not augur well for the future of such agreements. 'A statement approved by the A.S.T.M.S. executive reminded the T.U.C. that it has no constitutional right to make commitments on wages for individual unions.'[33]

The political aspirations of individual trade union leaders are largely matters of indifference to lay members. So long as officials meet or pursue legitimate union objectives they will be accorded a degree of autonomy to advocate the political aims of their choice. Thus some trade union executive bodies can contain all shades of political opinion. The giant A.U.E.W., for example, has been led by a right-winger (the late Lord Carron) and subsequently by a left-winger, Hugh Scanlon. The A.U.E.W. executive has always shown a wide range of political opinion.

Sometimes the union leader can incur the wrath of the rank and file by adopting bargaining strategies which they do not regard as appropriate. The members will have their own subjective assessment of the best way of pursuing objectives. The union leader, however, will sometimes be forced to amend or modify strategy to further longer-term interests. He will usually have greater knowledge at his disposal through meeting managers, employers' associations and officials of government departments. During negotiation, for instance, he may settle for what he knows is the limit of the employer's ability to concede, the utmost that can be gained. But, to members not involved in the proceedings, this may seem a betrayal. Again, the union leader may feel that the long-term interests of the union are best served by complying with incomes policy even though his members may have given him no such mandate. Individual members may oppose productivity bargaining only to find that full-time officials often advocate their acceptance.

As already noted, the union can keep deviants in line by a system of sanctions such as fines, removal of benefit and expulsion. Their coercive force, however, does not match that of the sanctions of the work-group, where physical immediacy is all-important. Work-group sanctions range from ridicule and sarcasm to outright ostracism. These sanctions are applied when group norms and values are transgressed; the purpose of these norms and values is to maintain the cohesion of the group. Immediacy of sanction helps explain the unanimity of the vote at work-place meetings. Sometimes a member will disagree with the majority feeling, but this will rarely be shown, as deviation is seen not in terms of the merit of the objection but as a threat to group cohesion. Work-place voting also illustrates, in addition to the fear of sanctions, the success of the collectivity's ideology.

Where the member wishes to vote differently he is reminded that aberration detracts from 'solidarity'. As solidarity is often pursued as an end in itself the member will usually sink his difference and contribute to making the vote unanimous.

The trade union collectivity, like any other, must adjust to meet the challenge of a changing environment. Decreases in the manual work force, increases in the white-collar section, the unionization of female workers, company takeovers and mergers, all have their effect. The environment sometimes causes collectivities to clash. With trade unions this is evidenced in jurisdictional and 'poaching' disputes. A union may seek to increase its membership because of the increased power it can thereby wield, as well as the additional contributions involved. Sometimes it can only do so by taking members from another union. This is not always done through conscious intent; technological change may make what was one union's territory more appropriate for another. On the employers' side, industry-wide bargaining can bring different employers in the same industry together to negotiate with unions, but when they pursue their own individual company interest they clash with one another through competition for markets.

Trade unions do not clash with one another as often as employers must necessarily do, but the fact that they clash at all raises questions about the appropriateness of phrases such as 'the trade union movement'. The 'movement' is in reality a collection of collectivities which have combined to further interests which they have in common; but where differences occur it is evident that what is really being pursued is the interests of individual institutions and not those of any 'movement'. Nevertheless common areas of interest have held a movement of sorts together – although a loose one. From time to time certain changes in the political, economic and legal environment can serve to weld this loose alliance more closely together. The Industrial Relations Act, 1971, provided a clear example. Opposition to the Act was under way before it even became law. The T.U.C. and most unions were united in developing strategy and tactics to deal with problems arising under the Act while pressing for its repeal. But even during this period of increased 'solidarity' of the 'movement' there were differences; these developed around problems such as registration and appearances before the National Industrial Relations Court – which will be dealt with later in this book.

To speak of a person's membership of a collectivity is misleading.

31

It is more appropriate to talk of a person's position in relation to several collectivities which seek – with varying degrees of success – to impose constraints upon his behaviour:

> . . . the 'collectivity' may mean very different things according to the goal being pursued and the level at which action is appropriate. It may change as the collectivity at one level considers that effectiveness for the group concerned would be best served by upward – or downward – reference to a different level. The relevance and importance of these different levels of collective organization tends to fluctuate according to which goals are most immediately pressing and which level is perceived as most effective for their satisfaction.[34]

Formal descriptions of the British industrial relations system give little hint of the complex of collectivities which operate within the institutional structure. Behaviour that is apparently irrational starts to make sense only when considered in terms of the nature and functions of the collectivities involved. They do not function in isolation but in an environment which history, society, industry and technology have provided. This environment has in the past been altered by struggle, concession and compromise – rarely as a result of rational planning. Unfortunately, this is still largely true today. There have been brave attempts to proceed in a planned manner – which will be discussed later in this book – but such endeavours have been concentrated on largely structural matters in the vain hope that behavioural change would follow. As change has traditionally been slow and gradual, perhaps this indicates the trend for the future. A planned streamlining and updating of the system, rather than a sweeping, comprehensive overhaul, will no doubt prove less traumatic to those involved.

2

The Legacy of the Law

To the uninitiated layman, one of the most extraordinary phenomena of recent years has been the vehemence of trade union opposition to attempts to regularize industrial relations in the UK through legislation. The Labour Government's White Paper *In Place of Strife*, and the Conservative Industrial Relations Act, for example, were fought with every appearance of venom even by trade unionists like Victor Feather, the General Secretary of the T.U.C. at the time, who were normally regarded as moderates. The explanation for what would appear an irrational response is to be found in the history of the trade union movement and more particularly, how the trade unions have perceived the role of the law. Seen through union eyes, the law has persistently denied its members basic human rights and, even when ameliorating laws have been passed, interpretations by the judiciary have regularly thwarted its intentions.

British Ministers of Employment have too readily looked across the water at America and Europe, even the Soviet Union, where legislation banning strikes has been successful. They would have been better employed turning the pages of British history to understand why the trade union movement has seen the law as a weapon to be used against them, not as a shield to defend their interests.

Several important attitudes evident today on the part of both management and unions were formed as far back as the industrial revolution. Britain was the first country to develop a capitalistic system but, as with most advances, many mistakes were made, many wounds were inflicted, and some scars left. Marx and Engels, describing how capitalism might be destroyed, nonetheless paid a striking tribute to its dynamic nature:

The bourgeoisie, during its rule of scarce one hundred years, has created more massive and more colossal productive forces than

33

have all preceding generations together. Subjection of Nature's forces to man, machinery, application of chemistry to industry and agriculture, steam-navigation, railways, electric telegraphs, clearing of whole continents for cultivation, canalization of rivers, whole populations conjured out of the ground – what earlier century had even such a presentiment that such productive forces slumbered in the lap of social labours.[1]

Unfortunately, although early capitalist endeavour did so much to improve the *means* of production it altered the *relations* of production in a much more distressing manner:

It has resolved personal worth into exchange value, and in place of the numberless indefeasible chartered freedoms, has set up that single, unconscionable freedom – Free Trade. In one word, for exploitation, veiled by religious and political illusions, it has substituted naked, shameless, direct, brutal exploitation.[2]

This was the background against which the early struggles between capital and labour took place.

COMBINATION

With changing production methods, from a domestic to a factory system, there came into being large numbers of workmen. Disputes there had been under the domestic system, but the important point about the factory was that disputes now involved greater numbers of people. With domestic production there were differing *individual* needs; the factory system gave birth to *class* needs. The grouping together of people in workplaces and towns meant that an attack on the wages and conditions of one was also an attack on the wages and conditions of many. This phenomenon gave workmen a tremendous potential bargaining strength *vis-à-vis* their employers but it was a potential which the state sought to ensure was never realized or, if realized, was illegal to act upon. This gave rise to the Combination Acts of 1799–1800.

These Acts made it an offence for workmen to combine with each other for the purposes of demanding increases in wages or alterations in the hours worked. Differing motives lay behind this legislation. The government of the day had to contend with a great deal of unrest at home while the Continent had witnessed, just a decade earlier, the French Revolution, with both its radical changes and excesses. This story, it was feared, might be repeated in England, Ireland (which had just seen a rebellion by the United Irishmen) and the Colonies, if the downtrodden working people were permitted to use their strength to the full in combination:

> Two ideas inspired this legislation. First, workmen's unions were regarded as a political danger, for the government was still nervous of Jacobins. Secondly . . . Parliament considered that the masters of industry must be given a free hand and therefore that their workmen ought not to combine against them.[3]

There also existed the economic philosophy known as *laissez-faire*. This French expression may be translated as 'do as you like' or 'leave things alone'. It was the term applied to a school of economic thought which insisted that employers should be given a free hand and the state should abandon attempts to regulate trade. The tough and independent early capitalists felt that they could manage well enough to survive the rigours of free competition without reliance on government intervention. The main emphasis of *laissez-faire* was on relations between nations, but employers sought and obtained another perspective to this doctrine. It meant, they insisted, that masters and men should be left alone to construct between them a 'free bargain'. However, as with our latter-day 'free collective bargaining', it was anything but 'free'. Employers had great financial and material resources to see them through periods of industrial strife – workmen had none.

Economists and historians hold, in general, that *laissez-faire* triumphed during the first half of the nineteenth century. In terms of capital and labour the Elizabethan Act, authorizing magistrates to fix wages, was repealed in 1813. The following year that section of the Elizabethan Statute of Artificers which enforced apprenticeships was also repealed. This was merely the formal acknowledgement of the triumph of employer power – the masters were able to claim and exercise freedom from state control in practice before 1813. The Combination Acts provide an illustration. Their terms were so drawn that they could theoretically have been applied to employers; in practice, they were used almost exclusively against workmen. They were used in such a way, moreover, as to dispel any illusions of fairness – men were punished harshly for the slightest infringement. Thus a bootmaker called Alexander had his wages halved by his employer; he then, with six others, refused to work. All seven were prosecuted under the Acts and sentenced to fourteen days' imprisonment with hard labour.[4]

Francis Place, a master tailor of Charing Cross, fought long and hard for the removal of restraints on unions of workmen. By virtue of great tactical skill – he was very proficient in collecting evidence and ensuring that it was received in the right quarters – he and his friend Hume (a radical M.P.) secured the passage of a Bill repealing the Combination Acts in 1824; but the struggle was far from over. A wave of strikes followed, and in 1825 an alarmed Parliament passed a less permissive statute which permitted trade unions to exist but visited them with numerous penalties if they tried to do anything to change their situations. Once more we find the law being used against workmen only, although it could equally have been applied to combinations of employers.

THE COURTS

Section 3 of the 1825 Act laid down a number of loosely worded definitions of criminal offences concerning pressures brought to bear on employers by way of industrial conflict involving violence. These were 'threats', 'molestation', 'intimidation' and 'obstruction'. The overwhelming majority of judges did not confine the application of these offences to circumstances where violence was involved but sought, instead, to widen the extent of the definitions so as to cover most instances of what would today be termed legitimate union activities. For example, in a case in 1832 it was held that a *threat* to strike was 'molestation'. Judges vied with each other in finding ingenious ways to restrict union activity. One well-known example is the case of the Tolpuddle Martyrs.

These six men were natives of Tolpuddle in Dorset. In 1834 they were prosecuted for the offence of taking an oath to their union. They could not be proceeded against under the Combination Acts as these had been repealed. In those times joining a union involved many unusual rituals (skeletons, masks and robes were used) which could bring workmen into breach of several old laws. The one used to sentence these unfortunate men was the Unlawful Oaths Act of 1797, originally passed following the Nore Mutiny. They were given a sentence of seven years' transportation and hard labour in Australia. After widespread indignation and protest they were released, having served four years. This iniquitous use of an old statute did not exhaust the weapons of the Judiciary. The activities of trade unionists could be threatened with legal action on grounds of civil and criminal conspiracy. In addition the objects of a trade union could render them in 'restraint of trade': 'Some judges in the nineteenth century even thought that the existence of any association in restraint of trade was criminally "indictable at common law as tending to impede and interfere with the free course of trade" . . . the same restraint of trade doctrine deprived unions of any lawful civil status.'[5]

Union agitation helped to bring about the Trade Unions Act, 1871. Section 2 of this Act ensured that the purposes of a trade union should not render any member liable to criminal prosecution merely because they were in restraint of trade. In addition, the Criminal Law Amendment Act, 1871, restricted the definition of 'threats' and 'intimidation', making a mere threat to strike no longer a statutory offence. But some judges were of the opinion that although statute law said one thing, the common law said quite another. Mr Justice Brett, for example, ruled that the Act did not abrogate the common law so as to permit an act to be done with improper intent and amounting to an unjustifiable annoyance and interference with the employer's business (*R* v. *Bunn* (1872). In this case, some London gas workers had threatened to go on strike unless a fellow worker (dismissed for union activities) was reinstated. A conviction was secured against them on a charge of criminal conspiracy and they received a sentence of twelve months' imprisonment. In spite of the 1871 Act, criminal conspiracy had slipped in again through the back door.

Once more a judge had sought and found a way round a statutory protection granted by Parliament after much union agitation and endeavour. Yet again the legislature was compelled to step in and cover a loophole discovered by an all-too-willing court. The result was the Conspiracy and Protection of Property Act, 1875. Section 3 of that Act provided that an agreement or combination by two or more persons to do or procure to be done any action in contemplation or furtherance of a trade dispute should not be actionable as a conspiracy if such act, committed by one person, would not be punishable as a crime. At this stage it is easy to appreciate how the divisive 'them and us' attitude was given birth. Trade unionists could hardly be expected to strive for the success of an enterprise or factory in the face of untrammelled employer attacks on their wages, conditions and basic institutions. The state, through the law, had declared its bias towards the master.

When Parliament enacted progressive legislation, it did so only after demand, agitation and protest on the part of workers, reformers and liberal political figures. Advances were not acknowledged as such by the work force; they were seen more in terms of *concessions*. The political make-up of government was vastly different in 1875 from what it had been in 1800; but the damage had been done. The state had given laws which favoured the employer and shackled the unions. The courts had enforced such laws. When the state had been pushed into changing parts of the law, the courts had managed to find fresh ways to circumvent the changes. Struggle and conflict were the essence of this relationship. Workers had but little respect for employers, for the state, and significantly, for the law:

> In 1800 trade unions were utterly illegal. The fact remains today a critical feature of their legal situation. The explanation of this paradox will provide us with the key to the peculiar structure of our law concerning trade unions and industrial conflict. The most powerful influence on that law . . . has been the unions' struggle to emerge from that illegality.[6]

TAFF VALE AND THE RIGHT TO STRIKE

More shocks for the unions lay ahead. Earlier they had been denied an essential right, viz. to organize. Having eventually won this right, they were then denied the prospect of legally using their new-found strength. The 1875 Act had apparently cleared this hurdle. A new obstacle appeared, however, in the form of an attack on something as basic to a union as its right to organize – union funds. In the Taff Vale Railway Case of 1901 the House of Lords decided that a registered union could be sued in its own name *in tort*, i.e. a branch of civil law. This meant that, in an action for damages, union funds could be proceeded against. Prior to this case unions had felt safe from a financial point of view. They were not corporations and the Trade Union Act, 1871, did not confer corporate status upon them. This had meant that union funds could only be proceeded against by means of a 'representative action', i.e. one taken against a few members on behalf of the rest. Such an action could have failed for several reasons (mostly procedural), a fact which made the unions feel secure.

This security was shattered by the Taff Vale Case. The majority of the Law Lords held that, while it was true that a trade union was not a corporation or a legal entity distinct from its membership, nevertheless the privileges conferred upon registered trade unions by the Trade Unions Act, 1871, implied a correlative liability on the part of such a union to be sued in its own name for any tortious acts committed on its behalf. Professor Wedderburn notes:

> Nothing did more to embitter relations between the courts and the workers than the Law Lords' decision that a registered union could after all be sued. . . . The Taff Vale case became part of working class culture, part of the way 'they' treat trade unions if they can. Such feelings have not died.[7]

Trade unionists throughout the land expressed great alarm at the decision. Unrest was widespread and there was much agitation by trade unions and workers for Parliament to intervene and redress this state of affairs. With the victory of the Liberals in 1906 the Trade Disputes Act of that year was passed. The Act was a response to the findings of the Report of the Royal Commission on Trade Disputes and Trade Combinations, under the chairmanship of Lord Dunedin. The Commission considered not only the Taff Vale decision but also a difficulty in the Conspiracy and Protection of Property Act, 1875. This was that the protection given to those acting 'in contemplation or furtherance of a trade dispute' against prosecutions for *criminal* conspiracy did not extend to actions for *civil* conspiracy.

These situations were covered by the 1906 Act. Section 1 provided that an act done by two or more persons in contemplation or furtherance of a trade dispute should not be actionable unless the act done without any such agreement or combination would be actionable. Section 3 provided that an act done by any person in contemplation or furtherance of a trade dispute should not be actionable on the ground only that it induced another person to break a contract of employment. This gave the union official or shop steward who called a strike, for example, an 'immunity'. Their action could still be considered an inducement to breach of contract but it was not actionable; they could not be proceeded against in the courts. Pickets were given protection – to peacefully persuade any person to work or not to work – from actions for inducement by Section 2. The Taff Vale situation was covered by Section 4, which ensured that an action against a trade union or against any members or officials of such unions in respect of tortious acts alleged to have been committed by or on behalf of the union should not be entertained by any court.

One point concerning Section 4 is worthy of note. Though unions were protected, their officials and members individually were not. In addition, though Section 3 gave protection against inducement to breach of contract of employment, it was framed in terms which precluded the use of unlawful means. This had meant that if any worker called on others to strike in an orderly, peaceful manner, the inducement could not be a matter for litigation. (We shall return to this point later.) On the other hand, if any worker had forced others to come out on strike by, for example, threats of violence, then the statute offered no protection against any legal action which might be taken.

After 1906, the law concerning the exercise of collective power between unions and employers seemed fairly well settled. Trade unions had won the right to combine, to exercise their power, to have their funds protected and to ensure the security of their members from legal action in regard to trade disputes. The tale of the relations between workers, employers and the state had been one of struggle, concession, reaction and yet more struggle. It can be readily appreciated, therefore, that the typical stance of trade unions has been defensive, parrying increasingly subtle attacks on their hard-won rights.

An analysis of trade union reaction to the law might usefully draw on Abraham Maslow's theories of motivation, particularly his work on the hierarchy of needs. The work of Maslow is dealt with in Chapter 6 in relation to managerial assumptions about man's basic motivations.[8]

In Maslow's hierarchy, man's most basic need is seen as being physiological, concerned with survival, such things as food and shelter. Once this need was met man looked for security and safety, some assurance that there would be persistence of basic needs in the future. He might then aspire to higher needs.

The Industrial Revolution tended to make physiological needs dominant. Squalid working conditions, insufficient wages, long hours of work and little leisure time served to make these basic demands uppermost in the consciousness of the working population. The exercise of collective bargaining power through combination and the work of certain reformers, helped to achieve satisfaction of most basic needs. Safety needs then became dominant. By and large, people prefer order to chaos, the known to the unknown.

The more sophisticated forms of trade unionism which took shape in the 1850s (such as the establishment of Mechanics' Institutes), indicated a desire to progress towards meeting higher needs, such as social ones. However, every attack on organized labour, whether on combinations, industrial action, funds or the like, only served to throw workmen back on their basic needs. Instead of co-operation from the working population in helping to run both industry and the country, we find caution, wariness and often distrust. Why do trade unions adopt defensive attitudes? Why do they not co-operate with employers and government to a greater degree? Questions such as these are constantly asked. Yet trade unions and workers do sometimes evince initiative and co-operation with employers and government! The industrial peace secured during the Second World War, and co-operation in the wage freeze of the post-war Labour Government, are clear examples. Part of the answer lies in the fact that guarantees in regard to trade union organization and activities were given during these periods. Shop stewards, for example, were given certain protections during the war in the exercise of their duties. In short, the safety needs were met and workers were able to turn their attention to higher things.

It could be argued that, in Maslow's terms, safety needs were only met, so far as is possible to completely meet them, with the introduction of comprehensive legislation governing redundancy agreements.

Sometimes when safety needs seem fairly well satisfied certain circumstances threaten their existence and trade unionists close ranks in defence of them. One such instance was the case of *Rookes* v. *Barnard*,[9] in which the House of Lords held that a threat by persons that contracts of employment would be broken unless the employer concerned conceded their demand, was a threat to do something unlawful, as it constituted the tort of intimidation. Thus the persons concerned, when sued for civil conspiracy, could not rely on the protection given by the Trade Disputes Act, 1906. This decision meant that, while anyone could *induce* a breach of contract of employment where a trade dispute was in existence and not be proceeded against, the same person could not *threaten* the employer with the inducement without being guilty of tortious 'intimidation'. Earlier in his judgement in the Court of Appeal,[10] Lord Justice Donovan stated:

> If that be the true position, as I think it is, then the situation is reached . . . that a strike is not unlawful, but the threat to do so is. In other words, the policy which workmen should pursue in order to avoid liability is to strike first and negotiate afterwards.

The House of Lords did not agree with the Court of Appeal finding, and the resulting decision rocked the trade union movement as seriously as had the 1901 Taff Vale decision:

> What startled the trade union world was that, after the Trade Disputes Act, 1906, and more than half a century of case law, in which the courts had shown a deepening understanding of the vital role of the trade unions in running British industry and their need to enjoy freedom of economic action to protect the legitimate interests of their members, there still remained coiled in the common law the possibility of an action against union officials for crushing damages and costs for threatening strike action in breach of contracts of employment, whether to remove an objectionable employee . . . or to pursue any other industrial purpose, like a claim in respect of wages or any other terms or conditions of employment.[11]

Once more the legislature was forced to intervene to protect unions in the exercise of basic duties, and the result was the Trade Disputes Act, 1965. This stated that an act done by a person in contemplation or furtherance of a trade dispute would not be actionable in tort on the grounds only that it consisted in threatening that a contract of employment would be broken. The decision in *Rookes* v. *Barnard*, however, still applied where the threatened breach involved a contract other than one of employment.

The unions had once more been forced into defence of the safety needs; and it is hardly surprising that they felt threatened again with the introduction of the Industrial Relations Act, 1971 (this Act will be examined in Chapter 5). What proved surprising was the fact that there were people in government who expressed some amazement at

T.U.C. hostility to the Act, in spite of the fact that the trade union movement had received setbacks with many legal interventions into the industrial relations sphere. When such a watertight statute as the Trade Disputes Act, 1906, had been breached (as late as 1964) who could honestly say what lawyers and judges might be able to do with as complex a piece of legislation as the 1971 Act?

Not all legislation governing the work situation was punitive or restrictive towards the unions. Some Acts confer positive benefits. The Factories Act (1961) deals, among other things, with health, heating and ventilation, sanitation, welfare provisions such as drinking water, safety requirements concerning the guarding and maintenance of certain types of machinery, the notification of accidents and industrial diseases and with the employment of women and young persons. Certain statutes deal with specific industries. These include the Mines and Quarries Act, the Merchant Shipping Act, the Agriculture Acts and so forth. The Offices, Shops and Railway Premises Act (1963) extends similar provisions to those of the Factories Act into areas from which the protection of such Acts was formerly excluded.

Some statutes have made significant changes in the contractual of relationship between employer and employee. During the Industrial Revolution, for example, employers could hire and fire at will. Freedom of contract in this sense applied to employers but not to workers. The owner had property rights in his land and capital which were regarded as sacred – and denied to labour. This is not the case today. A manager cannot dismiss an employee as a result of a passing whim. He must give the worker a certain minimum amount of notice (Contracts of Employment Act, 1972). The worker may receive compensation for being made redundant, the amount depending on length of service (Redundancy Payments Act, 1965). Under the Terms and Conditions of Employment Act, 1959, an employer may be required to observe terms and conditions not less favourable than those established for his trade or industry by collective bargaining.

The worker is also now protected against unfair dismissal. The 1971 Industrial Relations Act first gave workers protection against unfair dismissal. Sections 22–26 of the Act deemed every dismissal unfair until the *employer* established otherwise, and the maximum permissible ceiling for recovery of compensation was made higher than under the common law. The provisions of the 1971 Industrial Relations Act were expanded by the 1974 Trade Union and Labour

Relations Act which extended fair dismissal to include situations where the employee refused to join a union or refused to remain a union member where a trade union membership agreement exists. The 1974 Act also lowered the qualifying period. This means that those who have been in employment for over twenty-six weeks are now protected against unfair dismissal. The 1975 Employment Protection Act also extended the unfair dismissals legislation to enable dismissed workers to obtain written reasons for dismissal and to enable industrial tribunals to award the reinstatement or re-engagement of dismissed workers.

These enactments may be said to establish a certain 'property' right for the individual worker in his job. This 'property' right has been widely extended over recent years. Notably, the 1975 Employment Protection Act, which not only increased protection for workers in the event of unfair dismissal, but also extended the rights of workers to maternity leave, time off for public and trade union duties, and increased protection in redundancy situations. Similarly, the 1974 Health and Safety at Work Act provides increased protection for the worker in the field of health and safety. The 1975 Industry Act has also extended workers' rights, through their trade union, to company information, and can involve workers, through their union, in planning agreements relating to their enterprise. These major recent areas of legislation are examined more fully in Chapter 5.

Not only does the organized labour movement in this country avoid resort to the law where possible, often it does not need the support of the law to gain its ends. Legislation on the hours of work of women and young persons, to quote one example, was once welcome, but today most unions feel they could enforce these by collective bargaining and not only by reference to, say, the Factories Act, 1961. This Act restricts the hours of work of women and the employment of women on certain jobs when machines are in motion. Many female trade unionists realized that when the Equal Pay Act 1970 came fully into force by December 1975, the next stage was to work for the repeal of protective legislation on matters such as hours of work. Equal pay should also mean equal opportunity and there cannot be equal opportunity to earn higher wages when men are permitted to work certain shifts (and longer hours) while women are not. The 1975 Sex Discrimination Act, which is examined in Chapter 5, failed to remove the discrimination against women in employment contained in the 1961 Factories Act. The Equal Opportunities Commission which was established under the 1975 Sex Discrimination Act is, however, required to issue reports to the Home Secretary on the discriminating provisions of existing legislation. The fact that some trade unionists can even advocate such repeal indicates the confidence which they have that collective strength could fill the gap left by the law should such repeal become reality.

The tendency to advocate reform by way of legislative enactments has lost favour with the unions. As Professor Clegg points out, the union movement was dominated before the First World War by the coal and cotton unions who, together with the railway unions, worked hard at furthering protective legislation on matters such as hours of work but: 'The distribution of trade union membership has greatly changed since then, and over the last twenty years further change in these areas of legislation has appeared to most unions as a matter of marginal adjustment.'[12] The same author also correctly notes that the great bulk of the law which might impinge upon union-management relationships lies outside the scope of industrial relations.[13]

In general, strikes involve a breach of the contract of employment, but most managements do not therefore take their workers to court. They have to conduct relationships at the workplace when the court action is over; they realize that the presence of victor and vanquished in the same factory is inimical to good industrial relations. Also, as Professor Wedderburn observes,[14] most workers, refused their wages, would go first to their shop steward and not to a solicitor. The law is avoided for practical as well as historical reasons. Greater resort to law could not help but bring conflict at present. Most judges and lawyers receive little or no training in industrial relations and labour law. At the time of writing only a handful of British law schools even include labour law on the syllabus. Consequently judges and lawyers can only attempt to fit industrial relations situations, of which they have no practical experience, into legal categories – and the result is very far from perfect.

With such little resort to the law by present-day management and workers, it would seem pointless to attempt to reform British industrial relations solely by legislative processes. Britain had its Industrial Revolution before other countries. Being first in the queue, we made the first mistakes – we did not have the benefit of hindsight! A possible answer lies in the speed of change. The best structures in the world will not work unless people wish them to. But behavioural and attitudinal changes take time. Changes in structure must be designed to aid this process, not confound it. As the process is gradual it seems logical that structural and institutional change should also be gradual. The law must be geared to the realities of industrial relations situations and not simply the demands of a logical, tidy system such as codification or a 'New Deal' implies.

3

Collective Bargaining

We have described the part which the law has played in the formation of attitudes, particularly those of the trade union movement. We have also drawn attention to the somewhat haphazard growth of the trade union movement in contrast to developments on the continent. If there is one way in which management and unions meet face to face, in almost daily confrontation, it is through the processes of collective bargaining.

Collective bargaining is the most dynamic area of industrial relations. It is here that the nature of the relationship between workers and employers, in regard to terms and conditions of employment, is determined. The individual employee has virtually no bargaining power *vis-à-vis* his employer – except in those rare areas where his skill is personal to him and essential to the enterprise. Technological change has made such examples few and far between. Standardization of jobs and the division of the tasks into relatively simple work processes has continuously reduced premiums on personal skills and abilities and, it follows, on individual bargaining power. Individual employees have naturally sought to pool their resources in order, through the exercise of collective strength, to achieve a position where they can negotiate effectively. Collective bargaining happens where they delegate power to their collective representatives to negotiate terms and conditions of employment with an employer or employer representatives.

In Britain there is conflict between the formal collective bargaining system, operated by trade unions and employers' associations, and the informal system where at plant level shop stewards and managers negotiate additional terms and conditions applicable to particular situations.

THE FORMAL SYSTEM

In the formal system representatives of one or more trade unions meet with representatives of one or more employers or employers' associations to negotiate collective agreements concerning such matters as minimum rates of pay, the length of the working week, overtime premiums and holidays – these are known as 'substantive' agreements. They also negotiate 'procedural' agreements – these establish procedures for reaching substantive agreements and for handling disputes within the industry or establishment. The most common type of collective agreement in Britain is the industry-wide one. Traditionally employers have concentrated on bargaining with trade union representatives on an industrial basis, negotiating about the pay and conditions of workers in particular industries and not particular occupations. Sometimes 'industry-wide' means confined only to one area of the country, if the entire industry is based there. More usually the term also means national. In the U.K. there are over 500 industry-wide arrangements for some 14 million manual workers, out of a total of 16 million. There are some 7 million non-manual or 'white-collar' workers, 4 million of whom are covered by such arrangements. Thus the number of workers covered by industry-wide agreements is greater than the membership of the trade unions, which is just over 10 million.[1]

The formal system presents a tidy, coherent picture. Collective representatives decide terms and conditions. Procedural agreements indicate the manner in which these substantive agreements are to be amended, interpreted or applied. Disputes procedures may be included in the same agreements, providing for the orderly and peaceful resolution of grievances, or they may be in separate documents. This model of precision, unfortunately, is marred by an awkward reality – viz. the informal system.

THE INFORMAL SYSTEM

Where terms and conditions are standard throughout an industry the application of industry-wide agreements presents few problems. However, instances of such standardization are becoming increasingly fewer. Companies within the same industry have generally met the challenges of a changing social and technological environment in various ways, leading not only to different methods of working but also different ways of accommodating the needs of their employees. The industrial relations situation, therefore, in individual plants or undertakings is usually quite different from what is envisaged at industry level. Wages and overtime provide clear examples.

The wage agreed at industry level provides only the minimum basis for the average pay-packet. It bears no resemblance to actual earnings or 'take-home pay'. The premium rate to be received for overtime working is normally an industry-level matter but the *amount* of overtime is a matter usually decided in individual plants in the industry. Bonus or incentive schemes in particular plants also lend an air of unreality to industry-level rates. In addition, managers often come to *ad hoc* arrangements on an assortment of pay matters giving increases which could never have been envisaged at industry-level. The Donovan Commission called the gap between minimum rates and actual earnings 'wage drift', noting that the main elements of 'drift' from agreed rates were piecework or incentive earnings, company or factory additions to basic rates, and overtime earnings.[2]

Wage drift indicates a number of problems. The settling of terms and conditions within factories or plants means a marked loss of control – and hence authority – on the part of trade unions and employers' associations. Then there is the problem of disputes procedure; the transfer of authority to the workplace can often mean resolution of grievances on the basis of factory expedience rather than common standards for the industry. Declining union authority can also be witnessed by the increase in unofficial and unconstitutional strikes. This extreme de-centralization of authority has at times tended towards indecision and virtual anarchy in some industries. It is interesting to note that it took place under the eyes of management; the fact that it happened almost imperceptibly may be traced to over-adherence to the assumptions of the formal system: 'The assumptions of the formal system still exert a powerful influence over men's minds and prevent the informal system from developing into an effective and orderly method of regulation.'[3]

The growth of plant bargaining has added a new dimension to the collective bargaining process – the shop floor. It has also meant the inclusion of new parties. Traditionally the process involved trade union officials and employers' representatives; now we must add shop stewards and factory management to the list. The phenomenal growth of plant bargaining can be seen from two of its aspects – the type of dispute handled in the workplace and a staggering increase in the number of shop stewards. E. E. Coker[4] has compiled some interesting statistics from various sources, using definitions of 'basic' and 'frictional' disputes, to show the incidence of plant issues. (These definitions were attributed to K. G. Knowles.) Basic disputes were those concerned with wages and hours of work (appropriate for handling by unions); frictional disputes were those concerning questions such as working arrangements, rules and discipline (appropriate for handling by shop stewards). These definitions do not include disputes from other sources therefore the percentages given below do not add up to 100.

	Sources of strikes in the period	
Period	Basic	Frictional
1911–1925	69%	22%
1927–1947	54%	39%
1945–1957	48·5%	48%
1957–1965	49%	45%

It has always been difficult to discover the number of shop stewards in Britain. There is a very high turnover in the job, and unions do not always issue credentials to every worker called upon by his colleagues to exercise the duties of a shop steward. Nonetheless, some figures have emerged which indicate an amazing increase in their numbers. In 1960 the T.U.C. estimated that there were about 3,000 full-time officials and 175,000 shop stewards. When the Commission on Industrial Relations examined the position in 1973[5] they found no marked increase in the number of full-time officials, but they discovered that the shop steward population had increased to 350,000. As shop stewards are concerned largely with workplace matters it seems reasonable to regard this increase in their numbers as proof of the predominance of plant bargaining in the present-day collective bargaining scene. The growth of the shop steward movement was an important factor in the development of shop-floor bargaining; had they been incorporated into the formal system when they emerged as an effective shop-floor force the modern plant bargaining scene would undoubtedly be more orderly and peaceful.

SHOP STEWARDS

Shop stewards as a definable category of worker representative emerged first in the skilled trades towards the end of the nineteenth century. There were, however, workers' representatives in other industries who carried out some of the functions of stewards before this time. For example, in coal-mining a 'checkweighman' was appointed in each lodge under the provisions of the Coal Mines Act, 1860. As miners were paid by output, they had been demanding since 1845 a representative to check the weight of their output.[6] This they received – and more – in the shape of the checkweigher. He also acted as a channel of communication between the men, their union and management; in time, he took on the additional burden of processing grievances. Even earlier examples of shop-floor representation were provided by the Friendly Ironmoulders' Society and some unions in the cotton industry.[7] These early employee representatives did much to relieve full-time officials of such time-consuming chores as collecting dues and checking membership cards.

Developments in the engineering industry, however, placed much greater responsibilities on shop stewards, shop delegates and employee representatives – as they were variously called. Incentive payments, bonus schemes and piece-rates, towards the close of the nineteenth century, brought an unprecedented demand for workers' representatives with on-the-spot knowledge of the production processes involved, together with an understanding of relevant payment structures. Technological change in this period brought increasing pressures to bear on the work force by way of increased machine-speeds and more detailed work measurement. The help that trade unions could extend to their members was limited. They were organized largely on an occupational, not an industrial, basis; therefore their local organs were their branches and not individual workplaces.

During the First World War, unions were further removed from the problems of the workplace by the 'industrial truce' declared between themselves and employers at industry level. This was, however, the period when workshop representation was most needed. The introduction of dilutees and the emphasis on greater production in the interests of the war effort brought an outbreak of disputes at shop-floor level. The shop steward population increased dramatically to fill the representational gap. An important factor in this increase was the security of employment given to stewards by both statute and conditions of full employment. Trade depressions between the wars took their toll of the shop steward population, but the Second World War brought a renewed need for their services, a need not confined only to engineering. Again, the steward was given some protection by statute against dismissal when conditions were those of full employment; another 'truce' was also evident between unions and employers.

In the period since the war, technological advance has spread over wide areas of industry, serving to make the shop steward a permanent feature in most companies. Mass production and automation have brought problems to the modern shop steward which his predecessors could not have envisaged. Continuous-production processes, shift-working, bonus and incentive schemes, manning levels, overtime allocation, redundancy and discipline – to mention but a few – continually tax the ability of the steward. Increases in the shop steward population since the war have taken place in conditions of relatively full employment; there have been periods of unemployment but even these have done nothing to erode the position he has established as a major force in industrial relations.

Today, the duties of the typical shop steward are a far cry from those of the former collector of dues and checker of membership cards, although both these functions still remain an important part of his task. In some undertakings, the steward still collects union dues personally; but increasingly companies are turning to the 'check-off'. This is an arrangement whereby the company deducts the worker's membership contribution from his wage and pays it directly to the union – approximately one out of every five trade unionists in Britain is covered by check-off agreements.[8]

When one considers the ease with which most companies with computerized accounting systems could extend this facility, it may seem surprising that so few trade unionists take advantage of it. The main argument against this system is that manual collection helps consolidate personal contact between the representative and his members. Some trade unionists also treat the check-off with a degree of suspicion; management may ease their burden for them but in doing so they put unions under an obligation to reciprocate in some way. In the event of disagreement, management will then possess an additional sanction – they may withdraw or threaten to withdraw the check-off.

These objections, however, weigh little compared with the advantages of this system. The relief of the burdensome chores of collecting dues would give stewards extra time to pursue the more pressing interests of their members. This would result in much greater, and more meaningful, personal contact with members. It is unlikely that management would seek to destroy their industrial relations goodwill by withdrawing this facility; even if they did so, stewards could easily revert to manual collection. The check-off applies mainly in the public services and nationalized industries, though there is an increasing tendency to use it in the private sector. It is to be hoped that this tendency will be accelerated in order to provide more stewards with sufficient time to face the growing complexity of the tasks before them.

The recruitment of new members and maintenance of existing membership levels forms an important part of the steward's duties. Each new member means for the union an extension of its influence, and an increase in its finances through contributions. Some stewards were assisted in their recruitment function by the establishment of 'closed shop' agreements with management. The popular image of the closed shop is that of a union seeking to coerce a worker into membership – whether he likes it or not – by threatening him with the loss of his job if he does not comply. The popular image, however, tends to exaggerate the purely negative aspects of the position without any consideration of the positive; and it only envisages one type of closed shop. Dr W. E. J. McCarthy in his book *The Closed Shop in Britain*[9] shows that the question of the closed shop is much more complex than many people think; and that the closed shop itself can take several forms.

The closed-shop situation arises where employees come to realize that a particular job is only to be obtained, and retained, if they become and remain members of one of a specified number of unions. The pre-entry closed shop exists where management agree with union representatives that prospective employees must undertake to join the union before commencing employment. The post-entry shop exists where the worker commences employment but must join the union if he is to continue in the job. A labour-supply closed shop happens where the union becomes accepted by management as the sole or main source of new recruits for the work force, e.g. newsprint workers in London. The labour-pool shop is an arrangement whereby employers, in co-operation with the union, agree to form a recognized pool of labour confined to workers which the union finds acceptable. Promotion prospects may be dealt with by a promotion veto shop. Here the union insists that entry to a particular job must be contingent upon the next senior man, at the time of promotion, being a member of the union; if not, he will be passed over in favour of the next senior man who is.

The main *union* argument in favour of the closed shop is that without it there would be many 'free-riders'. Trade unions, stewards and work-groups have frequently worked long and hard at establishing favourable terms and conditions, often incurring personal loss and sacrifice (e.g. through strikes). A free-rider is someone who has done nothing to effect favourable terms and conditions but who is nonetheless prepared to enjoy the benefits. Collective agreements, it must be recalled, cover more workers than are to be found in trade unions. If a worker is prepared to enjoy the benefits, the argument goes, he should be prepared at least to contribute financially to the struggle – thus some closed-shop agreements tolerate non-membership provided the required contribution is either paid to the union or to charity. Another argument in favour of the closed shop is that it ensures solidarity:

> The union must control the working personnel of the group – and all the members in the group must feel that their interests are common rather than individual and must be willing to sacrifice individual advantage to the common good. Hence, to maintain these principles, the union must determine who shall be members of the group and must be able especially to determine who shall come into the shop. This is the real basis of the demand for the closed shop and the abhorrence of scab or non-union workers.[10]

The above quotation is from an American commentator. In Britain the main closed-shop demands emanate from stewards and work-groups – two out of every five trade unionists are covered by the closed shop but the vast majority of closed-shop agreements are informal in nature and rely ultimately on work-group sanctions for enforcement. Where trade union control proves effective the closed shop can help in establishing stable and effective organization, and some employers see advantages in it as ensuring that they are talking to effectively organized representative bodies; there is the implicit hope that the closed shop can maintain discipline in order to secure the enforcement of agreements. The Donovan Commission treated this view with some caution: '. . . the closed shop is widespread in motor-manufacturing, ship-building, coal-mining and the docks, the four industries in which strikes in breach of agreement have been most common in recent years.'[11]

Against the closed shop, it is argued that it reduces the freedom of the individual. He has no choice but to join the union – the alternative is loss of employment. Once in the closed-shop situation, circumstances may arise in which he differs in his attitudes from the rest of the work-group. Then he will be subjected to work-group sanctions – the ultimate result being, again, loss of employment. The economic argument against the closed shop holds that by restricting entry to, for example, a skilled trade it creates manpower shortages damaging to the economy. It is argued, also, that it hinders re-training and the re-deployment of labour to areas where it is most needed, thus reducing the ability of industry to meet the challenges of technological change. In spite of these arguments the Donovan Commission did not recommend the prohibition of the closed shop by law, stating that its negative aspects could be contained in other ways. The Conservatives, however, ignored this advice and made the closed shop illegal by Section 5 of the Industrial Relations Act, 1971.

The closed-shop provisions of the 1971 Act were some of its least successful – which suggests that no amount of legal prohibition will halt closed shops. The 1974 Trade Union and Labour Relations Act repealed the 1971 Industrial Relations Act. The closed-shop situation was complicated by several sections of the Act which we shall examine in detail in Chapter 5. At the time of writing, these sections of the 1974 Act are in the process of being repealed. The Government is in favour of voluntary arrangements whereby the T.U.C. would undertake to establish its own appeals machinery for individuals excluded or expelled from union membership; and industries, such as the Press, can embark on their own attempts to reach agreement to exclude certain categories of employees from trade union membership.

The shop steward forms an essential part of a complex communications network. As comparatively few union members attend routine branch meetings, he will normally form the only link between the shop floor and the union. He is responsible for communicating union policy to the members and for keeping the union informed of the feelings of members in the workplace. His main communications function is to keep management informed of the feelings of his members and to convey the results of dealings with management back to the shop floor. Management, in the normal course of events, meet full-time union officials infrequently and this poses another task for the steward – he must convey current management opinion to his full-time official where it affects important terms and conditions of employment.

Grievance processing constitutes another important part of the steward's job. Members look to him to present their grievances to management and to pursue them to a conclusion. The steward will rarely receive much guidance from industry-wide procedures, as most of them cannot deal with the details of workplace situations. Sometimes industry-wide agreements lay down guide-lines for dealing with domestic grievances but the help they offer is usually too general in nature; individual workplaces are left free to establish their own procedure agreements within the framework of industry agreements. Sometimes these take a written form but more often they are based on informal understandings and custom and practice.[12] Even when written, these agreements are still normally too general to cope with all workplace problems and much improvisation takes place to cope with specific issues. The inadequacies of procedure agreements tend to lead to an insecure system of workplace relationships and an over-reliance on personal dealings:

> One effect of this extremely flexible system is to lay emphasis on the quality of personal relationships at domestic level. Another is to maintain and reinforce the custom of relying on unwritten, informal understandings between shop stewards and management in particular plants. This in turn results in both sides tending to regard their local grievance procedures as instruments by which they can obtain concessions from each other, rather than arrangements which have any absolute validity in themselves.'[13]

We shall be returning to this theme in later parts of the book. If change is taking place in such a way as to 'lay emphasis on the quality of personal relationships' between the manager and the shop steward, it is necessary to examine in detail all facets of this encounter, educational, social and cultural.

The foremost duty of the shop steward is the negotiation of pay and conditions of work with management on behalf of his members. As already noted, industry-wide agreements usually lay down only minimum rates, leaving any adjustments to the parties at domestic level. Many industry agreements do not even mention some of the topics covered by plant bargaining. This situation leaves the typical shop steward with a wide range of bargaining to conduct on behalf of his members. This includes wage-related issues such as piece-work rates, bonus and incentive schemes, merit gradings and payment for work of an unsocial nature (dirt money); working conditions such as the distribution, pace and quality of work, machine-manning levels and transfers from one job to another; matters such as the level and distribution of overtime, breaks in working hours and stopping and starting times; disciplinary matters such as suspension and dismissal; and general employment issues such as redundancy and short-time working.[14]

It is easy to see that the duties of shop stewards have become extremely complex and will become increasingly so in the future. Stewards will only be able to cope adequately with the problems facing them if they are given sufficient education and training. Unfortunately, education and training facilities are far from adequate:

> . . . the provision of education and training for trade unionists tends to be rather sparse. Certainly this is true of education and training for shop stewards for which the vast majority of trade unions are not able to cater. Some university adult education departments, W.E.A. districts and technical colleges are working in this field but the shortage in the provision of funds often means that these bodies are not able to meet all the demands made upon them by industry and the trade unions.[15]

The C.I.R. in its Report 'Industrial Relations Training'[16] advocated, among other things, that employers should adopt a joint responsibility with trade unions for the training of shop stewards, and should contribute financially to the provision of training services. Good industrial relations could aid the efficiency of an enterprise and is therefore a management concern. Training should be related to the needs of the workplace. Industrial relations training should distinguish between 'union' subjects and 'industrial relations' subjects – between 'union' skills and 'industrial relations' skills.

The T.U.C. did not agree with these conclusions. It accused the C.I.R. Report of being 'management-oriented'. Responsibility for the education and training of shop stewards rested, said the T.U.C. Education Committee,[17] not with management but with the trade union movement. It denied the distinction made between 'union' subjects and skills and 'industrial relations' subjects and skills. Reliance on management interests, it alleged, led to:

Over-exaggeration of the argument for relating training to the actual circumstances of those being trained, leading to recommendations that the training of shop stewards should be totally related to the industrial relations situations of the individual enterprises in which they are employed, and organized mainly on an in-plant basis.[18]

Shop stewards, said the Education Committee, are union officers and as such their relationship with employers and management must always be influenced by union organization, rules and policies. Their training must be undertaken within these perspectives – not with individual company interests in mind. The T.U.C. could not accept that the Government's interest in trade union education should be vested in the Secretary of State for Employment. Shop steward education and training should continue to be developed on a co-operative basis between the trade union movement and the further education and adult education sectors of the public education service.

Whichever way the debate goes, one thing is certain. The demands made on shop stewards' abilities and skills will increase rather than decrease in the future. Education and training facilities are inadequate at present and will become even more so in future unless some major intervention – whether from unions, employers, the Government, or all three – is made to provide the facilities, and the finance, necessary to cope with the problem.

THE NATURE OF WORKPLACE BARGAINING

Allan Flanders, in his evidence to the Donovan Commission, stated that workplace bargaining was 'largely informal, largely fragmented and largely autonomous'. Informality arises from the fact that unwritten understandings and custom and practice hold sway at shop-floor level. Fragmentation is evidenced by different groups getting different concessions at different times. Autonomy is indicated by the lack of external controls on workplace bargaining. The growth of the shop steward movement was not the only reason for the development of workplace bargaining – there were other factors. These will be examined in the following pages.

Trade Unions

By their very nature trade unions could have little effective control over the shop-floor situation. Trade union officials, for example, are too few in number and the geographical area to be covered is too large. Even if there were enough officials they would still be hampered by multi-unionism in individual workplaces. Most committees, negotiating or consultative, have as members shop stewards from more than one union, severely hampering the official who only has authority over stewards from his own union. Most union branches are not based on workplaces but on geographical areas; this means that members attending branch meetings are representative of not one but several workplaces. In addition, branch meetings have very low attendance levels – the Donovan Commission stated that attendances were on average 'somewhat less than ten per cent' of branch membership.

All of these factors tend to militate against trade union control over workplace bargaining, making it virtually non-existent in the vast majority of undertakings and plants. Trade union officialdom still largely clings to the illusions of the formal system, but some have made efforts to meet changing conditions by recognizing shop stewards and their functions, and by providing facilities and training for them. Some effort must be undertaken to accommodate shop stewards within formal union structure if order is to be substituted for chaos in workplace bargaining but, argues the Donovan Commission, greater union discipline over stewards is not the answer: 'Trade union leaders do exercise discipline from time to time, but they cannot be industry's policemen. They are democratic leaders in organizations in which the seat of power has almost always been close to the members.'[19]

Employers' Associations
Employers' associations are the main participants in the charade of industry-wide bargaining. Before 1914 they could justifiably claim that the agreements which they negotiated with trade unions at industry level had industry-wide application – being relevant to the majority of concerns in their respective industries. This is not the case today. In most of private industry the rates negotiated at industry level are simply minima and the subjects covered do not apply to every workplace in the industry. Many of the subjects relevant to the individual workplace are not even mentioned at industry level; e.g. the rights, duties and responsibilities of those required to administer the agreement at plant level. However, employers still normally stay with their respective associations because of the other services and

advice they offer, although some large companies have found it necessary to leave because of the limitations imposed by industry-level agreements.

Management

Management has played a large part in the growth of workplace bargaining by its preference for informal agreements and tacit understandings with shop stewards and work-groups. Industry-wide agreements did not help matters. Rarely do the rates of payment for work to be performed apply throughout an entire industry. Usually different companies in the same industry use different machinery and different methods of working; naturally, this involves different rates of pay. As the industry-wide agreement is normally valid only where standardization exists throughout an industry, most individual plants and concerns have had to negotiate additional payments in excess of standard rates in order to reconcile production demands with the aspirations of their respective work-groups. As methods differ not only between one plant and another but also between one department and another, this has tended to create chaotic payment structures.

If this had been accomplished on a planned basis there would be fewer problems today. Unfortunately, managers in general tended to settle such matters on an *ad hoc*, informal basis with little or no thought for the repercussions on common rules and regulations in whichever industry they happened to be; and the shop stewards, concerned with short-term objectives, were happy to acquiesce. This can be illustrated by considering the question of overtime working. Overtime can often be both useful and necessary. It may be required, for example, to cover periods of excess demand, holiday coverage and the like. Industry-wide agreements normally lay down the rate or premium at which overtime working is to be remunerated. The formal system thus presents a picture of necessary, planned overtime being paid at common rates. But work-groups soon come to realize that overtime pay can give earnings well in excess of the basic wage; so they use various forms of pressure to maintain overtime levels. Management, by conceding to actual or threatened pressures, may then sacrifice common industry standards to avoid industrial strife and achieve more immediate objectives. Thus they tend to use overtime not in a planned, logical manner but simply as a means of giving an acceptable level of earnings to the workers involved.[20] Once an acceptable level is reached, it is maintained by dealing with shop stewards on the amount and allocation of overtime.

Management thinking has also hindered the containment of shop-floor bargaining within manageable proportions. For a long time managers have been preoccupied with the principle of 'joint consultation', which has been defined as '. . . . the means whereby management and employees may together consider, and where appropriate determine, matters affecting their joint or respective interests'.[21] This formal definition is somewhat at variance with reality because of the words '. . . and where appropriate determine . . .'. Professor Clegg's definition indicates the real nature of the subject: 'In joint consultation managers give information to representatives of their workers and discuss their plans with them but retain the sole responsibility for the final decision.'[22] The former definition indicates what joint consultation ought to be, the latter demonstrates what it is in practice.

Adherents of consultation saw it as distinct from the process of collective bargaining. Consultation required, it was felt, a 'unitary' view of enterprise – management and workers were part of a team which had as its common interest the good of the enterprise. Partnership and teamwork were therefore the hallmarks of joint consultation. Collective bargaining, on the other hand, required a 'two-sides' attitude – strong negotiators sought to wrest concessions from one another in the interests of those they represented. Conflict and compromise were the hallmarks of negotiation. Advocates of consultation therefore attempted to increase its scope – and limit or decrease the scope of collective bargaining. Joint consultation was accordingly advocated at the expense of workplace bargaining: 'Influenced as they were by a doctrine such as this, it is understandable that British personnel managers did not generally recognise the consequences of the growth of workplace bargaining.'[23] Since the 1950s joint consultation has been on the decline in this country – while workplace bargaining has been on the increase. However, joint consultation still has a wide *theoretical* acceptance by unions and employers, and to help close the gulf between advocates of consultation and advocates of negotiation the Industrial Relations Code of Practice advised:

Consultation and negotiation are closely related by distinct processes. Management and employee representatives should consider carefully how to link the two. It may often be advantageous for the same committee to cover both. Where there are separate bodies, systematic communication between those involved in the two processes is essential.[24]

Work-Groups

Shop stewards receive only formal authority from trade unions – where they are mentioned at all. Some unions issue credentials, others merely acknowledge the stewards, after workplace elections, by dealing with them. Many unions give both formal and implicit recognition. The authority which the shop steward wields in dealing with management, however, comes not from the union but from the 'work-group'. These are comprised of workers who have similar interests and aspirations with regard to their work. Workers in the same department may form groups for differing purposes, e.g. social and recreational, but they are properly termed work-groups by industrial relations commentators only insofar as they seek to affect terms and conditions of employment:

> In work-groups the task is the primary reason for the group's existence. The task affects the relation between people . . . work-groups engage in purely sociable behaviour such as jokes, games and gossip. The social relations formed involve only part of the personality and members may know little of one another's life outside. However an important part of the personality is involved, in that livelihood, career and identity depend on work, and there can be considerable intensity of feeling over both cooperative and competitive relationships.[25]

Elton Mayo and his researchers – in the Hawthorne Experiment – first noted the existence of the informal system of relationships in the workplace, as opposed to the formal structure of the company. More recently Argyle has stated: 'The group may have a different pattern of communication, incentive, leadership, or division of work from that officially laid down, because it suits the members better.'[26] What distinguishes one work-group from another is the particular values and norms created and maintained. Sometimes the steward may be able to lead concerted group action, at other times he may only be able to muster minimal support. A lot depends upon whether or not his aims accord with group values and norms. If they do not, the work-group may throw up an unofficial leader to take his place, going over the steward's head direct to management. Such cases are not unknown, but in general the shop steward will be sensitive enough to group feelings to know where his limits lie. A strong-minded and persuasive steward may be able to influence the group to some extent, but research by Lord McCarthy[27] shows that members do not by any means slavishly follow the lead of their stewards.

The shop steward is not the leader of a single work-group. Within a steward's constituency there may be an average of about sixty members.[28] But this membership may contain several work-groups. A study by Goodman and Whittingham[29] involving nineteen shop stewards in six different factories indicated that the median number of groups under each of the stewards was five – the mean average was three. One steward represented ten groups, another one nine. Thus it is correct to describe the shop steward as a leader of work-groups. A work-group may change its membership in differing circumstances, e.g. process and maintenance workers on shift may act together as a group but if reversion to daywork comes they may divide into separate groups. Again, fitters may form a definable work-group but when working in different departments they may identify with groups they are working beside. A work-group can often consist of men from different unions.

In view of the complexities of work-groups and their inter-relations with one another, it would be unrealistic to demand of shop stewards that they should exercise greater control over them. To even attempt recognition of work-groups in domestic bargaining structure would be an extremely difficult matter as groups can change their composition for different purposes. Goodman and Whittingham have suggested expanding the steward's role to bring him into a formalized plant bargaining structure; in doing so they anticipated the possible objections of full-time officials:

> ... many full-time officials are overworked and cater for thousands of members. . . . If they are to spend more time on the more important aspects of their job, they might be advised to delegate, where necessary and possible, responsibility to their stewards. This would overcome the problem of giving better service to their members, while being unable to persuade them to pay adequate union dues to provide it. . . . They (the members) would see the benefits of membership at first hand, rather than regarding trade unionism as something centred beyond, and remote from, their workplace.[30]

The Foreman

If management draws up the various agreements with the unions it is the foreman who is expected to implement the decisions of management at shop-floor level. Ostensibly this places him in a position of some importance, yet several factors have combined to detract from much of his formal authority. In the small concern he is in a position where he can influence relationships by personal dealings, but in large plants the process of bureaucratization makes this virtually impossible – instead he must conduct workplace relations through impersonal rules handed down from senior management levels.

The foreman is responsible for the day-to-day work of the shop floor, but increasingly in the large firm specialists have removed several areas from his control: 'Planning and costing, work study, systems for safeguarding the agreed rights of the labour force, all mean that men outside the foreman's control are vitally influencing the scope of his work and his freedom of action.'[31] Where joint consultative machinery exists, it largely serves to erode communication links between the foreman and shop stewards, as most consultative bodies do not include foremen. The foreman then usually hears of management decisions – when they have already been made – from the shop steward. Most grievance or disputes procedures include a reference to the foreman at their lower levels, but in practice managers often 'short-circuit' procedures by inviting the steward to discuss matters with them without going through the appropriate machinery. Stewards are often advised by their union: 'Don't try to jump over the foreman. Settle your grievances with him whenever possible. In any case never take anything over his head without keeping him informed. Good working relationships with the foreman strengthen a shop steward's hand not only in dealing directly with the foreman, but in raising issues with higher management.'[32] Regrettably, this advice is rarely taken.

Foremen are generally promoted from the shop floor but few will actually attain the ranks of senior management. This does not augur well for the future. It means that senior managers will have little conception of workplace feelings and needs. The foreman is in the front line of management and has a wealth of experience in shop-floor dealings. Therefore if top management continue to by-pass the foreman, they will be alienating a valuable pool of knowledge and experience. Workplace bargaining between managers and shop stewards has tended to relieve foremen of many of their former tasks, i.e. overtime allocation. But as management seek to wrest back some control over domestic bargaining, this will surely mean the return to the foreman of some of his former tasks. If this happens to any great degree foremen, whose training is inadequate at present, will desperately need industrial relations training to equip them for the tasks that lie ahead.

Custom and Practice

Even the most comprehensively drawn agreement cannot provide for each and every workplace situation. There are sure to be gaps and areas of ambiguity. Where the collective agreement, works rules and methods of working provide no answer, workers will tend to get on with the job in the manner they think fit – not necessarily the most efficient manner. Once they have habitually undertaken a certain course of action for a period of time, they may regard it as 'custom' based on 'practice' acknowledged by the workers concerned (the abbreviation C.&P. will be used to denote this in the following pages).

The main legitimators of C.&P. are managers – they may lay the basis of C.&P. either by errors of commission or errors of omission.[33] The foreman, being the level of management nearest the shop floor, may – sometimes quite unwittingly – play a major part in extending the contract of employment through C.&P. Where his authority is limited, he may openly make concessions – having few sanctions at his disposal, he may seek to offer inducements to the work force. On the other hand, he may simply acquiesce in the continuance of a particular practice only to find that workers come to regard it as 'customary'. Take the question of tea-breaks. If a particular contract of employment – whether through a collective agreement, company rules or *ad hoc* agreement – specifies only one tea-break per working period and the workers habitually take two, the second break can become C.&P. in the workers' eyes if the foreman does not stipulate to the contrary. Even where the contract of employment specifies a precise period, this could be exceeded in practice and over a period of time the lengthened break may be defended as C.&P. These are examples of errors of commission.

Errors of omission arise largely through either ignorance or negligence. Take once more the example of the exceeded tea-break. If a foreman is entirely ignorant of this abuse he may nonetheless find that by the time he is aware of it things may have gone too far;

workers will have grown accustomed to the excess period and defend it as C.&P. The same thing can happen where the foreman knows of the abuse and disapproves but does not make a determined effort to enforce the specified break – his negligence may be taken as assent in establishing the excess as C.&P. Most foremen would no doubt regard C.&P. as something to be blamed on the work force without realizing that some C.&P. can be contained within the regulations and rules of the plant. By errors of commission or omission the foreman becomes a kind of 'legislator' – extending employees' contractual rights to the point where they become 'new law'. As with courts of law, C.&P. has a hierarchy of precedent-making authority: 'The higher the manager who sets the precedent for C.&P., the greater its likelihood of becoming an established rule'.[34]

The levels of management above the foreman may therefore be said to play the crucial part in legitimizing C.&P. The departmental manager may perpetrate gross acts of commission or omission in the interest of peaceful relations without being aware of the broader implications of his actions for collective regulation. More senior levels of management, being further removed from the shop floor, may make similar interventions without considering the detailed implications of their actions on the shop floor. This partly explains the readiness of shop stewards to 'short-circuit' procedure in order to have questions considered by senior managers and not foremen or line managers. Professor Wedderburn observed that a court of law may be prepared to enforce a custom where a contract of employment is silent on the point raised, provided the custom is 'reasonable, certain and notorious.'[35] This means that certain C.&P. would not stand up in court; those unknown to managers could not meet the criterion of 'notorious'. Much C.&P. would not be considered 'reasonable'. However, legal arguments are unlikely to persuade workers to refrain from pursuing C.&P. Management, too, do not like to expose their plant C.&P. to the courts. The importance of C.&P. would probably even be denied by boards of companies who do not wish to give shareholders and the public at large the impression that they have lost certain areas of managerial control to C.&P. Certain areas of C.&P. could be eliminated by comprehensive plant agreements, but greater vigilance would be required from all levels of management to ensure that it did not re-emerge during the life of such agreements. Where C.&P. has predominated for a long period of time, it can prove costly for management to reassert authority over terms and conditions of employment. The productivity bargains entered into in the 1960s were in many cases no more than the buying out of established customs and practices. More sophisticated management communications systems can play an important part in preventing the establishment of certain practices where these have been due to management ignorance or negligence.

It is easy to postulate theories for resolving conflict between the formal and informal systems – it is difficult to apply them in practice. A major starting-point would be the admission by those involved in the formal institutions that they no longer hold a position of pre-eminence in collective bargaining. Comprehensive factory or plant agreements establishing the rights, responsibilities and facilities of those required to administer the informal system, together with procedures based on the realities of domestic bargaining, would help resolve much of the conflict. But the understanding and skills required to administer workplace bargaining will not follow simply from institutional changes – they must be striven for:

> In general, management and stewards have not yet come to terms with each other on the same durable basis that has been found for employer–union relations at higher levels, where the rights and obligations of the parties are reasonably well-defined and respected, and where this full mutual acceptance is accompanied by subtle understandings of relative bargaining strengths and bargaining needs. New skills have to be learned in the workplace, just as they had to be learned for collective bargaining at the national level. . . . Bargaining and conflict can no more be avoided here than at any other level of industrial relations. They can, however, be contained within the bounds of agreed institutions which facilitate more rational settlements, provided always that the necessary skills are acquired for operating them.[36]

Strikes and other Industrial Sanctions

No discussion of the processes of collective bargaining would be complete without some reference to what is frequently described as the 'English Sickness'. It is a common fallacy to think of Britain as a strike-prone country. While our strike record leaves much to be desired it is by no means the worst in the world. A good deal depends upon the way that strikes are recorded in terms of their effects. If one looks at strikes in terms of the number of stoppages then the U.S.A., for example, is better off than Britain because it has fewer stoppages in proportion to its work force. Again, fewer stoppages do not mean less financial damage to the economy – American stoppages, on average, last four times as long as British ones. The important fact is that, because of their outstanding productivity, America can 'carry' strikes in a way which we cannot.

Strikes must be evaluated in terms of the relevant collective bargaining system. In the United States, to take one example, collective agreements are drawn up at plant level. Much thought, preparation and negotiation go into the making of agreements. The final result is a detailed, comprehensive agreement appropriate to the nature of the particular plant. The agreement will last for a specified period – usually about two years – and will be legally enforceable. The parties normally agree that during the life of the agreement there shall be no resort to strikes or lock-outs over matters covered in the agreement. Rises in the cost of living during this period are covered by means of agreed 'escalator' clauses. When the agreement expires, massive strike action is often evident where the parties cannot agree over the terms of the next collective agreement. Nonetheless, there are several advantages in the American system. There are generally no stoppages during the period of the agreement. American managers can say with certainty what their wages bill will be for the specified period, with the qualification of the escalator clause. The American manager, therefore, possesses a great advantage over his British counterpart, viz. predictability.

In Britain a distinction is sometimes made between disputes of 'right' and disputes of 'interest'. Disputes of right are those concerned with the interpretation of industry-wide agreements and are commonest among white-collar workers. Disputes of interest concern claims for improvements in terms and conditions of employment within the workplace; these are generally the preoccupation of manual or 'blue-collar' workers. In the United States disputes of right sometimes arise but disputes of interest are kept to a minimum until the collective agreement expires. Disputes of right and interest often become confused in this country. This arises from the fact that most collective agreements in Britain are 'open-ended', i.e. they have no definite termination date. Therefore, unlike American workers, British workers tend to raise issues which go beyond interpretation and present challenges to existing collective agreements which ultimately require their re-negotiation, a re-negotiation which thus takes place in a haphazard, *ad hoc* manner.

Collective agreements in Britain, unlike American agreements, are not normally legally enforceable. Voluntary agreements are traditional, and resort to the courts happens only in rare cases. Even if the tradition was changed and the parties suddenly desired legally enforceable agreements, there would be many difficulties to be overcome. Most British agreements are too loose and rambling in form to be capable of legal enforcement. In order to avoid confusion between industry-wide and plant agreements, the parties involved would have to treat negotiations in a much more comprehensive and detailed manner. American unions normally draw up agreements with the help of lawyers and accountants. This is not the traditional way to negotiate in Britain but something of this nature would be required if legal enforceability was to become widespread. The question of responsibility for breaches of legally-binding agreements would raise more problems. Trade union officials nowadays have little or no authority over the average workplace. In the event of a breach, however, officials might be held responsible, even though they had no control over those who caused it. Perhaps the officials themselves would be required to discipline those causing the breach in order to avoid responsibility at law. Perhaps one has to look outside the law to effect an improvement. Maybe licensed worker participation holds out a more realistic prospect.

The system of collective bargaining in Britain affects the nature of the strike problem. The overwhelming majority of strikes in this country – some 95%[37] – are 'unofficial', i.e. they take place without prior union approval. They are also generally 'unconstitutional', i.e. they occur before the appropriate dispute procedure has been exhausted. This highlights both the lack of authority of the union leadership and the inadequacy of disputes procedures in general. The majority of official strikes result from the breakdown of negotiations about terms and conditions at industry level. The causes of unofficial strikes are more diverse. The Donovan Commission's summary of the evidence presented to it about the causes of unofficial strikes is instructive. It shows that 50% concern wages or working arrangements; rules and discipline account for 29%; redundancy, dismissal, suspension, etc. 15%; and demarcation disputes contribute 2·6%. Of 1,052 unofficial strikes examined, the closed shop accounted for only 29 stoppages.[38]

A decrease in the incidence of disputes can be greatly assisted by legal intervention which provides remedies which trade unionists can use instead of striking. Legislation has, since 1971, protected workers from unfair dismissal. The development of the law relating to unfair dismissal is traced in Chapter 5. Moreover, the 1975 Employment Protection Act now provides trade unionists with an entitlement to forward warning of redundancies and a legal obligation on employers to consult with trade unions on the issue of redundancies. This legislation is also outlined in Chapter 5. It should go some way towards reducing the number of stoppages arising from redundancy issues.

The strike weapon is not the only sanction which workers can apply. There are others which involve less hardship to workers but which may often prove just as damaging to employers as strikes. One such sanction is the work-to-rule; this a *literal* performance of the contract of employment. A bus-conductor, for example, may find a rule stating that he must ensure that all passengers are safely seated before he signals to the driver to move on. In practice, the conductor will meet this requirement by permitting waiting passengers to board, looking up and down the bus, then signalling to the driver when satisfied that all are seated. Where a work-to-rule applies the same conductor will show each passenger individually to his seat, return to the waiting passengers and repeat the process with each one. The inconvenience caused is obvious; and the bus company will suffer financially as prospective passengers will then seek other means of transport. The conductor is still doing his job and will therefore suffer no loss of wages – as he would have done in a strike situation.

Employees may institute a ban on overtime. Although their level of earnings will be reduced they still receive basic pay. But the employer suffers where he requires overtime working, for example, to meet urgent orders, progress maintenance work and cover holiday periods. The British miners' overtime ban (which eventually turned into strike action) of November, 1973, proved particularly devastating to industry and the country as a whole.

The term 'go-slow' is self-explanatory, although in practice it is often indistinguishable from a work-to-rule, at least in its effect – once again the workers still receive their basic pay.

Most employers find that a certain level of co-operation is required at the place of work to keep things running smoothly. But if workers use the sanction termed 'removal of co-operation' things will not run as smoothly, work will be performed only at a minimal level and good working relationships will suffer in the long run; necessary overtime will not be worked, although employees will still claim their basic pay.

The 'guerrilla' strike is what the term implies. It can come suddenly, without warning and, unlike some normal strikes, it cannot be provided for by management preparation. It may last for a few hours, a day, or an indefinite period. In practice, it tends to last no longer than a day, thus involving minimal loss of pay for the workers involved.

THE SEMANTICS OF COLLECTIVE BARGAINING

As the reader will find throughout this book, the language of industrial relations is a main source of conflict. Words used are so often contrastive and polar. Much of the language of collective bargaining and collective sanctions therefore is expressed in quasi-military terms. The 'guerilla' strike has already been mentioned. Unions and employers seek to 'outflank' and 'outmanoeuvre' one another. Unions and employers meet with their respective colleagues before negotiations, to discuss 'strategy' and 'tactics'. There is talk of 'closing ranks' in order to gain 'victory' or avoid 'defeat'. The title of the preceding section might equally well have been 'The Weapons of Industrial Warfare'.

David Wilson[39] criticizes the unqualified use of the term 'free collective bargaining' by trade unions. He notes that unions have been to the fore in demanding state intervention in collective bargaining – with the exception of the wages sector. He argues that free collective bargaining ultimately means the absence of restraints in the struggle between capital and labour, and points to what might happen but for state regulation. In agriculture, catering, retail distribution and clothing, the union presence is so slight that these might very well be areas of 'sweated' labour but for Government regulation. Only 10 million of the 22 million U.K. working population are in unions, therefore the non-unionized might fare very badly if collective bargaining were truly free. In some areas – dustmen, teachers and municipal busmen, for example – the basic freedom to bargain with one's employer is negated by industry-wide bargaining.

Plant bargaining, he observes, is anything but free. What happens is a topping up of basic rates and benefits already established at industry level. Rarely do unions face employers across the table with the freedom to talk on all aspects of the contract of employment. He sums up the results of free collective bargaining: 'It has given riches to the strong and left the weak to fend for themselves, and it has done little to redistribute the wealth of the country. Three-quarters of the wealth is still owned by a tenth of the population.'[40] These are strong words but they convey meanings as imprecise as that of 'free collective bargaining'. Few if any wage-earners can be considered rich; even those in possession of posts with lucrative salaries did not get there by means of collective bargaining but rather by the operation of market forces. The general point is made, however, that adherence to an imprecise term has channelled union energies in a limited direction. More, not less, state intervention is necessary to protect the interests of the low-paid and the unorganized (a subject which is developed in some detail in Chapter 5). Collective bargaining has lamentably failed to influence these important areas.

Underlying assumptions play a major role in the formulation of imprecise terms and concepts. V. L. Allen[41] notes this of attitudes concerning strikes. Many commentators, he states, employ terms and formulae for resolving the strike problem which have no basis in reality. He claims that they do so because of adherence to a belief in the 'harmony of interests' between employers and employees. The basis of this belief is that they have interests in common which make them collaborators in the production process. The underlying assumption is that there exists an ideal or norm of industrial harmony between workers and employers: differences between the parties are but temporary aberrations, deviations from the norm. This often leads to a blatant misuse of terms. The problem of whether conflict is structural or perceptual will be treated in later chapters since it is a recurring issue.

One explanation of strikes – used by some politicians and a few industrial relations practitioners – is that they are caused by 'agitators'. The truth is that, although agitators may 'agitate', they do not 'cause'. The argument that many strikes are caused by poor communications is often heard from those attempting to resolve strikes; these people are normally advocates of 'fact-finding'. But there is little evidence that strikes are caused by ignorance of the facts or, if some are so caused, that elucidation will persuade workers to desist from continuing strike action. There are those who recommend better welfare and more humane treatment for workers as a means of resolving strikes. Yet welfare, wages and equitable treatment have steadily improved over the past fifty years or so but strikes have increased. There are those who still advocate applying the law to cure strikes – in spite of the overwhelming evidence showing the futility of this course of action.

These and other beliefs have been held for some time. Strikes have not decreased, they have increased – but still these beliefs persist. Allen traces this to the belief in industrial harmony; in the 'organic unity' of industry. Allen argues that the basis of capitalist production produces irreconcilable antagonisms:

> Strike action shows every sign of being endemic to capitalism. It is an historical phenomenon which has persisted through radical changes in living standards . . . it has defied all prescribed solutions, both prophylactic and punitive. Its historical persistence and its universal characteristics question any assumption which treats strikes as aberrations of a temporary nature or which poses them as being responsive to remedial measures.[42]

Allen's case is cogently reasoned and deals a heavy blow at the beliefs of those who maintain that there are not two sides in industry, but rather a malfunctioning unity which can be cured some day. The basis of capitalist production is antagonistic, having as its essential feature two sets of people – employers and workers – with mutually irreconcilable interests. If this becomes widely acknowledged then the energies and abilities of industrial relations' practitioners can be more efficiently utilized in *containing* rather than *curing* industrial strife.

WIDER HORIZONS

The environment in which collective bargaining takes place is changing at a rapid rate in this country. New demands are being made on the skills and abilities of negotiators. It is interesting to observe the response of the T.U.C. to changed conditions. Where formerly the T.U.C. tended to emphasize the importance of wage increases and fringe benefits, they have now taken a more sophisticated approach. Growing unemployment during 1970/71 made them re-think the nature of their demands. They concluded that the problem could be solved to a large extent by calling for a shorter working week and longer holidays. These demands have not been pressed because of the preoccupation of the Government and the T.U.C. with an incomes policy, but the fact that they have been emphasized at all shows an increasing awareness of the need for changes in approach to meet the challenges of the future.

The T.U.C. stress the essentials of collective bargaining:

First, it is a joint activity: each side must recognise the other's right to be present on equal and independent terms. Second, its purpose is to identify the respective interests of those represented in the collective bargaining so that interests held in common can be accentuated and means can be found to reconcile those interests that conflict. Third, it results in the joint regulation of the work situation by establishing a framework of rules and practice to govern relationships between workpeople and management.[43]

They acknowledge the demands made upon negotiators and call for a greater amount of information to be made available about the establishments in which employees spend so much of their working lives. Their 'shopping-list' is very comprehensive, going far beyond what the Conservative Government thought necessary in their disclosure of information provisions. The T.U.C. list ranges from information about manpower utilization, finance, costs and profits to trading and merger plans and the incomes of directors.[44] Other important changes in the collective bargaining environment include increasing state intervention, equal pay for women workers and incomes policy – all of which will be discussed in a later chapter.

It is a depressing fact that with unemployment rising at the time of writing and with little prospect of any immediate decrease, one of the major bargaining issues is redundancy. Economic pressures are forcing unions and management to move into the issues of manpower utilization and job security, where bargaining tends to be 'protective' on the part of trade unions. Thus the economic situation may well hinder their attempts to explore those frontiers of bargaining that recent legislation has opened up. Unions are currently seeking agreement with employers on redeployment, retraining, and consultative processes to be adopted in the event of a redundancy situation.

It is difficult to assess what the long-term impact of Britain's membership of the E.E.C. will be on industrial relations in general and collective bargaining in particular. One estimation is that British unions will provide a reformist counter-balance to some of the more revolutionary tendencies in the labour movement in Europe. The inclusion of British unions is likely to lead to increased activity against the multi-national corporation. The involvement of British trade union officials in Europe may gradually persuade them of the advisability of operating within a comprehensive legal framework.[45]

Anthony Banks, Head of the Research Department of the A.U.E.W., welcomed the number of statutory regulations covering such matters as freedom of movement and social security rights of migrant workers, and equal pay for women workers. He anticipated greater links between unions in Britain and in Europe; and more action against multi-national corporations.[46] There would be, he claims, a greater use of the international strike, but for political reasons:

> This is because one can recognise political ideals and common political attitudes far more easily than one can recognise common industrial interests . . . the big difficulty for a trade union is establishing the necessary international solidarity . . . (which) depends on a belief in a community of interests. . . . The willingness of American and Canadian workers to support each other springs obviously from their similarity of social and economic conditions. It is also no mere coincidence that such advance steps in international action, international liaison, that we have had so far have taken place in the motor car industry.[47]

Campbell Balfour argued[48] that one of the major developments would be the closer combination of employers through institutions such as the multi-national corporation and the countervailing combination of the multi-national union activity – although he noted that this was still in the conference and policy discussion stage. There would be greater harmonization of law and practice in regard to participation and consultation, but the question of comparison between different systems of industrial relations was more complex:

> We cannot point to any industrial relations system . . . and say, 'We will follow that example and cure ourselves', for each has its strong and weak points. We should also remember that the German system, with its low strike figures and productive workers, may function because they are German, and not because of the system.[49]

There will undoubtedly be much greater contact between trade union officials in Britain and Europe. This will serve to raise questions of parity. Workers in Europe enjoy more statutory public holidays than their British counterparts, but the Government in Britain is not required to equalize statutory holidays in line with the rest of Europe – this will be left to the process of collective bargaining. However, European workers have much better fringe benefits than British workers, and pressures will inevitably be applied to British employers by the unions to remedy this situation – adding a large increase to the wages bill. Increased worker participation will mean increased burdens upon British workers' representatives. If they are given more opportunity to exert a decisive influence in the running of their respective companies, it does not necessarily follow that they will have the knowledge to take advantage of it. There will have to be more union officials and more union research undertaken so that British trade unionists are better able to communicate with their colleagues in Europe and co-ordinate multi-national union activity. Whether the process of change is slow or fast, it will have a profound effect on British industrial relations and on the practice and behaviour of those involved in the system.

4

The White-Collar Worker

The interface in nineteenth century industry was very obvious – the owner or boss and his workers. As industry grew in size and complexity, two things happened. The boss found it increasingly difficult to control all the operations; and he found it necessary to appoint someone to carry out some of his functions. Hence the rise of the managerial type. As industry became more complex, other functions arose not directly related to purchase, production, sales and distribution. If a firm was to stay in business, there was a need to develop new products or new markets. The skills needed to perform these jobs were not manual but analytical. They called for research chemists, design engineers, market researchers and economists. As technology became ever more sophisticated and computers replaced wages clerks, so whole new Management Services departments burgeoned and flourished. All large firms today will have a whole range of functions concerned with accounting, personnel, investment appraisal and forward planning, technical groups and work-study departments. One way of describing these departments is to refer to them as the overheads. In modern capital-intensive industries they employ an ever-increasing proportion of the work force.

The significant feature about the emergence of the new class of managers and the new class of employees to apply the sophisticated analytical skills was that staff people now appeared on the scene. These people no more owned the factory than did those employed on the shop floor. They were, however, given more favourable terms and conditions of employment. Most importantly they were given more security. They were on a month's or three months' notice as opposed to a week or a day. They were paid a monthly salary, not a weekly wage or an hourly rate. They had more security when off sick. They tended to be recruited from the middle class, or the lower middle class.

Their status needs were more adequately met. They did not have to clock in. Tea breaks were not scrupulously timed but taken to suit the work situation. Supervision, even of junior clerical staff, was much lighter. Holidays could be taken at discretion, not just during the first fortnight of August. Given such preferential treatment, the 'white-collar workers' as they subsequently came to be called, not unnaturally identified themselves with the managerial class. They were bosses' men, in no need of unions to protect them from exploitation. Workers saw them as part of 'them' rather than of 'us'.

The situation now, of course, has changed dramatically. The fastest growing unions in Europe are the white-collar ones. In Sweden, one of the countries frequently held out as a paragon of good industrial relations, 70% of white-collar workers are unionized. Many factors have produced the change. Shop floor workers, with their greater opportunities for overtime working, incentive schemes and piece-work rates, together with successful bargaining by unions, were able to earn more money than many of the lower paid staff. And manual workers on contract work, for instance, were able to earn almost astronomical amounts. Staff still felt, though, that they had the advantage with their pensions, or sickness schemes, which allowed pay whilst off work, or more generous holiday entitlement. In time, however, as more and more shop floor workers were given these privileges ('rights' they started to call them, 'privileges' smacking too much of feudalism), differentials became harder to discern. As many firms abolished clocking, and the modern petrochemical plants started recruiting to their new refineries shop floor workers as 'staff', perhaps the privilege of coming to work in a collar and tie was not that important after all. Paragraph 42 of the Code of Practice which accompanied the Conservative Government's Industrial Relations Act 1971 recommended:

Differences in the conditions of employment and status of different categories of employee and in the facilities available to them should be based on the requirements of the job. The aim should be progressively to reduce and ultimately to remove differences which are not so based.

And in its first general report the Commission on Industrial Relations stated:

We have expressed the view in a number of our reports that the principles of organisation and collective bargaining are just as applicable to white-collar employees as to manual employees, though the forms of organisation and the procedures may need to be adapted to suit the special interests of the groups concerned.

With the growth of mergers and the closing down of obsolete plants (and obsolescence was now something which took place within a decade rather than a generation), staff became vulnerable to dismissal. That last prop, their security, was pulled away from them. A few firms are now fighting a rearguard action to preserve the distinction between staff and shop floor, hoping to negotiate individual contracts with the former, whilst resigned to collective bargaining for the latter.

What is important for the student of industrial relations to be aware of is that behaviour can be as much a function of environment as genetics. It has been interesting to take part in the establishment of productivity agreements. When managers are asked by some consultant what they hope to get out of the agreement, they often say *inter alia* 'staff attitudes'. The assumption behind such a statement is that there are two breeds of men, one designated 'staff' and the other 'shop floor'. Staff stand for everything that is noble and responsible, shop floor for everything that is devious and reactionary. Evidence in support is that staff can be trusted, they do not need supervising, they do not automatically put their hand out when they are asked to work overtime, they do not cavil about doing different jobs, they are work-oriented. Some managers, one would gather, believe it is ordained in the stars and there is little one can do about it.

One of the purposes of this book is to indicate that people respond in many ways according to the expectations held of them. We make quite arbitrary distinctions between staff and shop floor. One of the reasons why shop floor workers have always put out their hand when extra work is requested from them is that that has been the nature of the contract that management has made with them. What else does 'a fair day's pay for a fair day's work' mean? If shop floor have been given less job security than staff, it is not altogether surprising that they haggle over demarcation disputes which affect what they see as their bread and butter. The only property they own is their labour and skill. Why see it eroded? If, as a result of scientific management and job simplification, the job has been broken down into such a ludicrously simple module that a moron can do it (and there are many such jobs in British industry), it is not altogether surprising not to find a shop floor man work-oriented. If in the nature of things, with limited education and skill, opportunities for promotion and advancement are remote – and in British industry not many shop floor workers go beyond the rank of foremen – even the over-emphasized 'prospects' are not a very enticing bait.

It is amazing how quickly people learn to respond to expectations. The process can be seen at school. Pupils in the 'A' stream enjoy high expectations from their teachers. Pupils in 'C' streams are told that it's not their fault, not being very bright; they are not expected to get more than, say, 2 GCE 'O' levels. Invariably that is the level to which they perform. It is interesting to compare the results of 'A' streams in secondary modern schools with 'C' streams in grammar schools in the GCE, which show that the former achieve better examination results. One of the reasons is that the secondary modern pupils get the brightest teachers who continually urge their students on; the grammar school 'C' stream students get the teachers who are in transit and who have low expectations. A self-fulfilling prophecy soon becomes established.

So it is in industry. Staff behave responsibly not because they are genetically different but largely because different expectations are held of them. A good deal of nonsense is talked about 'staff attitudes' in any case. Commentators tend to refer to their positive virtues. Staff can be just as ingenious at manipulating their entertainment or travel allowances (combining business with pleasure) as workers at manipulating the work-study incentive scheme. And for every shop-floor worker who wheedles sick notes from his overworked doctor, there are many who have not had a day off in twenty years' service with their company. For the many workers who are late starters, there are many shift workers who make a practice of relieving their mates twenty minutes early for them to catch buses home. What bedevils much of the industrial relations scene, particularly for outside observers, is the tendency to rely on stereotypes.

It is not difficult for a self-fulfilling prophecy to become established. 'You can't get anything out of Johnny', says teacher. Nothing is got out of Johnny. 'You will not get those men to work on a Saturday afternoon', says the foremen, and they don't. 'I told you so!' is the triumphant answer. But the gifted teacher does get something out of

Johnny and the good foreman can get a higher output from his men. That is the art of good teaching or good management, and what makes both skills so extraordinarily difficult.

WHAT IS A WHITE-COLLAR WORKER?

To state that the arbitrary distinctions between manual and non-manual workers are being held up for questioning and analysis does not mean that all differentials have disappeared, nor that it does not help to distinguish between white-collar and blue-collar workers. Although they both belong to the species *homo sapiens*, their history, development and needs are different.

Terminology can be a problem. The pairs of terms 'manual and non-manual', 'works and staff', 'blue-collar and white-collar', have commonly been regarded as synonymous. But many jobs have both manual and non-manual aspects. As we have seen, many firms are treating all workers as 'staff'. What separates people is perhaps occupational category. The following categories have come to be recognized as white-collar workers: administrators, managers, supervisors, scientists, technologists, technicians, laboratory staff, draughtsmen, artists, musicians, the professions (teachers, doctors, accountants, lawyers etc.), clerical and administrative workers, computer programmers, shop assistants, salesmen.

In this chapter they will be referred to as white-collar workers. Some important facts need to be stated about them. Whereas they constituted only 8 per cent of the labour force in the U.K. in 1907 and in 1966 represented only 24 per cent, the proportion has been rapidly increasing and in 1974 accounted for about 40 per cent of the total labour force, of which women made up about 46 per cent. Already in the United States white-collar workers outnumber blue-collar workers. It is estimated that by about 1985 over 50 per cent of the U.K. work force will be white-collar. The degree of unionization amongst white-collar workers is still less than among manual workers. In Britain in 1970 only three out of ten white-collar workers belonged to a union whereas five out of ten manual workers were members. Membership of white-collar unions had increased from 2,623,000 in 1964 to 3,531,000 in 1970, which represented an increase of from 30 per cent to 37 per cent of all trade unionists. A conservative estimate would now put the proportion at 40 per cent. Figures for other comparable countries are interesting. Although in the United States white-collar workers outnumber blue-collar workers, only 13 per cent are unionized compared with 56 per cent of manual workers. In Germany white-collar workers are 24 per cent unionized as compared to 42 per cent manual; in Australia 30 per cent as compared to 81 per cent; in Norway 58 per cent as compared to 65 per cent; and in Sweden 70 per cent as compared to 80 per cent.[1]

One of the theories advanced for the relative slowness of growth in white-collar unionism, though the position is fast changing, is based on the different positions of white-collar and manual workers within the social stratification system. A detailed analysis of this thesis appears in *Social Stratification and Trade Unionism* by Bain, Coates and Ellis.[2] Many determinants of growth have been suggested, and some of them will be touched on in this chapter. Social stratification would tend to assume the need for identification with the boss class expressed in terms of nature of work, place of work, type of payment, type of dress worn, and educational background. Where some of these characteristics are less marked in other countries, e.g. in Sweden where there is a common educational system and in the United States where there is far more upward social mobility, one needs to look to other factors. These may include the standardization of the work situation, the erosion of the personal quality of the manager/managed relationship, and the reduction of promotion prospects. As we argue later, there is no single cause affecting the growth of white-collar unionism. The causes are various, and they differ considerably from country to country.

This growth has taken place during a period of decline in union membership in some of the basic industries such as mining, the railways, textiles. Such a change of membership has implications for the Trade Union movement.

The distribution of white-collar unions is very uneven. The proportion of white-collar unionism in the public sector of the economy is over 80 per cent, whereas in the private sector it is not much over 10 per cent. There are wide variations of union membership within the same occupational group in different industries – e.g. draughtsmen are 80 per cent unionized in vehicles, only 50 per cent in engineering and less than 6 per cent in chemicals.[3] There is also a tendency for craft unions and general and largely manual unions to develop white-collar sections, sometimes at the expense of exclusive white-collar unions.

It is moreover a fast-changing field. Diversification, merger and takeover are more common than in the blue-collar field. Many unions were once more specialized than they are now. The Clerical and Administrative Workers Union (C.A.W.U.) initially set out to cater for clerks; the Association of Scientific Workers for scientific workers; A.S.S.E.T. for supervisors and technicians. A.S.S.E.T. and A.S.C.W. merged to form the Association of Scientific Technical and Managerial Staffs (A.S.T.M.S.) and even extended its influence to embrace the Prudential Staff Association. The C.A.W.U. broadened its scope to become the Association of Professional, Executive, Clerical and Computer Staff (A.P.E.X.). Other unions prefer to represent staff in one particular industry, e.g. the Civil Service Unions, the National Union of Journalists, the National Union of Bank Employees, and N.A.L.G.O. In the mid-sixties N.A.L.G.O. changed its name from the National Association of Local Government Officers to the National and Local Government Officers Association, suggesting that the union was anxious to extend its recruitment activities.

White-collar unionism is frequently taken to include not only trade unions but staff associations and professional associations. Staff associations are bodies which exist to further the interests of their members, but are not autonomous self-contained unions, being largely dependent on the goodwill and financial assistance of the employer. They are internal bodies who have relations with only one employer. Apart from the Bank Staff Associations, they do not have relationships with the trade unions, with other staff associations, or with the Government. Because they are confined to one employer, they can offer no continuity of membership if an employee chooses to change his employment. Nor are they in a position to offer the kind of benefits such unions as, for example, N.A.L.G.O. provide (insurance coverage, legal advice, discount facilities, holiday service, a benevolent fund, building society arrangements). One major difference is that basically they accept the legitimacy of the power structure. They have no desire to change it. Employees who see themselves coming from the same social class as the managerial class are more prone to join staff associations. This is a problem which N.U.B.E. faces (who represent about 40 per cent of bank employees) because of the individual's perceived social status, characteristic of banking, compared with, say, railway clerks who have a low status classification and solidly support the Transport Salaried Staffs Association (T.S.S.A.).

Professional associations are primarily concerned with the need to protect and advance the standing of their profession to promote learning, to enhance its esteem, to ensure high levels of competence and standards of conduct. They are much more exclusive than manual unions in admitting people to membership. (A classic example of a restrictive practice is the right of barristers to appear as advocates in higher courts to the exclusion of solicitors.) They also attempt to exercise influence over terms and conditions of employment – in the form of minimum fees that qualified practitioners should be prepared to accept. Some professional associations, such as the British Medical Association, have exercised a negotiating function for their members, but most professional associations accept the claims to legitimacy of employers and are more concerned in resisting attempts to require their members to act unprofessionally or efforts to dilute the profession.

The B.M.A. is perhaps a little unusual in that the Government is effectively the employer of its members. Although the B.M.A. is obviously concerned with its status and professional standing through the sponsorship of scientific activities, it made unmistakably clear its other role in collective bargaining and joint consultation when, at its 1970 assembly, it passed a resolution stating 'the cardinal function of the B.M.A. is the negotiation of satisfactory terms and conditions of service for its members'. Nor has it hesitated to use militant action when it has felt its vital interests to be threatened. Like the miners, the doctors are in a monopoly position, controlling services essential for the well-being of the community, and therefore able to exploit their position in a more powerful way than, for example, teachers can.

REASONS FOR GROWTH

Let us now look more closely at the growth of white-collar unions, the factors that have encouraged it and the attempts which have been made to discourage it.

G. F. Bain identified four factors which led to increased white-collar unionism. One of the most potent, as we argue in this chapter, has been Government influence and legislation, starting with the Whitley Committee (set up in 1916 during the First World War to help forestall the industrial unrest that it was felt would occur in the post-war period). The Whitley Committee was asked to make recommendations 'for securing a permanent improvement in the relations between employers and workmen' and concluded that an essential condition was an 'adequate organisation on the part of both employers and workpeople'. It therefore recommended the establishment of joint industrial councils representing both trade unions and employers' associations to give regular consideration to workers' problems. This recommendation the Government accepted. As Henry Clay observed in his book *The Problem of Industrial Relations*: 'Whitleyism constituted a public and official recognition of trade unionism and collective bargaining as the basis of industrial relations that is perhaps surprising, when it is recollected that large groups of employers were still refusing to recognize the unions when the war broke out'.[4]

Conspicuously in this period the N.U.J. were recognized by the Newspaper Proprietors Association (1917), and the Engineering Employers Federation recognized C.A.W.U. (1920) and D.A.T.A. (1924).* The period was a short one. As economic depression descended, with falling wages and high unemployment, trade union membership declined and employers became tougher. After the recognition of D.A.T.A. in 1924, fifteen years elapsed before another major private employer was to concede recognition to a white-collar union.[5]

Even the Conservative Government's much despised Industrial Relations Act 1971 and the Code of Practice, by establishing that all employees had equal legal rights to join a trade union if they wished, made no differentiation between the rights of white-collar and blue-collar workers with regard to union membership, and thus acted as a spur to white-collar unions. The pamphlet of the Commission on Industrial Relations – Study No. 3 'Recognition of White-Collar Unions in Engineering and Chemicals' – urges management to produce policies to cope with the upsurge in white-collar unionism.

The other three factors noted by Bain were: that membership was higher when there was a greater concentration of employment; that sociologists claim bureaucratization to have encouraged it; but, perhaps most significant of all, that membership grew whenever employers recognized it.[6]

Employers' recognition has not always been easy to come by. His survey of employers reveal some interesting answers and assumptions. Some typical replies are recorded below:

* D.A.T.A. was known until 1961 as the Association of Shipbuilding and Engineering Draughtsmen (A.E.S.D.).

Every possible step is taken to ensure that staff do not reach the frame of mind which will make them think that membership of a union is appropriate.

Management's freedom to act without consultation in areas previously regarded as management's prerogative is restricted.

We regard our staff as being members of 'The Family'. There is no need for them to be represented by a union.

We already have a Staff Committee which provides the necessary facilities for staff to make their views known.

I do not see how management or a part of management such as foremen can be part of an anti-management organisation such as a trade union and still be an effective member of the management team.

And as the C.I.R. record in their pamphlet: 'Many employers, when faced with a claim for recognition feel they are to blame, that they have in some way failed and that the claim represents a vote of no confidence in them by their white-collar employees.'

The assumption behind such management statements as 'that a trade unionist's loyalties are to his union rather than the organization for which he works' requires further analysis. A nurse's first loyalty is to her patient, a Civil Servant's to the Service, and it is only at times of extreme provocation and when this primary loyalty is felt to be exploited that it is temporarily transferred to the union. It is neither permanent nor unthinking.

At first sight it is somewhat paradoxical that companies who for years have encouraged their hourly-paid employees to join appropriate blue-collar unions, because of their advantages in dealing with people who can speak with authority for all employees in a certain category, should take a contrary view when it comes to their white-collar workers.

There is no gainsaying the steps which management have resorted to in order to discourage union membership, either through forms of bribery (increased benefits during union drives) or threats (lack of promotion) or the establishment of staff committees or, if must be, Staff Associations.

One of the most formidable devices for discouraging staff unionism was the Foremen and Staff Mutual Benefit Society. The Engineering Employers Federation and the Shipbuilding Employers Federation encouraged member firms to join F.S.M.B.S. The F.S.M.B.S. is a friendly society, founded in 1899, and had as its purpose the provision of pensions, sickness benefits and life insurance to all foremen and like grades of staff in the shipbuilding and engineering industries. The Society had two kinds of members – employers and ordinary members. The employers paid at least half of the total contributions of each ordinary member.

The Society used to have a rule stating that an ordinary member may not belong to a trade union. So if a foreman wished to join, he had first to relinquish his union membership. Alternatively, if he wished to join a trade union after he had become a Society member, he had to resign from the Society, in which case he forfeited his claim to the contributions which his employer had made on his behalf.[7]

Even an enlightened company in the chemical industry in 1973, balloting its members about their views on white-collar staff unionization, felt obliged to circulate a confidential memorandum to heads of departments saying that it saw staff unionization 'as an unhelpful development' because unions for white-collar workers 'fundamentally do not share the company's interests and objectives'.

It is perhaps worth examining the attitudes and fears which lie behind such statements – 'challenging management's prerogative', 'can be part of an anti-management organisation such as a trade union', 'equivalent to a vote of no confidence in management'.

It is true that industry can never be administered solely in the interests of its employees and therefore conflict is inherent in any industrial organization. But can it honestly be said that unions such as N.A.L.G.O. who have a vertical membership, embracing a hierarchy of grades (which in many ways militates against hasty and militant action), are anti-management? Or can the same be alleged against the Civil and Public Services Association, who are very conscious of their image as public servants? The challenge to 'managerial prerogative' is, as we have argued elsewhere in this book, a phenomenon not confined to those people who are unionized but part of a world-wide movement against all authority systems, secular or religious.

Staff unionism has arisen, as we have suggested, in many cases as a result of changes management have made in their individual contract with their employees. It is all very well maintaining that unions are superfluous because of personal treatment. But the movement has been away from the private office to the open plan and the typing pool, to larger groups, to computerized operations, to reduced promotion prospects, to (perhaps unwittingly) a wider gap between employees and boss. How can you talk of loyalty to your boss when you rarely see him? The process of bureaucratization (the drift from personalization to standardization) encourages the growth of unionism, and a vicious circle sets in, since unionism, through its demands for even treatment and more formal channels of communication, further increases the trend towards bureaucratization. In its desire to help the weakest, unionism can easily encourage the lowest common denominator! The emphasis is on the role rather than the occupant. Reward becomes related not to performance but to job grade and position in the hierarchy. Salary levels are not an outcome of a personal discussion with your boss but rationally assigned by a remote authority. One of the grievances sometimes expressed by managers in the public sector is that whether the employee merely does sufficient to get by or performs superbly, if he is on the same job grade, he gets the same amount of money. Even the pace of his progress is determined by nationally determined annual increments. There is no process that allows the 'high flyer' to progress faster through the grades. Monetary reward can only come through promotion to a higher grade.

As one of Bain's respondents put it:

> The real disadvantage is that any minimum scale of salaries and conditions tends to destroy incentive, initiative and ability, and can result in levelling down. . . . We feel strongly that although we would recognise a staff union if it is the wish of the majority of the staff – we would not negotiate over salaries of staff as such negotiations might well lead to the underpayment of the efficient and the overpayment of the inefficient.[8]

Unionism, it must be admitted, does limit management's capacity to interchange staff with quite the same freedom; it sometimes affects management's capacity to recruit what they regard as the best staff. The Civil Service does not normally recruit for its posts on the open market: promotion is from within. It would be difficult, however, to prove that the Civil Service is worse served than other parts of the public sector, such as local government, where posts are put out to advertisement.

Employers like to believe that employee loyalty is unitary – to themselves – so that membership of a union must produce a conflict of loyalty. But if, as a result of mergers, takeovers or technological change, redundancy or changed occupation become the fashion rather than the exception (and experience tells us that few jobs in the future are going to provide a lifetime's work), what use is unitary loyalty to a company when the employee is out of a job?

Another employer objection is that unions are so politically motivated as to be disruptive. It is true that many white-collar unions are affiliated to the T.U.C., some of these unions pay a political levy which sustains the Labour Party, and the Labour Party is pledged to an extension of nationalization. Two points need to be made. One: public sector industries still have to be managed. Two: many of the white-collar unions do not fully subscribe to the political levy. Under the Trade Disputes and Trade Union Act 1946, union members were able to contract out of paying the political levy, and at the end of 1969, 20·3 per cent of members were contracted out. Many white-collar unions e.g. N.U.B.E., N.A.L.G.O., C.P.S.A., do not establish political funds. T.S.S.A. is one of the few white-collar unions which sponsors Parliamentary candidates. Even in a union as allegedly militant as A.S.T.M.S., as many as 44 per cent of its members have contracted out of paying the political levy. White-collar unions are also much less prone to unofficial action, being far more disciplined in honouring agreements.[9]

Employer opposition to white-collar unionism moreover overlooks some of the differences that separate white-collar and blue-collar workers, and even some of the sectional interests present within the white-collar unions themselves. A.S.T.M.S. makes no secret of its claim to maintain differentials even though such a policy goes against contemporary Government thinking. Not many people like to see an erosion of what they have come to take for granted, be it the divine right of Kings, managerial prerogative or superior working conditions. Those white-collar workers who espouse socialism have mixed feelings about the narrowing of differentials. They fear management are having it both ways by assuring them at one moment that they cannot have as large a pay increase as their hourly-paid counterparts because their holidays are longer, and by then increasing the holidays of manual workers to white-collar levels, telling them that this is a natural and progressive change. White-collar workers' feelings towards blue-collar workers vary from envy to slight aloofness deriving from what they feel are their more professional standards and attitudes.

There is a pecking order within the unions themselves. Higher grade employees often form their own separate unions, such as the British Association of Colliery Management; whilst within N.A.L.G.O. the Society of Town Clerks and the Association of Local Government Finance Officers are almost autonomous for negotiating purposes. Membership of a union does not imply lack of loyalty to the objectives of the employing organization. In the case of white-collar workers the amount of responsibility they hold, the interest and pride they maintain in their work, are sufficient safeguards against anti-management action. But if their fundamental security is threatened through technological change or any other cause, they tend to behave like any group similarly situated.[10]

Firms must expect the trend to grow. Even possible Common Market legislation makes it more likely. The critical question firms need to ask themselves is under what terms do they wish to meet the challenge – as a rearguard action, fighting every inch of the way and thereby building up resentment, or with a reasonably open approach, neither pushing employees into it against their will nor putting inordinate obstacles in their way, but satisfying themselves about the appropriateness of the union, since there can be considerable competition for members amongst unions? Consultative Committees, which have been one way in which firms have allowed staff a safety valve for airing their discontents, are unlikely to bear the weight of future demands. Staff unions are pushing out the boundaries of what is negotiable, including such matters as pensions, sabbatical leave for long service employees, improved allowances for travel. Most consultative committees have very restricted terms of reference as to what may be *discussed*, let alone negotiated. They do not usually allow for negotiation rights as their name implies.

One of management's main fears is that recognition of a staff union encroaches on that diminishing area of unilateral decision-making. If the movement towards unionism is to grow, however, is it not better for it to be through ordered systems and procedures?

WOMEN AND THE WHITE-COLLAR UNIONS

As women form 46 per cent of white-collar workers and as they move towards equal pay and opportunity with the implementation of the Equal Pay Act and the Sex Discrimination Act, will they adopt a more positive attitude towards staff unionism than they have up till now? The statistics of female labour are well known. In the tobacco industry, for instance, they form 60 per cent of the labour force, but only 20 per cent of the supervision and less than 5 per cent of management. This is a function of much higher turnover for women, lack of comparable training facilities and education, and differing attitudes to work because of their dual role. It is tempting to think that equal pay and equal opportunity will change matters, but it is worth looking at women's attitudes to the manager/managed relationship, and to their felt need for a trade union to support their position. An interesting study carried out in a chemical company by the Tavistock Institute of Human Relations highlighted this difference between men and women.

The study was designed to investigate white-collar workers' attitudes to staff representation in a large company which at the time of the study only made provision through the medium of Staff Committees. By means of a very comprehensive questionnaire, staff were asked whether they wished their interests to be promoted through the medium of improved staff committee machinery, through a staff association, or by trade union representation. The questionnaire explored staff's attitudes to the three systems. The results were analysed in such a way as to differentiate between male and female response.

The study took various groupings of junior and senior staff. Males employed in scientific work, research and laboratory assistants showed a majority in favour of granting the trade unions bargaining rights. Female staff in the same group showed an entirely opposite trend, favouring improving the Staff Committee procedure. In addition, the questionnaire showed them antagonistic to the option of trade union representation. A similar pattern showed itself for junior engineering and technical staff. The scores in favour of improving Staff Committees and rejecting trade union representation were heaviest of all in the clerical, administrative and commercial grades, where numerically women were most heavily represented. The response of the women in these grades seemed to be totally irrespective of job, whereas with the men, the option they chose was related to occupation; this suggests that some sex factor was operating.

Many women do have different expectations from work – they want an income and to get out of the house for a while – but they are frequently not so committed to work that they feel trapped and bored as many men do. Work is not a central life interest. Many employers with part-time labour have a much more flexible attitude towards the work force, organizing the work round them rather than fitting them to the work.

One should not attempt to derive too much from such a study but it does reveal a major discrepancy between men and women in their ideas about staff representation. Is it that women prefer to conceal their views? Do they dislike being organized? Do they prefer a more individual contract in the manager/managed relationship?

Another interesting statistic the study threw up contradicts the common assumption that young people are much more radical and therefore would be strongest supporters of the trade union option. The responses were the contrary. The trade union alternative was most popular amongst the 40–49-year-olds and least popular amongst those up to 19 years of age.

THE FUTURE

What is the way ahead? As always, a number of factors need to be taken into account. The movement towards single status is likely to continue. There will still be employees who are resistant to narrowing of differentials and some unions, despite their overall desire to maintain equality of treatment for their members, are willing to go along with maintaining differentials. The sensible way is to maintain those differentials which make sense – such as letting a salesman have a car and a reasonable expense allowance and more flexible hours of working, conditions which would be totally inappropriate for a fitter. But there is no need to maintain clocking unnecessarily and there is little rationale in making distinctions in sick-pay cover, holiday entitlement or pensions. As one junior member of staff of a chemical company remarked when he had problems of housing (a matter with which senior staff received some assistance): 'We're just not supposed to have domestic problems at our level.'

The evidence is that the narrowing of the gap over these differentials is best effected gradually. The exercise needs to be carefully costed. There is little point in a company's adopting such a scheme if it bankrupts itself in the process. On the matter of staff unionism, just as the Industrial Relations Act proved ineffective in achieving its ends, so legislation commanding no widespread support which forces white-collar workers, hostile to unions, into unions would be likely to prove counter-productive. People not committed can find ways of defeating the system.

Again, one detects a difference between the 'shop floor' view and that of the union official. In an issue of the Industrial Society Journal the executive secretary of the Association of Professional Executive, Clerical and Computer Staff (A.P.E.X.) asserts:

What the unions are after is nothing short of democratisation of a part of industry which on too many occasions, has shown an unacceptable face in dealing with its employees. . . . The union has also tried to transform the power structures and decision-taking processes inside companies.[11]

One suspects that, as with blue-collar workers, the white-collar workers' main interest is that expressed by the shop stewards employed by contractors working on the Shell Stanlow site. When interviewed about union involvement in managerial prerogative, most of the shop stewards insisted that 'we do not want to tell management how to run their business. All we want is to be consulted over issues which concern us'. The most immediate issues which concerned them, and in which they sought involvement, were the recruitment and selection of staff and matters of redundancy. With white-collar workers the issues may be more concerned with promotion prospects, travel allowances and such matters. Central to the issue of involvement is a point that we have discussed earlier, namely whether an industrial organization is to be considered as a unitary system or a pluralistic one. The unitary system sees the firm as having one source of authority and one focus of loyalty; the other sees the firm as a pluralistic society containing many separate interests and objectives (and therefore conflict as endemic). Management's attitude towards white-collar workers has been within a unitary rather than a pluralistic frame of reference. But changing to a wider frame should not be regarded as a first step towards a palace revolution. As we argue in Chapter 9 on Industrial Democracy, it is, significantly, the politicians and the professional trade unionists who see it as a form of social control. The worker on the floor or the technician in the laboratory are more concerned with exercising some influence over those areas which most immediately affect them.

It is possibly a mistake to see white-collar unionism as something separate and distinct from other forms of unionism; once organized their demands are much the same. Maybe the differences are those of degree, not kind. It is not necessarily a matter of class or status or

93

prestige. Some high prestige occupational groups such as airline pilots and musicians are highly organized. Nor is it accurate to make a clear-cut distinction even between professional associations and unions, although the popular image is of one group concerned with the pursuit of status of the profession, the promotion of specific subjects of study, and qualifying the competent, and the other solely interested in promoting the economic interests of its members; trade unions and professional associations are both concerned with job regulation (they both try to shape the rules by which their members work), though one does it by unilateral regulation and the other by collective bargaining.

Growth of white-collar unionism, as Bain argues, follows the same lines as other forms of unionism; it not only enables them to represent their members, but also equips unions with power over them. When unions become institutionalized, membership ceases to be small and selective, and becomes large. Other forces start to operate. Unionism remains no longer a voluntary system of individuals who choose to conform. Rather conformity becomes obligatory, either through social pressures (custom and practice or subtle forms of coercion) or even by quasi-legal coercion through the operation of a closed shop. Given a free situation there are some manual workers who would elect not to join a union. Some employers may feel they are genuinely protecting and preserving the individual freedom of their staff by keeping them from such a fate. If the individual contract which they have cultivated over the years persists, it may be that, given freedom of choice, individuals will elect not to join unions. Technological and other forces are making the individual and personal relationship more difficult to sustain. If the move to unionism grows, better industrial relations are more likely to ensue if management responds positively than if they make last-ditch stands, which create bitterness and resentment.

5

State Intervention

In Britain, in contrast to many European countries, the State has traditionally adopted a policy of non-intervention in the collective bargaining process. In keeping with our concepts of freedom, it was felt that harmonious working relationships would best be served by leaving the parties concerned free to construct voluntary agreements and procedures within the limits of the law. As we point out in Chapter 9 on industrial democracy, the employers feel change can best be accomplished through voluntarism rather than by legislation by the State. The unions too prefer 'social contracts' to the kind of system imposed by the Industrial Relations Act 1971. Laws of course, are seldom neutral. Both unions and employers are selective in their attitudes to legislation. Much as the Government may have wished to stand aside, the public interest and the need to develop a total economic policy have obliged them to intervene in support of the voluntary bargaining process.

State intervention in the collective bargaining field has been on the increase since the 1960s. Protective legislation for workers in factories, offices, shops, railway premises and particular industries has already been noted in Chapter 2, as were more direct interventions such as the Contracts of Employment Act 1965. Particular problem areas such as the docks, ship-building and the motor industry have been the subject of investigations initiated by the State. Inflation and a worsening balance-of-payments position can only mean more attempts by the Government of the day to influence the nature of industrial relations in this country – whether for good or ill. It therefore seems irrelevant to question the *fact* of increasing State intervention (as many trade unions and employers do), but it is relevant to examine the *nature* of such interventions.

This chapter therefore examines in detail some of these areas of intervention. It traces intervention by the State in the pay field, and shows how the State has traditionally intervened through the establishment of Wages Councils and in the area of equal pay to protect workers where the voluntary processes of collective bargaining have failed to develop.

Other interventions have been through the development of Whitley machinery, joint industrial councils and, more recently, protective employment legislation.

INCOMES POLICY

We begin by examining incomes policy and the allied question of low pay. Incomes policy is an area where the State has intervened in recognition that parties to the collective bargaining process were either unable or unwilling to regulate pay settlements voluntarily in a manner the State saw as necessary.

The State has intervened in the collective bargaining process on several occasions since the mid 1960s by attempting to alter the rate of wage and salary increases through incomes policy. However, incomes policy has a much earlier history and worked relatively well during the period from 1940 until 1950.

During the Second World War an unofficial policy of restraint was followed. The Government undertook to stabilize price levels by means of subsidies and the unions in turn made only modest and infrequent pay demands. Overtime and piece-work earnings rose rapidly but much of their inflationary potential was offset by high taxation. But circumstances in wartime were necessarily abnormal. A sense of patriotism was reflected in high production levels and an acceptance of compulsory arbitration for the settlement of disputes.

Compulsory arbitration existed for a period after the war as, to a lesser extent, did the patriotic spirit of self-sacrifice. Thus in 1948 the Labour Government's White Paper 'Personal Incomes, Costs and Prices'[1] met with a favourable reception from both trade unions and employers' associations. Considerable restraint was exercised for almost two years; in many industries wage demands fell off completely during this period and in others increases were minimal. But earnings at plant level continued to rise, leading to feelings of frustration in industries – such as the railways – where earnings levels were relatively standard. This, coupled with rising prices towards the end of 1950, led to the collapse of wage restraint.

The Conservatives tried a novel approach with their 'price freeze' in 1956. After considerable discussion, the Government obtained a promise from employers' representatives to stabilize prices and make concessions on pay only where they could get increased efficiency in return. The employers, for their part, took a firm stance, but national strikes in the shipbuilding and engineering industries threatened a devaluation crisis and the Government finally gave way in late 1957 by persuading employers to make offers. In 1961 the Chancellor of the Exchequer, Selwyn Lloyd, announced a 'pay pause' in the public sector. The Government undertook to resist wage demands in the State industries and private industry was asked to follow suit. Some employers did try to conform but the unions refused to co-operate. The pause ended in March, 1961, to be followed by the 'guiding light' in 1962, in which the Government advocated that wages and salaries should increase only by what productivity and stable prices would permit. It envisaged a rise in productivity of 2–2½ per cent a year and stated that pay increases should therefore be kept within these bounds. A National Incomes Commission ('Nicky') was established with the aim of developing a long-term policy. The unions, however, refused to co-operate with the Commission, preferring to work instead with the National Economic Development Council ('Neddy'), which included T.U.C. representatives. 'Neddy' persuaded the Government to change its 'guiding light' to 2½–3½ per cent a year.

When Labour returned to power in 1964 they were faced with an acute balance-of-payments problem and immediately sought their remedy in incomes policy. The Head of the new Department of Economic Affairs, George Brown (as he then was), succeeded in gaining the consent of the T.U.C. and employers' representatives – together with the Government – to a 'Declaration of Intent' on productivity, prices and incomes. This was supposed to commit them to 'urgent and vigorous' action to raise productivity, keep increases in incomes in line with national output, and maintain a stable price level. There was to be a 'norm' for increases in wages, prices and rents of 3–3½ per cent a year.

Exceptional pay increases could be granted in certain circumstances, one of which was increased productivity. This exception was used by many employers to grant pay concessions based on productivity bargains – many of them being simply fabrications to beat the norm: 'The mad scramble for productivity at any price in 1968 and 1969 made only a very modest contribution to economic growth, but managed to do a lot of damage to the incomes policy'.[2] Even the presence of the National Board for Prices and Incomes (established in 1965) had little impact. In the first two years of the policy, wages and prices continued to rise and weekly earnings rose by 8 per cent.

In the midst of yet another sterling crisis in 1966 a wage freeze was imposed under the Prices and Incomes legislation. The freeze lasted for six months and was followed by another six months of 'severe restraint'. When this ended it became clear that a wages explosion was impending and further price increases were on the way. Powers given to the Government under the legislation were not renewed in 1969, and by 1970 it became clear that the prices and incomes policy had failed.

When the Conservatives came to power with the 1970 General Election they did not at first seek a compulsory incomes policy, hoping instead for voluntary restraint in accordance with an 'invisible norm'. The Government attempted to keep increases down by displays of opposition to union demands in the public sector. Pay rises were kept to 8 per cent, and price increases to 5 per cent, in 1971; but in 1972 the death-knell of the policy was sounded by the miners' national strike. The Government then turned to legal compulsion. The first two stages of its policy – Stages 1 and 2 – attempted the restraint of prices and incomes, but they were loose enough in construction to permit increases to be granted by employers, under union pressure, in terms of shorter working hours, increased holidays and so forth.

Stage 3 of the policy, however, closed the loopholes that had become evident. Pay increases were limited to 7 per cent of the average pay bill per head of the applicable group for the preceding 12-month period or £2·25 per week per head. Negotiators and others concerned with pay determination could choose which of these limits to apply to the group. The Stage 3 Code also covered such matters as hours of work, holidays and assorted fringe benefits in order to prevent 'hidden' concessions from breaching the pay limit. Certain exceptions were recognized and claims under this heading could be referred to the Pay Board set up under the legislation. There was a flexibility margin of 1 per cent to cover matters such as productivity bargaining.

It is important to consider why the Government's incomes policy was never popular with the trade union movement. The policy followed a series of meetings between the T.U.C. and the Government at which there had been fundamental disagreement about the direction of incomes policy.

The main stumbling block in these negotiations was clearly the 1971 Industrial Relations Act, the effects of which are described later in this chapter. Co-operation and involvement by the trade union movement could have been won by the Government but only at the expense of sacrificing one of the main pillars of their policies. In addition the T.U.C. feared that the incomes policy could become a permanent feature in industrial relations. The policy was initially for a three-year period but was renewable annually. Many trade unionists considered that the policy was designed to establish the framework of a permanent system of pay controls which would ultimately erode their authority as wage negotiators. To a trade union movement which had failed to persuade the Government as to the faults of the 1971 Industrial Relations Act, the Conservative Government's incomes legislation looked like another attempt to curb trade union power.

The T.U.C. expressed its opposition at a Special Congress in March 1973.[3] Opposition was not towards incomes policy in general but towards a policy which appeared directed mainly at limiting pay settlements. The T.U.C. proposed to the Government that an effective incomes policy could be built on strong price controls, rent and food subsidies, protection for the low paid and those on fixed incomes, and a redistributive taxation system. These are proposals that appear later as the basis of the Social Contract but would have been unacceptable to a Conservative Government.

The Government attempted to hold back prices and profits. But some profits rose considerably, anyway, and prices of many food-stuffs increased because of exceptions in the Code such as increased input costs and prices. Rises in world food prices and the oil crisis brought increasing inflation towards the end of 1973. Stage 3 came under attack from the miners in particular. Their overtime ban in November, 1973, became a national strike in early 1974 and eventually brought down the Conservative Government. The minority Labour Government elected in its stead quickly settled with the miners, using certain powers of exemption granted to the Secretary of State for Employment under Stage 3.

Labour had concluded what became known eventually as the 'social contract' between the Government and the T.U.C. The T.U.C. agreed to advise unions to moderate wage claims provided the

99

Government took action to restrain prices of certain basic foodstuffs by means of subsidies, repeal the Industrial Relations Act and permit the legal controls under Stage 3 to lapse. The Labour Government also undertook to consider action in regard to problems of 'social justice' concerning, for example, the position of old-age pensioners and the low-paid sections of the working population. Unlamented, Stage 3 eventually lapsed in November, 1974, and incomes policy became one aspect of a wider Social Contract.

Free collective bargaining did not last long under the Social Contract. The State found itself under more and more pressure to intervene as settlements grew in size to compensate for previous restraint under the Conservative Government's pay policy and the effects of rapid inflation.

The lack of success of recent legislative pay policies and the general reluctance of the Labour Government to introduce statutory pay policies led to a desperate search by the Government, T.U.C. and C.B.I. for alternative strategies to deal with the problem of large wage settlements affecting the increasing problem of inflation. The Government started discussions with unions and employers in early 1975 and a flat rate £6-a-week policy for all for one year, with no increase for incomes over £8,500, a policy first suggested by the T.G.W.U., became operative from August 1975. A voluntary policy for one year was accepted by the T.U.C. at their Congress in September[4] of that year.

The return to free collective bargaining that was promised under the Social Contract became a £6 norm, with the implied threat of direct State intervention if the norm was breached. Intervention by the State in the incomes field, as the previous pages suggest, has not been particularly popular, yet is likely to become a more permanent part of the industrial relations scene.

The major problem of State intervention in the pay field is that whatever policy is implemented it disrupts the dynamics of the collective bargaining process. Chapter 3 showed that collective bargaining has become a very sophisticated and flexible process of reconciling general, economic and social factors along with specific managerial priorities and trade union objectives. If the Government intervenes and does not allow the normal processes of collective bargaining to take place, it inhibits the necessary response to economic and social change and imposes severe constraints on normal industrial relations. Once intervention is removed and normal bargaining is allowed to operate, large settlements can result as groups compensate themselves for losses incurred during the period of constraint. This is the dilemma of Government intervention in this field. The Social Contract may have secured some control of prices but how long can any particular norm withstand the pressures of unions having to contend with rising prices, and can a Government absorb the effects of large settlements that tend to follow a return to free collective bargaining?

The lessons of the past seem to indicate that incomes policy cannot work without the co-operation of the union movement and the ability of the Government to control price rises. Nonetheless demands are often made on the unions to alleviate the problem by dropping wage claims and tightening belts until some later date when employers are better able to grant increases. The trade unions can justifiably counter that they are not responsible for creating inflation, they are merely *responding* to changes in the economic environment: 'Workers have . . . been faced with both higher food prices and rising prices of manufactured goods due to factors other than their own actions. To this extent, wage claims are defensive reactions on the part of the unions rather than the prime movers in creating cost inflation.'[5] British industry in general is working with outdated plant and equipment. The unions are not required to plan long-term capital investment for industry, so they can hardly be blamed for this. As noted earlier, management played a major role in increasing the power of the work-group at plant level and it is, therefore, a management task to promote efficient payment and industrial relations systems in companies and plants – thus reducing the inflationary 'wages drift'.

State intervention in the collective bargaining process through incomes policy may increase in the years ahead. But the imposition of legal restraints will never be enough to make incomes policy work. The lessons of the past are clear. There can be no progress without the co-operation of unions, workers and employers and this will only be forthcoming where incomes policy can be *seen* to work. As price control is vital to the success of incomes policy, it may well be that the necessary evidence will be continually obliterated by inflation.

LOW PAY

It is in the specific area of low pay that we find the longest history of direct State intervention. The State, since 1909, has operated statutory wage regulation machinery in those areas where the voluntary collective bargaining processes have failed to develop.

101

From the 1880s public attention was increasingly focused on the social evil of 'sweating'. Tailoring, shirt-making and boot manufacture became identified as industries where employers were paying starvation wages. This public concern resulted in investigation by a House of Lords Select Committee which confirmed allegations of 'sweating' in these industries.

Almost twenty years were to elapse, however, before the Government reacted to the House of Lords report. Additional evidence of 'sweating' from other enquiries led in 1909 to the passing of the first Trade Boards Act.

The Act initially covered tailoring, paper-box making, lace and net finishing and chain-making industries. It ensured, for the first time, that wages were to be fixed by a body composed of representatives of employers and workers in equal numbers with the addition of independent persons called 'appointed members'. The rates fixed were made enforceable by law.

In 1917 the Whitley Committee recommended that the scope of the Act be extended to other industries where collective organization was weak or lacking and thereby preventing the formation of collective bargaining arrangements. The Government responded by passing a second Trade Boards Act in 1918, which empowered the Minister of Labour to intervene and establish a trade board where he was of the opinion that no adequate machinery for the effective regulation of wages existed in a particular industry. By 1938 there were fifty Trade Boards covering over one and a half million workers. Agricultural workers were covered in England and Wales by the Agricultural Wages (Regulation) Act, 1924; later by the Agricultural Wages Act, 1947; and subsequently by the Agricultural Wages Act, 1948. Scottish agricultural workers were covered by the provisions of the Agricultural Wages (Regulation) (Scotland) Act, 1937, by later statutes in 1940 and 1947; and subsequently by the Agricultural Wages (Scotland) Act, 1949.

The Trade Boards legislation was replaced by the Wages Councils Act, 1945, which was amended in 1948 and finally replaced by the Wages Councils Act of 1959. The Act gave the Minister of Labour power to establish Wages Councils by Order where collective bargaining machinery did not exist; or where it was likely to cease to exist or remain inadequate; and finally, where he considered that effective machinery did not exist or was likely to cease to exist or be adequate and a reasonable standard of remuneration could not be maintained. In the first set of circumstances the Minister could make an intervention on his own initiative – in the latter two he was required to call upon the assistance of a Commission of Inquiry.

A Wages Council consists of representatives of employers and workers in equal numbers, together with not more than three independent members, one of whom acts as a chairman. All members are appointed by the Minister and, with the exception of the independents, he is required to consult with organizations representing the employers and workers involved. In practice the Minister may accept their suggestions for appointments but he is not bound to do so. A Wages Council is empowered to make proposals for submission to the Minister concerning the fixing of minimum rates of pay and holidays. The proposals must be considered by the Minister who may accept them or refer them back with his observations, but cannot amend them. Accepted proposals are embodied in wages regulation orders made by the Minister.

A Wages Council is not intended to be a permanent feature in any particular industry. It is formed to establish only minimum rates and conditions and the parties are free to negotiate agreements giving more favourable terms. Where they can do so by means of effective machinery of their own, the Wages Council may be considered no longer necessary.

Some advance has been made since 1959 in the abolition of Wages Councils. Under the 1959 Wages Council Act the Minister could, on his own initiative, abolish or vary the field of operation of a Wages Council. Alternatively there could be a joint application from employers' and workers' organizations, which represented substantial numbers of the people concerned, on the grounds that they could provide adequate machinery for the effective regulation of terms and conditions in the particular industry. The Minister was then required either to make an order to give effect to the application or refer the matter to a Commission of Inquiry for investigation and report.

The 1971 Industrial Relations Act made several changes to the 1959 Wages Council Act which greatly assisted the processes of abolition of Wages Councils. The most important change was that application for abolition could be made by any organization of workers representing a *substantial* proportion of the numbers concerned. This meant a strong move away from the stipulation of joint employer and worker applications. Also, the justifiable grounds for abolition no longer insisted that adequate voluntary collective bargaining machinery must have been set up which could replace the Council's activities. The Commission on Industrial Relations was the body which examined proposals for abolition or variation in the operation of Wages Councils. Consideration of the operations of Wages Councils became a major feature of the work of the C.I.R.

With the repeal of the 1971 Industrial Relations Act, the C.I.R. was disbanded and responsibility for considering proposals concerning Wages Councils reverted to *ad hoc* commissions of enquiry and under the 1975 Employment Protection Act has now become one of the responsibilities of the Advisory Conciliation and Arbitration Service.

The 1975 Employment Protection Act further assists the process of abolition by providing the Secretary of State with power to change a Wages Council into a Statutory Joint Industrial Council. This was first proposed by the Commission on Industrial Relations[6] as a half-way house on the road to abolition. The S.J.I.C. would have many of the duties of a Wages Council except that it would not include independent members. It could prove a useful stimulus to effective voluntary collective bargaining. The Act also extends the scope of Wages Councils to cover the terms and conditions of employment generally and enables Wages Councils to make their own wage regulation orders and determine the operative date of settlements. This removes the need for the Council to obtain Government approval to its orders.

Thus State intervention in this low-pay area has moved from the establishment to the promotion of abolition of Wages Councils. However, there are still almost $3\frac{1}{4}$ million workers covered by forty-nine Wages Councils.[7] Wages Councils have not proved the great spur to voluntary collective bargaining that was originally intended. Moreover, they have had very limited success in improving the position of the low paid.

A change by the State in the direction of Wages Council operations may be necessary if they are to fulfil their role of developing collective bargaining. Over the years a number of suggestions for reform have been proposed. The 1968 Royal Commission on Trades Unions and Employers' Associations briefly examined Wages Councils and suggested several procedures for speeding up abolition, most of which were adopted in the C.I.R.'s examination of Wages Councils.

The T.U.C. has also been concerned at the failure of Wages Councils to promote effective collective bargaining. The 1969 T.U.C. conference for unions represented in the Wages Council sector[8] suggested that Wages Councils could extend their functions to co-operate with Industrial Training Boards in considering issues of productivity and training. It also proposed that Wages Councils should produce an annual report, and the T.U.C. suggested the possible abolition of independent members of Wages Councils.

Many of these suggestions are useful areas for the State to consider in the development of Wages Councils. A more exacting framework could be provided within which the independent members of Wages Councils could operate. Their role could change from the passive to active intervention. Why should bodies like A.C.A.S. be mainly concerned with abolition? Independent members with adequate servicing by the State could provide an on-going examination of areas within their Councils where collective bargaining could develop. Similarly independent members could encourage the development of jointly agreed disputes and disciplinary procedures within their sectors.

Successive incomes policies have provided for exceptional rises for the low paid. Wages Councils have not fully explored the implications of incomes policies.

The T.U.C. also proposed a more effective inspection system. This could be useful to unions. There may, however, be a case for extending responsibility for inspection to the trade unions themselves. At present there are approximately 140 inspectors to inspect 462,000 establishments[9] – which is hardly effective inspection. If information about infringements of Wages Council orders were made available to unions on the Wages Council, this could be of assistance to unions attempting to organize in these sectors and could provide added protection in those Wages Councils where abolition is no more than a remote possibility.

Wages Councils as the main instrument of State intervention in the area of low pay have not been particularly successful. This is partly because low pay is not simply a Wages Council problem. Pockets of low-paid workers can exist within industries with highly developed collective bargaining systems, and low pay owes more to geographical area, sex and age distribution of employees than to whether collective bargaining is in existence.

A number of solutions to the problem of low pay have been canvassed. The Royal Commission on Trade Unions and Employers'

Associations, the C.I.R.[10] and a number of trade unions have tried
to focus public discussion on the need for State intervention through
universal minimum wage legislation. Support for this form of intervention has never been widespread within the trade union movement
and the likely cost has caused successive Governments to react
cautiously to such proposals. Moreover, of course, the issue of minimum wage legislation tends to distract attention from other ssuesi
like training, productivity and trade union organization within these
low-pay areas.

The problems of low pay are more likely to be tackled in a piece-
meal manner. The Social Contract gives priority to raising low pay,
and the low paid are likely to benefit from threshold agreements and
flat rate incomes policies.[11] The State has also intervened in one area
where low pay has been a continual problem and where collective
bargaining has failed to assist. This is the area of female employment.

EQUAL PAY

The concept of equal pay for female workers is not new. It was first
mooted by the T.U.C. in 1888 and formed the subject of a Convention
of the International Labour Organization (I.L.O.) in 1951. The principle is embodied in Article 119 of the Treaty of Rome – which established the European Economic Community. The subject has been
talked about for some time but little action seems to have resulted.
Even the situation in Europe leaves much to be desired – e.g. in
France by the 1960s the differential between male and female earnings
was over seven per cent, while in Germany much discrimination was
evident, often in the distinction between 'heavy' (suitable for men)
and 'light' (suitable for women) work. If European experience is anything to go by the mere passing of a statute will not be enough and
much will depend on the extent to which the matter is pursued
through the ordinary channels of collective bargaining.

The problem was to get both sides of industry to begin to tackle
the matter. This the Labour Government did in passing the Equal
Pay Act, 1970 – virtually its last action before its electoral defeat.
Although the Act was passed in 1970 it did not come fully into force
until 29 December 1975 – although the Secretary of State was
empowered to bring it wholly or partially into effect on 31 December
1973. Individual employers had approved the principle but would not
implement it voluntarily because of the fear that their competitors

would not follow suit. The position had now been made clear – *all* were required to conform to a time-table established by law.

Women are to receive equal treatment with men in relation to terms and conditions of employment where they are doing 'like' work or where their work is rated – e.g. by work study or job evaluation – as being equivalent (section 1). 'Like' work is defined as work of the same or a 'broadly similar' nature. The Statute refers not only to equal pay but also to equal treatment. Provisions establishing equality in this respect – where it is not mentioned expressly – become an implied term in the individual contract of employment. A claim may be made to an industrial tribunal for arrears of remuneration or damages in respect of a failure to comply with an equal pay clause (section 2). Arrears may be claimed up to a period of two years. The Industrial Court is empowered to remove discrimination in collective agreements, employers' pay structures and statutory wages orders which contain any provision applying specifically to men only or to women only and which has been referred to the Court. The Act specifically excludes equal treatment for men and women in respect of pensions.

Equal pay does not necessarily mean equal earnings. If women wish to get increased earnings by way of shift premiums, for example, they normally come up against the provisions of the Factories Act which specifically limit the amount of hours (including overtime) which they can be permitted to work. Protection of women by such legislation may have been necessary in the past but there are many areas today in which trade unions feel they are strong enough to dispense with laws of this type and instead provide protection for women workers through the exercise, if necessary, of bargaining strength. The problem of removing protective legislation – and thereby increasing the earnings of women – has not yet been tackled systematically but there is clearly a need for something to be done, perhaps by the Government in consultation with the unions.

Equal pay will not, in practice, mean equal opportunity: 'The statute deals to some extent in equal *treatment*; but it does not set out to provide equal *opportunity*. Advocates of women's liberation will no doubt argue that it should have aimed at the latter.' If equal pay is to prove meaningful in practice women must be given full equality, including equality of opportunity. This means, for example, equal promotion and training prospects.

This is one reason why the Sex Discrimination Act was brought on to the statute book in 1975, to complement the Equal Pay Act. The Sex Discrimination Act is designed to make discrimination on the grounds of sex or marriage unlawful and will have particular effects in the area of employment, plugging some of the gaps in the Equal Pay Act.

The Equal Pay Act imposed the obligations and set the time-table but it was for collective bargainers to ensure that the promises of the Act became reality. The State assisted by allowing certain flexibilities for equal pay in incomes policy. Both the previous Conservative Government's pay code and the wage restraints of the Social Contract allowed for increases outside the limit to cover progress towards equal pay.

It is clear that there can be no simple solution which will remove pay discrimination against women. The Equal Pay and Sex Discrimination Acts can only be partially successful, they can do little to solve the problems that arise from differential male and female activity rates in the labour market and their effect on wage scales, problems that arise from the concentrating of female labour in specific employment sections, and problems that exist because of differentials in actual earnings.

The Equal Pay Act also by-passes the argument about concepts of equal pay. Should equal pay mean that men and women should receive equal pay for work of equal value, or should it mean equal pay for equal work? This latter view is much narrower yet the Act leaves room for either interpretation.

The Act goes some way towards alleviating low pay among female workers. Real advance in this particular sector may have to await more dramatic changes in society's attitudes towards the work undertaken by women.

SUPPORT FOR VOLUNTARY COLLECTIVE BARGAINING

This chapter has so far traced the development of State intervention in some of the major areas where the collective bargaining process has either failed to provide adequate pay protection for particular groups of workers or has failed to satisfy the State's intentions in the economic field. We now explore some of the areas where State intervention has been designed mainly to support and encourage the processes of voluntary collective bargaining.

The State provides a support function for collective bargaining by means of Fair Wages Resolutions of the House of Commons. The first such Resolution was made in 1891, the second in 1909 and the one at present in force in 1946. The main purpose of the Resolution is to ensure that employers who have been given Government contracts pay their workers 'fair' wages and extend 'fair' conditions of employment in every place where the contract is being executed. 'Fair' means what has been established in the trade or industry in the district by representative joint negotiation or arbitration. In the absence of these methods of establishing basic terms and conditions, 'fair' will then mean not less favourable than the general level of wages, hours, and conditions observed by other employers whose general circumstances in the trade or industry in which the contractor is engaged are similar. Another provision of the Resolution is that contractors must recognize the freedom of their workers to join unions. The contractor is also responsible for the observance of the Resolution by any sub-contractors engaged in the execution of the contract. The Government has extended the principle of the Resolution by recommending to local authorities that they should include like provisions in their contracts. This practice has been generally accepted although some local authorities use their own form of fair wages clause which sometimes differs from the one used in Government contracts. The corporations which run the nationalized industries also, as a general rule, require the insertion in their contracts of a clause based on the Resolution. A further extension of the principle of the Resolution may be found in Statutes which provide assistance to industries and public authorities by way of grant, loan, subsidy, guarantee or licence.

Another example of State support for collective bargaining is furnished by Section 8 of the Terms and Conditions of Employment Act, 1959. Under this section representative trade unions or employers' organizations may invoke the adjudication of the Industrial Court where it appears that an employer is failing to observe terms and conditions of employment not less favourable than those established by agreement or award for the industry in which he is engaged. If the Industrial Court finds this to be the case it will make an award requiring the employer to observe the appropriate terms and conditions. The award takes effect as an implied term in the contracts of employment of the workers concerned and of other workers of the same description employed from time to time by the employer in question.

This protection has been continued by the 1975 Employment Protection Act. This Act provides that a complaint may be made to the Advisory Conciliation and Arbitration Service (rather than the Industrial Court) that an employer is observing terms and conditions of employment less favourable than the recognized or general terms and conditions for the industry.

WHITLEYISM

In the context of State support for the collective bargaining process we need to look at the development of industry-wide agreements and the promotion by the State of machinery for negotiation at industry level. Industry-wide agreements flourished in the circumstances brought about by the First World War, and the Government, not wishing to see a re-emergence of strife after the war, set up the Committee on the Relations between Employers and Employed – known as the Whitley Committee, its Chairman being J. H. Whitley, M.P.

The Committee issued five reports between 1917 and 1918. Its recommendations had far-reaching effects on the construction of post-war industrial relations, the main ones being: (a) that joint industrial councils should be formed in well-organized industries; (b) that works committees, representative of both management and workers, should be appointed in individual establishments; (c) extension of the statutory regulation of wages in badly organized trades; (d) the setting up of a permanent court of arbitration; and (e) that the Minister of Labour should be authorized to hold inquiries regarding disputes.[12] The Committee emphasized that there should be adequate organization of both employers and employees in order to achieve a permanent improvement in relationships between them. The Whitley Report thus gave an important boost to the development of the formal system of collective bargaining. It was widely accepted by both sides of industry. In some industries the advice given helped to consolidate joint arrangements which had already been established; in others it provided valuable guidelines where no such machinery had previously existed – it served to substitute order for chaos.

Joint Industrial Councils were set up in many industries. They consisted of representatives of employers' associations and workers meeting at regular intervals to discuss, *inter alia*, ways of utilizing the knowledge and experience of workers, the settlement of general principles governing terms and conditions of employment, and methods of fixing and adjusting wages. Between January 1918 and December 1921 seventy-three J.I.C.s were established, together with thirty-three Interim Industrial Reconstruction Committees. The latter were attempts by the Ministry of Reconstruction to establish some form of representation in badly organized industries where development was insufficient for the formation of a J.I.C. But progress was hindered by inter-war trade slumps and depressions, so that by 1938 there remained in existence only thirty-eight J.I.C.s. The Second World War, however, provided a new impetus to joint negotiating arrangements and by 1960 there were some two hundred J.I.C.s or bodies of a similar nature.[13] The State itself had played a major part in this development. After the Whitley Report, the Government introduced Whitley Committees into the Civil Service, and in the period following the Second World War the statutes establishing nationalization placed an obligation on the boards of the new State-owned industries to form joint consultative arrangements with their respective employees.

DIRECTIONS OF REFORM

The previous chapters have shown that the worker of the 1960s was covered by extensive protective legislation introduced by the State. By the early 1960s it was becoming increasingly obvious that despite State intervention there were considerable deficiencies in the British system of industrial relations. A small unofficial strike in one section of the motor industry could quickly ripple through the industry causing widespread lay-offs and lost orders. Productivity generally in industry was considerably lower than that of our competitors and it had become a favourite national pastime to focus on one disaster in industrial relations after another. By the early 1960s both major political parties had become committed to fairly drastic revision of the system of industrial relations.

The Donovan Commission,[14] which sat from 1965 to 1968, made a number of far-reaching proposals for the reform of industrial relations in Britain. It analysed the nature of the conflict between the formal and informal systems of industrial relations. It proposed the factory-wide agreement as the main instrument of reform, with industry-wide agreements being limited to those areas that they could *effectively* regulate. It advocated an Industrial Relations Act, one of the provisions of which would be a requirement that companies of a certain size should register their collective agreements with the Department of Employment and Productivity (now the Department of Employment). This measure was designed to emphasize that the primary responsibility for industrial relations in a concern lay with its board of directors and to indicate those aspects of domestic industrial relations which should be covered by company and factory agreements.

An Industrial Relations Commission should be established under the Act to assist in the reconstruction of industrial relations. It could investigate and report on matters pertaining to the registration of agreements and deal with matters such as union recognition. It should have a full-time chairman and other full-time and part-time members. Its membership should include people with practical experience in industrial relations.

Trade unions should have full corporate personality and should be required to register. There should also be legal requirements in regard to admission, discipline, disputes between members, union elections and shop stewards. Unions could help in reducing multi-unionism by accelerating the tendency to merger and amalgamation between unions. Unions should conclude agreements on factory rights of representation in order to reduce competition for members between unions in the same workplace. Unions should consider establishing constitutionally recognized committees at workplace level to perform many of the functions carried out by unofficial 'combine' committees. The T.U.C. could help matters, claimed the Commission, by advocating the principle of 'one union for one grade of work within one factory' as a guide for the future development of union structure at plant level.

Employers' associations could assist reform by helping their members to develop orderly and efficient industrial relations systems within their undertakings. There should be more amalgamations between associations, particularly in regard to the smaller ones. The C.B.I. should consider widening its scope to include companies presently excluded from membership such as banks, insurance undertakings – who are 'commercial associates' – and associations from areas such as the retail distributive trades.

Employees should be protected by law from 'unfair dismissal'. The object of this proposal was to encourage employers to improve their voluntary arrangements for dealing with dismissals. Dismissal should be justified only where there existed a valid reason for it connected with the capacity or conduct of the worker or based on the operational requirements of the undertaking. Certain reasons should specifically be invalid, viz. trade union membership or activity, race, colour, sex, marital status, religious or political opinion, national extraction or social origin. An employee who felt that his dismissal was unfair could complain to a tribunal seeking either compensation or, if both parties agreed, reinstatement.

The Commission hoped that recognition of the informal system would lead to a voluntary reappraisal by employers and workers of their methods and procedures in relation to one another. They did not place much reliance on legislative change to bring about reform. The problem was to get the parties to enter into an efficient system of plant bargaining and collective bargaining generally. When this had been done there might then be a part for the law to play:

> If the reform was largely successful, so that relations in most companies of any size were carried on within the framework of clear and effective agreements, and yet stoppages in breach of those agreements remained a common occurrence, it would be possible to consider enacting some penalty against trade unions or workers responsible for such stoppages (and, of course, against managers and employers where they were responsible).[15]

With this in mind the Commission did not advocate making collective agreements enforceable at law: '. . . to make the present inadequate procedure agreements legally enforceable would be irrelevant and would divert attention from, and hinder, action to remedy the real causes.'[16]

IN PLACE OF STRIFE

In January, 1969, the Labour Government produced their White Paper entitled *In Place of Strife*.[17] The Government agreed with the Donovan thesis on the conflict between the formal and informal systems of industrial relations. But where Donovan relied on voluntary action the Labour Government sought to add certain 'penal clauses'. These gave the Secretary of State powers to order a 'cooling off' period and, in the case of official disputes, to order a ballot of union members.

The White Paper proposed the establishment of a Commission on Industrial Relations (C.I.R.). This body was to be primarily concerned with the reform of collective bargaining and would deal with such matters as the promotion of suitable company-wide procedures, disciplinary practices and dismissal, redundancy procedures and rules about shop steward duties and facilities within the firm: 'The C.I.R. will also be required, by reporting on references by the Secretary of State, to tackle other problems that are not now the direct responsibility of any public agency, so that its work will represent a novel extension of public involvement in industrial relations in this country.'[18] The C.I.R. was to be without legal 'teeth' as it was essential for its operation that it acquired the confidence and co-operation of both sides of industry by persuasion and not legal compulsion.

It was to be given indirect authority, however, on the question of inter-union disputes. Where the T.U.C. was unable to get a solution to particular problems of this nature through its own machinery, the matter would be referred to the C.I.R. If the unions concerned did not accept the C.I.R.'s findings the Secretary of State could issue an Order to back the C.I.R.'s recommendations. Employers and unions who refused to comply with the Order would suffer financial penalties.

There was to be protection for employees against unfair dismissal. The Industrial Relations Bill would ensure that dismissal could be justified only where there was a valid reason for it connected with the capacity or conduct of the employee or based on the operational requirements of the enterprise – without such reasons it would be unfair. An employee who considered his dismissal to be unfair would have the right to appeal to an Industrial Tribunal which could award either compensation or reinstatement.

The trade union movement was opposed to the proposals concerning the 'conciliation pause', strike ballots and inter-union disputes. The Labour Government had, in general, followed the Donovan findings but it soon became clear (during 1969) that the Government, unlike Donovan, intended to rely primarily on legal enactments – and penal sanctions – in order to achieve immediate restraints on certain trade union activities, while the main body of the White Paper was to be kept for an Industrial Relations Bill in the next session of Parliament.

These proposals caused a serious rift not only within the Labour Party but between the trade unions and the Government. It could be argued that a Labour Government could not have hoped to introduce legislation focusing mainly upon strikes[19] without engendering opposition from its traditional trade union supporters. No one had denied the need for reform but to the T.U.C. and many Labour supporters some of the Government's proposals went in the face of the Donovan report and by concentrating on the issue of strikes, seemed more designed to achieve electoral popularity. As Eric Heffer observed: 'It was an attempt to gain the support of the middle ground.'[20]

The T.U.C. demonstrated its opposition at a special congress in Croydon and produced its own *Programme for Action*[21] which undertook considerable improvement in the T.U.C.'s disputes machinery to embrace inter-union disputes, unconstitutional and unofficial action where there was a serious threat of damage to the economy.

In the face of union pressure and agitation from many Labour back-benchers, a series of 'crisis' meetings were held between the Prime Minister and Employment Secretary and the General Council. The Government, in the face of this pressure, dropped the penal clauses from their proposals and accepted the T.U.C.'s *Programme for Action* with the commitment by the T.U.C. to a 'solemn and binding' undertaking to do all in its power to obtain a solution to inter-union disputes, unofficial and unconstitutional action, where there was a threat of serious damage to the economy.

Shipbuilding and construction were the major industries where, because of their craft nature, inter-union disputes flourished in the 1960s. Since then there has been a sharp decline in inter-union disputes within these industries.[22] There are a number of reasons for this. Amalgamation of unions in these industries has been a significant cause and the T.U.C. can accept credit for its assistance in amalgamations and effective use of its disputes machinery and encouragement of demarcation agreements.

By 1970 Labour had created the C.I.R. with George Woodcock as its first chairman, and had taken action to secure the registration of procedure agreements (Donovan had called for the registration of collective agreements) but this was as far as it got with the White Paper. The diluted version of the White Paper which Labour had conceded under union and back-bench pressure was to have provided the contents of the proposed Industrial Relations Bill in the next Parliamentary session but in 1970 the Conservatives won the general election; and they had their own ideas on the reform of industrial relations.

FAIR DEAL AT WORK

Before their electoral victory in 1970 the Conservative Party's Political Centre had prepared the document entitled *Fair Deal at Work*.

This document had a long pedigree and derived from Conservative attitudes towards industrial relations that had been formed in the 1950s and 1960s. The proposals for reform ignored those of the Donovan Commission and suggested remedies similar to those rejected by the Donovan Commission and subsequently by the Labour Government.

Fair Deal at Work proposed that the pre-entry closed shop should be made illegal. Collective agreements made in writing were to be enforceable at law – this included existing agreements. New obligations were to be placed on trade unions. They should be required to register and if they did not they would suffer certain disadvantages; conversely, registration would bring positive benefits. Thus the Conservatives' central theme was emphasized – the main cause of Britain's industrial relations problems was the unregulated power of the unions. Legal sanctions should be used against unions which failed to keep their members to agreements.

It soon became clear to the Conservative Government that the proposed Bill would meet with a great deal of opposition from the trade union movement and some employers. The Government therefore published a 'Consultative Document' in October, 1970, for the benefit of unions and employers. Many employers made suggestions for changes in the Bill and its allied Industrial Relations Code of Practice but the unions argued that effective discussion with the Government on the Consultative Document was not possible since the Government, in publishing a consultative document, distinguished between negotiable and non-negotiable areas, the so-called 'pillars of the Bill'. It was of course these non-negotiable areas which the trade union movement found so objectionable, and on which they were denied negotiation.

THE INDUSTRIAL RELATIONS ACT 1971

The Industrial Relations Act became law in August, 1971. The stated purpose of the Act was to promote good industrial relations on the basis of four fundamental principles:

(a) Collective bargaining should be freely conducted on behalf of workers and employers with due regard to the general interests of the community.
(b) The development and maintenance of orderly procedures in industry for the peaceful and expeditious settlement of disputes by negotiation, conciliation or arbitration, with due regard to the general interests of the community.
(c) The free association of workers in independent trade unions, and of employers in employers' associations, so organized as to be representative, responsible and effective bodies for regulating relations between employers and workers.
(d) Freedom and security for workers, protected by adequate safeguards against unfair industrial practices, whether on the part of employers or others.

The Act made a significant distinction between trade unions; in fact the term 'trade union' was to be applied only to a registered union, i.e. 'an organization of workers which is for the time being registered under this Act'. Any organization of workers which had full power to alter its own rules and to control the application of its property and funds – provided it was also independent (not, for example, a 'staff' union) – could apply for registration. If the rules of the applicant organization met certain minimum standards laid down under the Act it could become a trade union. What was popularly known as a trade union, i.e. an unregistered union, was defined simply as 'an organization of workers' in terms similar to those of the Trade Union Act, 1913. Registered unions enjoyed certain advantages which their unregistered counterparts did not. For example, only a registered union could obtain an agency shop agreement, approved closed shop or sole bargaining agency.

A network of institutions was created for the processing of matters arising under the Act. Industrial Tribunals were already in use to deal with matters under such legislation as the Contracts of Employment Act, 1963, and the Redundancy Payments Act, 1965. A Tribunal was made up of a lawyer, as chairman, and two other members representing employer and employee interests respectively. These Tribunals were given additional jurisdiction by the new Act over matters such as unfair dismissal, cases of unfair expulsion by a union or employers' association or refusal by these to accept an otherwise suitable applicant into membership.

The Commission on Industrial Relations was established as a statutory body under the Act. Although it had no legal authority of its own its recommendations, in certain circumstances, could be enforced by an Order of the National Industrial Relations Court. It dealt with such matters as conducting ballots on agency shop issues and investigating the extent of bargaining units. The Act entrusted it with virtually unlimited investigative tasks: 'The Secretary of State, or the Secretary of State and any other Minister acting jointly, may refer to the Commission any question relating to industrial relations generally or to industrial relations in any particular industry or in any particular undertaking or part of an undertaking.'[24]

The National Industrial Relations Court (N.I.R.C.) was an entirely new institution. It had the same powers and status as the High Court but its style was more informal and it could hear cases anywhere in Great Britain. It had three members – a judge and two laymen with expert knowledge of industry. Contested points of law could be referred to the Court of Appeal – and, in Scotland, to the Court of Session. It had power to award compensation, to make an order declaring the rights of a complainant, and to issue an order requiring a party to take or refrain from taking a particular course of action.

A new office was created, that of the Chief Registrar of Trade Unions and Employers' Associations. His main task was to examine the rules of unions and employers' associations which sought registration to ensure that they met certain minimum standards. The Registrar was also empowered to receive complaints from individual union members and, where he deemed it necessary, to pass them on to the N.I.R.C.

An Industrial Relations Code of Practice was drawn up setting out what was considered to be good industrial relations practice for the benefit of those whom the Act covered. The Code outlined such matters as the responsibilities of management, trade unions, employers' associations and individual employees; employment policies, communication and consultation, collective bargaining, employee representation, grievance and disputes procedures and disciplinary procedures.

The pre-entry closed shop was made illegal by section 5 of the Act. Every worker, as between himself and his employer, had the right to join or not to join the *registered* trade union of his choice. He also had the right not to become a member of an unregistered trade union if that was his wish. This section made it an unfair industrial practice for the employer to prevent him from exercising his rights in regard to union membership and union activities; or otherwise penalize or discriminate against him on grounds of union membership.

Section 11 made possible the establishment of an agency shop. This was an agreement made between one or more employer and one or more registered trade union whereby it was agreed that every worker to whom the agreement applied must either belong to an appropriate trade union; or, in lieu of membership, pay a sum equivalent to the contribution to union funds; or in the case of a conscientious objection pay an equivalent amount to a charity agreed upon by the workers and the union. Where the employer was unwilling to agree to an agency shop, and the matter could not be solved by conciliation, either the union or employer could apply to the N.I.R.C. The Court was empowered to order a secret ballot under the supervision of the C.I.R. If two-thirds of those who voted in the ballot were in favour of an agency shop the employer was then required to operate it.

With the exception of certain excluded cases, e.g. registered dock workers, every employee who had two years' or more continuous service and who was not of retirement age had the right to protection against unfair dismissal (sections 22–29 (inclusive)). The burden of proving that a dismissal was fair lay with the employer. He could only do so by proving that it was reasonable and on one of four grounds, viz. capability or qualifications, conduct, redundancy, or that there could be no continuation of employment without contravention of a duty imposed by or under a legal enactment. The employee had the right to complain to an Industrial Tribunal which, if it found for him, could award compensation or try to secure his reinstatement.

All written collective agreements made after the commencement of the Act were presumed to be legally enforceable contracts unless the parties stipulated otherwise (section 34). However, the parties continued to express the wish for collective agreements to be binding in honour only; therefore a great deal of legal energy was expended on drawing up non-enforceability clauses – popularly termed TINA LEA (This Is Not A Legally Enforceable Agreement).

Sympathetic strikes were hit by the provisions of the Act (section 98). Where a strike at one factory is extended to another and those calling the strike knew or had reasonable grounds for believing that a contract (a commercial contract) existed between the two firms, an unfair industrial practice would have been committed where the strike-leaders' principal purpose was to induce another to break the contract or prevent its performance – provided the other person was an extraneous party in relation to the industrial dispute. In these circumstances it was also an unfair industrial practice to undertake any irregular industrial action short of a strike. Strikes or irregular industrial action short of a strike in furtherance of an unfair industrial practice – e.g. industrial action designed to force an employer to dismiss a person who refused to join a union – were prohibited by section 97.

Where industrial action was such that it constituted a serious threat to the economy, national security and public order, or was likely to expose a substantial number of people to serious risk, disease or personal injury, a cooling off period of up to sixty days could have been imposed by the N.I.R.C. after application by the Secretary of State for Employment – who could also apply for an order requiring a strike ballot. Refusal by those named in the Order of the N.I.R.C. to comply would have involved the imposition of fines for contempt of court.

Opposition to the Act from the T.U.C. was very strong. Many trade unionists saw the Act as crystallizing much of the hostility that they considered had long existed within Conservative ranks towards organized labour. The legislation placed an emphasis on the rights of the individual in the workplace that cut directly across bargaining arrangements and trade union organization on the shop floor built up through collective trade union strength.

The Act also ignored the quite considerable advances that the trade union movement had made since the 1968 Donovan report. The T.U.C. had accepted the need for reform in industrial relations and in the tradition of Donovan had emphasized the development of collective bargaining. The T.U.C. had instigated a series of 'Post-Donovan Conferences' to examine and develop collective bargaining. It had undertaken reviews and made recommendations concerning union rules and procedures for calling strikes, appointment and responsibilities of shop stewards, admission and expulsion of members of unions. It had also begun the long process of assisting unions in drawing up inter-union procedures and agreements.[25]

T.U.C. opposition to the Act concentrated on the issue of registration. The T.U.C. was not opposed to registration as such and indeed many unions were voluntarily registered under the 1871 Trade Union

Act. However, in the 1971 Act all the benefits of the Act flowed from registration. There was a philosophical objection also to registration. Trade unionists saw the Act as being concerned with shifting the balance of power within trade unions away from the shop floor; to be put on the register a union was required to satisfy the registrar about the content and operation of its rules and the union would have to conform to the basic principles of the Act. Moreover, the registrar would require union rules to 'adequately control the determination of union objects and procedures'. This would put severe restrictions on the role of the shop steward.

Chapter 3 shows that since the war, power has gravitated more and more to the workplace and the shop steward. Trade unionists feared that a result of operating the Act would be to reverse this post-war development and shift power back towards the union hierarchy. This would have drastic implications for the effectiveness of workplace bargaining. Moreover the shop steward would cease to be merely a representative of the work force and could become an officer of the union responsible for 'policing' the membership. The T.U.C. feared that registration would therefore require unions to alter their rules and internal procedures to create a centralized authoritarian structure.[26]

The Conservative Government hoped to see voluntary relationships flourish under the Act and stated that they did not envisage wholesale recourse to the law. The Act had been in existence only six months, however, before certain container employers in the docks sought the protection of the N.I.R.C. against the 'blacking' of their lorries by the Transport and General Workers' Union (T.G.W.U.). The N.I.R.C. made an Order to restrain this action, but shop stewards in the Mersey Docks ignored it. The Court required the T.G.W.U. to call off the 'blacking' or face fines for contempt. The T.G.W.U. contended, unsuccessfully, that it had used its best endeavours to have this course of action discontinued and submitted that they were not liable because the stewards concerned were acting outside union authority. Their failure to have the 'blacking' discontinued resulted in a fine. The Court of Appeal accepted the T.G.W.U. argument but when the case went to the House of Lords it was held that the T.G.W.U. was liable and the fines were reimposed – a total of £55,000. The Law Lords stated that although the stewards were not authorized to perform any act outside union rules or policy, it was union policy to retain work in connection with containers in the docks, and shop stewards therefore had implied authority to take industrial action in furtherance of that policy – including the 'blacking' of haulier firms. Far from promoting good industrial relations in the docks the Courts were advocating that the T.G.W.U., in order to purge its contempt of the N.I.R.C., should have disciplined or even disowned the shop stewards involved. The Law Lords had made a novel extension of the law of agency to the detriment of good industrial relations, even though Sir John Donaldson, in opening the N.I.R.C. in December 1972, had stated that the Court would reach its decisions not solely upon the basis of the evidence but upon the evidence weighed in the light of the Court's special knowledge and experience of industrial relations.

The T.U.C. required its constituent unions not to register or, if retained on the provisional register, to seek de-registration. In addition, unions were told not to use the machinery of the Act although it stated (after the T.G.W.U.'s case) that unions could appear at the N.I.R.C., but only in a defensive role – no constituent union was to initiate an action. The 1972 Congress suspended thirty-two unions for failing to de-register but eight unions subsequently did so and were readmitted. Twenty others were expelled at the 1973 Congress, including the Confederation of Health Service Employees and the British Air Line Pilots' Association.[27] The A.U.E.W. decided not to use the machinery of the Act (even in a defensive role) and called for a policy of total opposition to the Act, but this motion was defeated.

The A.U.E.W. was the most hostile union towards the Act and went so far as to call a national strike against it on 1 May 1973. In the Con-Mech (Engineers) of Woking dispute some A.U.E.W. members wanted the management to recognize their union but this was refused as the management felt that there was insufficient support for such a move. Strike action was then undertaken without giving prior notice (the A.U.E.W. was unregistered). The Company complained to the N.I.R.C. that this was an unfair industrial practice and were awarded £47,000. The A.U.E.W. refused to comply with an Order of the N.I.R.C. requiring the strike action to be lifted while the C.I.R. investigated the recognition claim and it was fined for contempt. The Court decided to sequester A.U.E.W. funds to ensure payment – still the union did not appear to defend itself. The matter did not come to a head, as an anonymous donor paid £65,000 to the Court to cover the fines and costs. Part of the money also went to two former A.U.E.W. employees who had been awarded compensation by an Industrial Tribunal for being unfairly dismissed by the union – the money had been withheld by the union, indicating clearly its total opposition to the Act.

The work-to-rule on British Rail in 1972 brought a further extension of the law. The Government had decided to impose a 'cooling-off' period but in order to do so it had to establish that this form of action was a breach of the contract of employment. The Solicitor-General, Sir Geoffrey Howe, claimed (successfully) that in the performance of a contract there was implied a general rule that performance must be undertaken in a reasonable manner and with reasonable diligence on either side. The object of the parties to the railwaymen's contracts was the running of an efficient railway system. Actions designed to reduce the railways to a state of chaos could not be a reasonable performance of the contract. Employees could be directed by the terms of their contracts of service to carry out duties other than those formally required, provided that these duties were within the reasonable scope of their employment. This was the only time that the Government used the 'cooling-off' period – a widespread use of this power had not been envisaged by the architects of the Act. 'In the United States, the only other country with any provision quite like this . . . there have been fewer than thirty cases . . . in more than twenty years, so that we need not expect many of them in Britain, although the Act provides a number of things to consider, like grave injury to the national economy, which the American law does not.'[28]

The 1971 Act is now history and the disruption that surrounded it has become part of trade union folklore. It is therefore worthwhile to examine the effects of the Act.

Many managers felt that the Act was superfluous from the very start as most unions with which they had to deal were de-registered and therefore could not have access to many parts of the legislation which could have helped union-management relations.[29] Certain procedures were tightened up, e.g. on recruitment, selection, discipline, and dismissal. Many companies were forced to examine their industrial relations policies in order to meet the Act's requirements – some for the very first time. The Act therefore played a useful persuasive part in sharpening management awareness of the need for industrial relations reform.

In general most employers in almost all industries managed to continue their voluntary arrangements without recourse to the law.

But many employers would also argue that the very existence of the law had an effect in various small but significant ways. They would argue that unions and shop stewards became more careful about giving proper advance notice of industrial action and that some procedure agreements have been more easily reformed than would have been possible without the law.[30]

Most managers preferred to play safe and stay within the law, making formal changes where they were required to do so by the Act – they wished to avoid the 'legalism' witnessed in the case of the T.G.W.U., the A.U.E.W. and the Railways. They could not have played a more dynamic part, anyway, as the other party to reform – the union movement – had in general declined to participate.

The Act had a rigidity disliked by both management and trade unionists concerned with the day-to-day business of negotiation. The Rail dispute high-lighted the difficulties faced by negotiators operating under the constraints of the Act. Effective negotiation did not take place during the 'cooling-off' period and the subsequent ballot of union members made trade union flexibility in negotiation extremely difficult. Their members had voted overwhelmingly in support of the union claim – could union negotiators then settle for much less?

Trade unionists and managers who study the arts of negotiation may view non-co-operation and non-registration as a successful policy. If trade unions had generally co-operated with the Act it would have made the T.U.C.'s subsequent negotiations with the Labour Government very difficult. The T.U.C.'s policy towards the 1971 Act was an effective bargaining strategy which enabled the T.U.C. to negotiate the almost total repeal of the Act.

Perhaps the main reason for the failure of the Act was that it was introduced without regard to the realities of industrial relations in Britain. It failed because it ignored the areas where improvement should be made in industrial relations, for example, industrial democracy and the need to develop effective strategies for both Government and trade unions to come to terms with the rapid expansion of the multi-national company. Moreover its insistence upon a new 'legalism' within collective bargaining constrained managements and unions from exploring the frontiers of negotiation and reaching agreements on such matters as information disclosure and manpower planning.

THE NEW LEGISLATION

In the face of Conservative opposition to any repeal or amendment of the 1971 Act, the trade union movement entered into negotiation with the Labour Party. The outcome was the 'social contract'[31] described earlier in this chapter. The extensive legislative programme of the Labour Government rested largely on policies formulated in conjunction with the T.U.C. in 1972 and 1973. Repeal of the 1971 Industrial Relations Act, a return to free collective bargaining, action on prices, pensions and rents were to be undertaken by a new Labour Government, which also promised legislation on health and safety at work and to introduce planning agreements and a National Enterprise Board into industry. In return, the T.U.C. accepted the need to restrain wages in order to combat inflation.

The 1971 Industrial Relations Act was to be specifically replaced by legislation covering industrial democracy and dealing with the legal rights of workers and trade unions. As a first stage in this process the Trade Union and Labour Relations Act, which repealed the 1971 Industrial Relations Act, was enacted on 31 July 1974. The N.I.R.C. was abolished on the same day, the C.I.R. and Registrar were abolished and the main provisions of the Act came into force from September 1974.

The 1974 Trade Union and Labour Relations Act kept certain of the 1971 Act's provisions. For example, it retained a code of industrial relations practice, and extended the provisions on unfair dismissal. The 1974 Act also continued several contentious issues. It gave the individual worker the right to appeal to an industrial tribunal if he considered he had been arbitrarily excluded or expelled from a union. The Act enabled an employer to dismiss an employee who refused to join, or resigned from a union where there was a union membership agreement, unless the individual had reasonable or religious grounds. The Act also gave every individual the right to terminate his trade union membership.

These particular parts of the Act have proved the subject of much Parliamentary debate. The Labour Government has approved of the T.U.C.'s decision to establish its own machinery to hear appeals from individuals who are excluded or expelled from trade union membership, and it is likely that industries covered by trade union membership agreements will enter into voluntary agreements to exclude categories of employees who may find difficulty reconciling trade

125

union membership with their occupational role. Such a proposal is already being considered in the print industry.

The Employment Protection Act came into force from November 1975, its provisions to be implemented by stages during 1976. It became the second stage of the Government's legislative programme in this field, to be completed with the advent of promised legislation on industrial democracy.

The main provisions of the Act concern employee rights. Sections 22–28 provide for guaranteed payments of up to £6 per day for workers during short-time working or temporary lay-offs not caused by an industrial dispute. An employee can appeal to an industrial tribunal if he considers his employer has failed to pay either the whole or part of the payment.

The Act also provides for up to twenty-six weeks' payment by employers to workers suspended on medical grounds. This provision relates to suspensions arising from a Government order or an order under the Health and Safety at Work Act, 1974.

Sections 34–52 provide female employees who have been employed for over two years with the right to paid maternity leave for up to six weeks. The Act makes dismissal because of pregnancy generally unfair and enables the pregnant worker to return to her employment after confinement on terms and conditions not less favourable than those which would have applied if she had not been absent. The employee may complain to an industrial tribunal if she considers her employer has failed to pay her. To assist employers the Act establishes a maternity fund similar to the redundancy fund into which the employer would make payments.

The Act provides for considerably increased protection for workers faced with redundancy. Section 61 provides, for the worker who has been employed for over two years and is declared redundant, the right to reasonable time off work to look for new employment or to make training arrangements. If the employer refuses this facility, the individual worker can complain to an industrial tribunal which can award compensation. Similarly, section 99 imposes a legal duty on employers to consult trade union representatives in the event of proposed redundancies and to notify the Secretary of State for Employment. The employer is now required to disclose to the recognized trade union the reasons for his proposals, the number of proposed redundancies and his proposed means of selecting employees for redundancy. A failure by the employer to notify can result in a reduced rebate from the redundancy fund and an industrial tribunal can make an award protecting workers from redundancy until consultations have taken place.

The Act also extends individual rights in relation to trade union membership and activity. Employees are now protected under Section 53 from victimization for belonging to a trade union or taking part in its activities. The Act also protects from victimization those who, on the basis only of religious belief, refuse to join a trade union. The employee is also now entitled in law to time off to carry out trade union duties or undergo training approved by his union or the T.U.C., if he is a trade union official. If he is not an official he is still entitled under Sections 58 and 59 to reasonable time off to take part in trade union activity and public duties.

The protections against unfair dismissal, retained from the 1971 Industrial Relations Act, are again extended by the 1975 Employment Protection Act. This Act now provides under Sections 71–80, an Industrial Tribunal with the power to award reinstatement or re-engagement and to increase an individual's compensation if such reinstatement or re-engagement is not possible. Additional awards can now also be made against employers who dismiss for membership or taking part in trade union activity or who dismiss because of discrimination on grounds of race or sex.

The Industrial Tribunal remains the main agency for hearing complaints arising under the Act. The work of Industrial Tribunals has expanded considerably in recent years. The Act also establishes a new Appeal Tribunal to hear appeals on issues of law arising from the decisions or proceedings of an Industrial Tribunal. The Appeal Tribunal hears appeals arising not only from the Employment Protection Act, but also the Sex Discrimination Act, 1975, the Trade Union and Labour Relations Act, 1974, the Contracts of Employment Act, 1972, the Equal Pay Act, 1970, and the Redundancy Payments Act, 1965.

The Act also follows the pattern set by the Government in the 1974 Health and Safety at Work Act, and reinforced by the 1975 Industry Act, by providing for a general duty on employers to disclose information to trade unions. Section 17 requires the employer to disclose information to trade unions which they require to assist them in bargaining. The Advisory Conciliation and Arbitration Service is to issue codes of practice to assist employers with this disclosure responsibility.

127

One of the most significant improvements provided by the Act is the establishment of an independent Advisory Conciliation and Arbitration Service. The Act formally established this service which had been functioning under temporary provisions since September 1974.

The State has traditionally played a role in assisting collective bargaining through conciliation and arbitration. The establishment of a conciliation and arbitration service independent of the State is, however, a new departure. The old conciliation services of the Department of Employment were closely identified with statutory or other Government-inspired forms of wage limitation which severely affected industry's willingness to use the services. During periods of pay restraints the State had sometimes withheld conciliation, even in major disputes, where a conciliated settlement could have breached a pay policy. The State had also weakened the effectiveness of arbitration by attempting to communicate its priorities in the pay field to arbitrators.

The establishment of this new service is therefore an area where the State has retreated from direct intervention and created new third-party machinery to assist the processes of collective bargaining.

The main function of A.C.A.S. is the provision of conciliation and arbitration. In addition, A.C.A.S. will provide industrial relations advice and issue codes of good industrial relations practice relating to the operation of the Act. Conciliation is provided where employers and trade unions cannot reach agreement through the normal stages of collective bargaining. A.C.A.S. may provide conciliation if requested by the parties to a dispute or A.C.A.S. can offer conciliation and advice if it is thought that this would be helpful. Before A.C.A.S. can respond to requests for conciliation, it is obliged to take full account of existing procedures and would not normally become involved where steps to resolve a dispute under an agreed procedure are still available to parties. A considerable amount of A.C.A.S.'s conciliation work is in cases of infringement of individual rights under industrial relations legislation. It has responsibility for initially conciliating in complaints of unfair dismissal. A.C.A.S. also conciliates in individual grievances arising from the Equal Pay Act, 1970, the Trade Union and Labour Relations Act, 1974 and the Contracts of Employment Act, 1972.

A.C.A.S. can also arrange to undertake arbitration in a dispute if requested by both sides. Arbitration usually follows attempts to resolve the dispute by conciliation. Arbitration can be undertaken by an independent person appointed from a list of people maintained by A.C.A.S. to act alone. Alternatively an *ad hoc* board of arbitration can be established to deal with a particular dispute, under the chairmanship of an independent member appointed by A.C.A.S. Such a board would also have one or more side members nominated by the employer and employees concerned.

Conciliation, arbitration and mediation (where third-party help is provided to assist a settlement) are all short-term remedies in dispute situations. It is clear that separation of these services from the direct influence of the State has done much to restore confidence in the service. In the first four months of its existence A.C.A.S. received about 55 per cent of requests for conciliation from unions, 20 per cent from employers, and 20 per cent of requests were joint requests, with A.C.A.S. offering its services in the remaining 5 per cent. The total number of requests for assistance went up by nearly 200 per cent, from 132 requests in the first two months of 1974 to 389 in the same period of 1975.[32]

Such short-term remedies in disputes leave many problems unresolved, since these services only focus on the effects, rather than attempting to examine the causes of disputes. Conciliation and arbitration may therefore mask a whole range of problems. Management or unions may misunderstand shifts that have taken place in procedures; there may be fundamental disagreement between parties about the principles of pay determination within the industry; or there may be implications within the dispute for trade union organization and management structure. These are not issues upon which conciliators and arbitrators are competent to comment. The establishment of A.C.A.S. does however represent a major advance in industrial relations, since not only does it provide conciliation and arbitration but these services are related to the other services which A.C.A.S. provides which are concerned with providing advice on industrial relations and assisting in the improvement of collective bargaining. The Commission on Industrial Relations represented the first major move by the State into the area of reform of systems of industrial relations. By uniting some of the traditional functions of the C.I.R. with conciliation and arbitration it is possible that considerable improvement could take place in those industries with problems in industrial relations.

The 1975 Employment Protection Act therefore marks one major reform by the State in industrial relations. Another important area where the State has intervened to provide new dimensions to collective bargaining is health and safety. The 1974 Health and Safety at Work Act grew from the Robens Committee's Report on Safety and Health published in July 1972. The Robens Committee urged reform of safety and health at work through the development of self-regulation by employers and employees.

The Act was the first piece of legislation to apply to all work-people. Between five and six million work-people who have never before been protected by legislation on safety and health matters are now covered by the Act. The Act placed a general duty on employers, reflecting their common law duties of care. An employer must now ensure the health and safety at work of all his employees. He must provide safe plant and systems of work and ensure that in using, handling, storing or transporting articles or substances there is no risk to health or safety. The employer must also provide the necessary supervision, training and information for safe working.

The Act makes provision for the appointment of workers' safety representatives. These would be appointed by recognized trade unions and they would have specific powers of inspection and access to information on health and safety matters. Employees have a duty under the Act to take reasonable care of the safety and health of themselves and other workers.

The Act established in October 1974 a Health and Safety Commission consisting of eight part-time members and a full-time chairman. The Commission must issue approved codes of practice and have overall responsibility for safety and health at work in all industries. It controls the new combined inspectorate which replaces the old inspectorates covering factories, mines and quarries, alkali and nuclear substances.

Other recent State intervention in the employment field has been through the 1975 Industry Act. The Industry Bill was published on 31 January 1975 and contained the Government's proposals to establish a National Enterprise Board with significant funds to control and direct key enterprises within the economy, to establish a system of voluntary planning agreements on the future direction, investment and manpower of firms, to widen and make permanent the powers of financial assistance to industry within the 1972 Industry Act and to provide for disclosure of information about the plans of major undertakings in manufacturing industries to Government and to the workers through their trade unions.

The Industry Act came into force in November 1975. The expansion of industrial policy in the ways set out by the Act provides a new dimension to collective bargaining.

The National Enterprise Board fills the gap left by the old Industrial Reorganization Corporation in focusing on the structural problems of existing industry. The N.E.B. is intended however to play a more positive role; it has power to take over and run firms and provide selective assistance to industry, particularly in the regions.

The introduction of planning agreements involving employers, trade unions and the Government could prove the key to successful industrial democracy. (Planning agreements are voluntary agreements about strategies for particular industries.) Industrial change is not an easy process but is made smoother if effective industrial democracy has involved all those in the enterprise in the key decisions of the industry. Planning agreements will take time to develop but will cover investment, employment, production development, pricing policy and their implications for industrial relations. The other major area of advance is the disclosure of information about certain specified activities to Government and trade unions, required from manufacturing industries. This means that the future strategic decisions of the firm will become a matter of joint control.

The Act contains a 'shopping list' of information to be disclosed. It includes information relating to members employed, capital expenditure, fixed assets, disposal or intended disposal of assets, acquisition of assets, productive capacity, output, productivity, sales and exports. As in the 1975 Employment Protection Act, the employer is safeguarded from having to disclose matters relating to national security or information given in confidence.

This chapter has examined the nature and extent of some of the significant State interventions in industrial relations. Future directions of reform are difficult to speculate on. The legislative framework introduced recently by the present Government is unlikely to be drastically altered, although it may be modified to include, for example, proposals on picketing. The future of Government incomes policy is far less certain and the chapter has highlighted some of the dilemmas faced by the State in this field.

One factor stands out in this examination of recent legislation.

Many criticized the 1971 Act for emphasizing the rights of the individual rather than the rights of the collectivity. Recent legislation may, however, warrant the criticism of over-emphasizing the rights of the trade union. The legislation that has emerged since 1973 has generally assumed a high degree of trade union organization. The necessary degree of trade union organization may be true of many industries where employees are no doubt now benefiting from the extended protection provided by their unions as a result of this legislation. Stable and extensive trade union organization is not true of the construction industry, or the hotel and catering industry. These industries are not renowned for their enlightened approach to employee relations. The lack of effective trade union organization may enable such employers to bypass some of their legal obligations.

6

The Challenge for Management

The focus in this book so far has been on the law, the growth of the trade union movement and employers' associations, and the system of collective bargaining as the process by which management and unions regulate their relationships.

In Chapter 2 we pointed out that one major source of conflict lay in the manner in which the law had been used at various times to defeat trade union purposes, and therefore led to suspicion of legislation itself, and even for a preference for using the machinery of collective bargaining for purposes where resort to the law would have been both possible and appropriate.

Although it may have helped in the short term to create an empire, through being 'the workshop of the world', it was not to Britain's long-term advantage to be the first country to experience the industrial revolution, particularly in its capitalist form. The excesses of the industrial development in that period led to a more thoroughgoing proletarianization of the British masses than in any other European country. It was from a study of the British working class that Marx and Engels derived their concept of the proletariat. The State itself, unwittingly perhaps, helped to perpetuate the separate working-class culture and consciousness with the introduction of the council house. Whole areas have been devoted to creating council house estates in a way which has not been paralleled in Europe or America.

Other countries, whose industrial revolutions took place some seventy or eighty years later than ours – Sweden is a good example – learnt from our history and were able to avoid some of the mistakes that all pioneers make.

We are, as a nation, pragmatic rather than intellectual. As suggested in Chapter 1, we developed no theory of industrial relations (any more than we developed a theory of education, where too the principle of voluntarism, which so characterizes employer/union relationships, prevailed over State responsibility and intervention) but allowed it to grow, like Topsy.

It is often argued that most trade union behaviour is reactive in nature, that it is in response to some action by management. It is critical therefore to look at managers' perceptions: what assumptions do they hold about work, about human motivation and about trade union behaviour?

When industry was small and the workforce under the sole control and day-to-day direction of the owner, the classic divisions of capital and labour, and property and work, were both harsh and obvious. The ruthless exploitation of the workforce, with labour treated as little more than a commodity, has been well-documented by historians and novelists.

The evils visited upon the working population by employers during the Industrial Revolution left however a legacy of hostility which management inherited. The establishment of the factory system eventually brought into being a class of employees who, like the workers, did not own the business – and who therefore did not create conditions – but upon whom workers looked with the same hostility as they had previously evinced towards owners. This new class were known as managers. They based their claim to authority on expertise, not heredity nor ownership. The hostility they met from the workforce was due primarily to the fact that in almost every respect they behaved little differently from the owners in whose interests they acted. They were also more privileged in their contracts of employment, higher pay, greater security and subsequently superior holiday, pension, sickness and welfare provision. They became very quickly identified as a part of 'them' in the we/them divide.

Even today the terms 'management' and 'employer' are used interchangeably by many. The Donovan Commission stressed the distinction: 'Those who settled our terms of reference no doubt chose the term "managements" deliberately, instead of the term "employers". For today most people are employed by a corporation, endowed by law with separate and independent existence.'

After World War II the notion of the management profession as standing between ownership and labour no longer held water, because the owners were not now known individuals. The new owners were typically the mysterious pension fund managers, and as J. K. Galbraith was pointing out in his writings and lectures, the modern corporation had developed to the point where decision-making was no longer the sole responsibility of a few senior managers but was spread through a complex organization.

The size of many companies serves to widen the gap between worker and management. In a small undertaking the manager is in a good position to establish personal working relationships; most issues can then be dealt with on an informal basis. Increase in size, however, inevitably leads to more complex methods for conducting relationships which involve more formal rules and procedures. Instead of being able to deal with each worker on an individual basis, management must establish ways of dealing with groups, sections and sometimes entire departments, in a uniform way.

The efficient operation of large organizations requires, to a greater or lesser degree, the construction of a bureaucracy – in some organizations it is, regrettably, to a greater degree. The main hallmarks of bureaucracy are specialization, a hierarchy of authority, a system of rules, and impersonality.[2] The term 'bureaucracy' is used here in the sense employed by social scientists, and not to denote certain extremes of over-organization. Increasing size is the most important factor in the tendency towards bureaucracy. Instead of a few people the concern will now employ hundreds, perhaps thousands. People with differing qualifications and talents are difficult to organize in achieving an objective. There will be differences of opinion, for example, concerning the best means of reaching the objective and about the nature of the contribution that different individuals and groups must make. The increasing complexity of work methods brings similar problems. Bureaucracy is an attempt to bring orderly organization and administration to bear in order to achieve stability in reaching objectives. Whether it is the best way of organizing people is open to doubt.

Specialization involves the allocation of specific tasks to designated individuals. Clearly defined jobs are laid down and individuals with particular qualifications are recruited to fill the posts. This ensures the continued existence of the job when the job-holder leaves. The main feature of specialization is its emphasis on fitting the man to the job – rather than the reverse. A hierarchy of authority is the result of different responsibilities and powers being allocated to various levels in an organization. A system of rules is established to ensure stable and uniform behaviour in the areas to which they apply. Impersonality is a key feature of bureaucracy. It is sought in order to provide for the exercise of authority in accordance with given rules rather than on the basis of arbitrary judgements and distinctions. These prerequisites for the existence of bureaucracies illustrate their essential nature. Their motive force lies not in individual self-fulfilment – where this happens it is purely an incidental – but in the continued survival of the organizational structure.

Whether managers operate in bureaucracies or in more task-orientated organizations, they manage on the basis of certain assumptions they hold about the nature of man and the nature of work. Many of these assumptions they do not consciously articulate. They are more commonly manifested in the way in which they manage their workforce. The introduction of piecework or incentive bonus schemes, of close or light supervision, have their origins in how they 'know' men will respond. Occasionally, assumptions will be expressed more overtly. Such expressions as 'A good spell of unemployment will sort this place out' or 'They're only here for the money' speak volumes.

SCIENTIFIC MANAGEMENT

Over the last fifty years or so various writers have tried to set down theories describing the nature of management, so that slowly a science of management is evolving. Some of these writers have had a considerable influence on the way managers think of their function. One of the earliest was Frederick W. Taylor, a consulting engineer employed by the Bethlehem Steel Company in the U.S.A. at the turn of the century. The work of Frederick W. Taylor has been a major influence on the development of industrial organization. He originated the concept of 'scientific management' (sometimes known as 'Taylorism'). Distrusting the pragmatic, rule-of-thumb methods employed by managers in regard to working practices, he endeavoured to bring greater precision to bear on the problems of organizing, co-ordinating and controlling industrial work. He advocated the separation of 'planning' from 'doing' so that 'planners', through the scientific study of working methods, could find the most efficient way of organizing work. Time and motion study was to be used to determine the most efficient way of working and then to lay down standards for the job. Operatives could then be suitably rewarded for meeting or surpassing standards. He devised detailed methods of work study, production flow and incentive payments,[3] which we describe in some detail in Chapter 8 on Productivity Bargaining. His work laid the basis for many modern techniques employed by managers including work study, production control, organization and methods study, payment by results and related incentive schemes.

Taylor felt that the main motivating force for workers was money. Workers would have few objections to increased efficiency once it was made clear to them that this was the best way of getting what they wanted most – bigger pay-packets. This barren assumption has prevented his theories maintaining the universal acceptance they once had. Peter Drucker notes both the positive and negative aspects of 'Taylorism':

> Scientific Management was thus one of the great liberating, pioneering insights. Without it a real study of human beings at work would be impossible. . . . Although its conclusions have proved dubious, its basic insight is a necessary foundation for thought and work in the field, . . . but it assumes – without any attempt to test or to verify the assumption – that the human being is a machine tool (though a poorly designed one).[4]

The conflict between organizational survival needs and the aspirations of workers was something which management found difficult, and often impossible, to control. Managers initially therefore readily took to the ideas of Taylor as it seemed to them that this was the only means of bringing order to industrial organization, and in many cases accorded with their own views. Preoccupation with Taylorism led to the neglect of the human relations field. This neglect proved a fruitful source of conflict. The failure of early management to consider the human needs of their employees led to the belief that such matters were not of primary concern as they were not capable of being subject to 'scientific' management.

The theories of scientific management largely went unchallenged till the work of Elton Mayo and his team of researchers at the Hawthorne plant of Western Electric. To say that, however, would be to do a disservice to the thinking of some employers in the United Kingdom, firms, to a great extent, but not exclusively, dominated by Quaker influence. Again we refer to this matter, in some detail, in our analysis of the background to I.C.I.'s productivity agreement in Chapter 8.

The management style of these firms would be regarded today as paternalistic. But the Quakers had some concept at least that the organizations which they ran served the employees as well as the owners and the customers, a concept which nowadays is becoming more widely articulated and finding its most extreme expression in industrial democracy. Nothing so adventurous was implicit in their thinking, but it was some advance to consider the workforce as something more than machine tools. If their life was to be dull and monotonous, they were at least entitled to as favourable an environment as could be provided.

This philosophy expressed itself in the provision of airy and attractive social amenities, medical centres, canteens, sports clubs, holidays with pay and pensions, even company housing. Such places as Bournville, New Earswick, Port Sunlight and Billingham, with their 'garden-city' layouts, are monuments to this kind of thinking. Nowadays people are inclined to be cynical about such manifestations, but it should be remembered that many of these advances were introduced between the wars during a time of depression, when there would have been every economic excuse for curtailing them.

These improvements in the life of the workforce were comparatively rare, and were the doing of enlightened and humanitarian employers. Nor did they go unappreciated by the workforce. They brought for the employers concerned, a bank of company loyalty they were able to draw upon in the post-war years from the older employee.

BEHAVIOURAL THEORIES OF MOTIVATION

Elton Mayo and his colleagues added a different dimension to management thinking since, like Taylor, they also attempted an analysis of the work situation but with an outcome totally different from his. In 1926 Mayo became Head of the Department of Industrial Research at Harvard University. His work involved a study of the social and psychological problems of groups of workers at the Hawthorne works of the Western Electric Company in Chicago.

Previous attempts to increase output at this plant by improving physical conditions had met with inconclusive results. Mayo at first attempted to do much the same but under conditions of scientific observation using a control group and an experimental group. One closely observed experiment, for example, was set up to examine the effect of illumination on output. Light sockets were dutifully numbered, bulbs of various wattage were used, and readings were taken recording output at varying levels of light intensity. As the light intensity was increased production went up. But when the light intensity was decreased production still climbed upward. In addition, control group output fluctuated with that of the experimental group. When conditions returned to normal, production increased even further. From this Mayo concluded that physical working conditions played little significant part, but that worker attitudes were all-important in stimulating motivation. The increases in output were not attributable to environmental change but rather to the fact that the workers, as a group, were being studied, and, what is more, they were aware that they were the subject of a study.

This gave them a sense both of their personal worth and their identity as a group. The researchers took an interest in them. They treated them as human beings, with views worth listening to, not merely as appendages of machines. Mayo also discovered, in the course of interview work, that grievances were often fabricated – though not always consciously – in order to air more general discontent. Such grievances were frequently resolved when voiced in the presence of a sympathetic listener. The formal structure of the company acknowledged workers as a category but failed to recognize them as individuals and groups.

This was accomplished by the workers among themselves; they had established an informal organization of their own. Groups within this informal structure set their own limitations on output, put their own interpretation on company rules, and protected their respective groups against deviants and outsiders by their own system of sanctions. Mayo therefore concluded that what workpeople needed was a 'sense of belonging' to a stable and cohesive group whose standards and aspirations were accepted by those within it. Groups had no place in formal industrial structure and so the task facing management was to recreate this sense of 'belonging' within the framework of productive enterprise.[5]

Because people responded to management interest there did develop, particularly after the Second World War, a school of management thought known as the 'human relations' approach – a sort of 'be-nice-to people' philosophy. At worst it degenerated into a series of rather empty routines. Secretaries to managing directors would have on their files the birthdays of each employee. Individually signed cards would be addressed and sent out.

As much of the 'human relations' approach was superficial and cosmetic, more fundamental studies of management behaviour were being undertaken, the most influential of them in the United States.

The reason for referring, in the next few pages, to some of the more prominent of the behavioural scientists, albeit in brief outline, is that their works are becoming widely known in management circles. They are opening up to managers opportunities for managing in a different way.

Abraham Maslow's studies led him to postulate that man was basically a needing animal, that there was a hierarchy of needs and that once a need was satisfied, it no longer motivated him. He then aspired to the next level of need.[6]

He defined man's most basic need as physiological – preoccupied with food, shelter, rest, water and air – and his highest need as self-actualization, the fulfilment of his potential. If a basic need, however, remains unsatisfied, this will be the individual's dominant motivation. A starving man will forgo his need for self-respect in order to get food. During the Second World War, particularly in the Far East where food was scarce, prison guards took pleasure in abusing prisoners-of-war by making them perform menial acts of obeisance to their captors in order to obtain extra rations. The lesson is that when you are on the breadline, bread is important.

The needs lying between the physiological and the self-actualization, in ascending order, Maslow designated as: safety needs (freedom from fear of deprivation, danger and threat, security for tomorrow as well as today); social needs (needs for affection and love, to belong and relate meaningfully to members of a group); and needs for self-esteem (the respect of others).

The significance of Maslow's theory for the industrial situation is that whereas managers have a natural expectation that their highest needs will be met through their work, the workforce by and large do not expect to aspire beyond the gratification of social needs. Even needs for self-esteem get blunted if you are known mainly through a works number. On the other hand, trade unionism can be seen as one way of meeting the social needs of people.

Perhaps one of the most influential writers on motivational theory is Frederick Herzberg,[7] whose name is associated with the concept of job enrichment. Herzberg considered motivational factors from the basis of two sets of needs which operate in everyone. The first he termed 'maintenance' needs, i.e. those concerned with avoiding pain or dissatisfaction. Factors based on these needs he called 'hygiene' factors, covering such issues as pay, pensions, welfare, working conditions, company policy, the nature of supervision. If these factors were not present to an acceptable standard, people remained dissatisfied and perhaps reflected their dissatisfaction in poor output and absenteeism. The adequate provision of these factors however did not provide psychological growth in an individual and a positive motivation to work and satisfaction in the job. Pay provides a clear example. An increase may remove a present source of discontent but it will achieve only a minimum level of commitment. The same is true of other hygiene factors, such as good working conditions and security of employment.

The second set of needs Herzberg described as 'motivational'. These are the needs for achievement, responsibility, advancement and recognition. The factors based on this need are to be found not in external sources but in the job itself. Work should not be organized in a dull and repetitive manner as this will only result in negative responses from workers, e.g. apathy, indifference or even open hostility. These needs can perhaps be satisfied outside work by way of sports, hobbies and other recreational activities. But if they are to be satisfied in the workplace then there must be 'job enrichment'. Jobs should be so organized as to engender more responsibility, more creative use of abilities and aptitudes, leading in turn to a sense of achievement. With continued proof of achievement there will follow a sense of self-development or growth. When recognition on the part of supervisors and management comes, the worker will acknowledge this as genuine because he will have proof that it is deserved.

Chris Argyris, Professor of Industrial Administration at Yale, has argued that rising educational standards have increased the expectations of individuals to the point where they no longer want mere jobs – they want work which requires both responsibility and the exercise of skill.[8] Education is supposed to develop the abilities of the individual to the full but its purpose is usually thwarted by the formal organization of work, since many jobs are tedious and repetitive and require little or no aptitude and skill. The individual employee who fails to obtain a sense of dignity and achievement from his work will tend to withdraw from areas of co-operation with supervisors; loyalty and commitment will disappear, and only the bare minimum of effort will be expended on his job. In these circumstances, pay becomes regarded simply as compensation for the employee's time which could be spent more fruitfully in some place other than at work.

Management can help alleviate boredom and dissatisfaction by making work more challenging, requiring greater skill and responsibility. Unfortunately, workers who have undergone boredom over a period of time tend to become set in their ways. They suffer a feeling of alienation from their work which can manifest itself in rigid attitudes towards change. They may prefer a low level of commitment rather than the challenge of increased responsibility. Management can help such workers by developing a greater sensitivity to their problems and needs. This may call for a change in the attitudes of senior and middle managers, a need to develop a high degree of interpersonal competence.

Douglas McGregor, Professor of Industrial Management at the Massachusetts Institute of Technology from 1954 until his death in 1964, noted the existence of two distinct approaches to the task of management, based on divergent sets of assumptions, which he termed Theory X and Theory Y.[9] Theory X states that the employee must be directed, controlled and motivated by management. Without this active intervention by management, people would be passive – even resistant – to organizational needs. They must therefore be coerced, rewarded, punished and driven; they must be the subject of constant surveillance and supervision. Behind this theory lie traditional assumptions concerning the average employee. He is regarded as inherently lazy, unambitious, afraid of accepting responsibility and indifferent to organizational needs. Theory X managers arouse defensive attitudes in workers, who will react by attempting to circumvent the system of rules imposed by management. This in turn serves to reinforce the assumptions which determine management's approach.

Theory Y, on the other hand, states that the essential task of management is to arrange organizational conditions and areas of operation so as to give employees responsibility and the opportunity to exercise skill and creativity in their work. This can lead to satisfaction, a sense of achievement and individual commitment to organizational goals. The assumptions behind Theory Y management are that motivation, the potential for development, the capacity to assume responsibility and the readiness to direct behaviour towards organizational goals are all present in people – management does not put them there. It is the responsibility of management to make it possible for people to recognize and develop these human characteristics for themselves.

Rensis Likert, Professor of Psychology and Sociology at the University of Michigan, reinforced McGregor's conclusions by arguing for increased utilization of the 'human assets' of organizations.[10] They form easily the most important part of a firm's total assets, yet they are often depreciated because of concentration on other assets, e.g. financial ones. Cost-cutting, increased productivity, tighter supervision and strict controls may improve the value of formal assets – on the balance sheet at least – but too often this happens at the expense of the human side of the enterprise where intangibles such as co-operation, goodwill between management and workers, and loyalty to the organization, are eroded. In these circumstances the employee will extend only the minimum of commitment – work will be of the lowest level of quality and quantity which can be produced without dismissal.

Likert, after extensive empirical studies, classified four sets of management systems. These he defined as:

System 1   Exploitive-authoritative
System 2   Benevolent-authoritative
System 3   Consultative
System 4   Participative-group

Where System 1 is in operation a rigid set of rules and norms is imposed on the worker, channels of communication are very restricted, motivation is based on coercion and the dictates of management must be explicitly obeyed. The most desirable situation is System 4 because it is the least wasteful of human assets. Workers, in an atmosphere of trust and goodwill, can feel free to make suggestions to their supervisors and to participate in discussion and decision-making. An air of co-operation prevails. Workers are given all the responsibility they are capable of assuming and loyalty to organizational goals is secured. Change in management style is therefore viewed as the motive force in changing the behaviour of people in the organization, bringing the position as close as possible to System 4 and thereby utilizing human assets to the best organizational advantage.

Burns and Stalker have defined two systems of management, viz. 'mechanistic' and 'organic'.[11] They did so as a result of extensive research in the electronics industry. The mechanistic system is distinguished by the presence of a rigid hierarchy of authority and the strict definition of jobs. Communication in the hierarchy usually takes the form of orders. Each level in the hierarchy is responsible to the level immediately above and controls the function of the level immediately below. The respective roles of managers are clearly laid down in terms of function, responsibility, rights and privileges. The worker is unable to view his task in terms of organizational goals because these have been translated into definite jobs with rigidly defined boundaries. He is paid to carry out a certain job and he will thus tend to see the completion of his job as an end in itself rather than a stage in achieving organizational objectives. The mechanistic system is best suited to operating in stable environmental conditions in which frequent change and new challenges are unlikely.

The organic system is distinguished by a loose and flexible delineation of responsibility, and job definitions are not broken down into specialized tasks but are instead more closely related to organizational goals. Thus the full range of each individual's skills and abilities is available as a direct contribution to the objectives of the organization. Responsibility is delegated to the persons best suited by knowledge and experience to exercise it, and it is never given or fixed in the static manner of the mechanistic system – it can change with the nature of the particular objectives which may be pursued from time to time. This means that when new problems crop up it is not always necessary to create new posts – where possible responsibility for dealing with the problems is shifted to those who can cope with it. By its very nature, therefore, the organic system is best equipped to deal with conditions of rapid change.

However, some firms are unable to cope with the change from stable to rapidly changing conditions by developing from a mechanistic to an organic system. Managers who favour the mechanistic approach seem to be primarily interested in the maintenance of the *status quo* and their energies are usually spent ensuring this stability. Both systems have their problems. The main problem of the mechanistic system is its failure to keep pace when stable conditions disappear and rapid change comes. The organic system, on the other hand, can experience difficulty in maintaining the cohesion of its members. Rapid change may throw up so many challenges that employees long for the security of the mechanistic order where they would at least have the security of a defined job. With rapid change, employees are never quite sure of what the organization expects from them – there is no such uncertainty in the mechanistic system. Dale and Michelon note:

> Very few people, however intelligent or unintelligent they may be, can be happy in an *entirely* unstructured job – that is, one in which their objectives and the extent of their authority and responsibility are entirely undefined – at least not where they must work in co-operation with other people, as they naturally must in an organisation.[12]

It was suggested earlier that the reason for quoting from the more influential of the behavioural scientists was because managers have been exposed to their ideas and thinking and had an opportunity to experiment with them. The pertinent question is what effect has that exposure had in practice? What evidence is there that managers do see things in a different way? And to what extent can this be attributed to the work of the behavioural scientists?

Managers as a class – and British managers particularly – are pragmatic rather than intellectual. Their most likely reaction to any innovation, whether it be an investment/financial tool such as discounted cash flow, an incentive bonus scheme based on work study, or an appraisal scheme linked to 'management by objectives', would be to ask 'does it work?'

The scientific management offered by F. W. Taylor appeared to offer a way out of the problems which beset management at the time. Certainly the introduction of work study yielded a significant reward in terms of productivity. The influence of the behavioural scientists is much more difficult to assess. Most of their work is not at the level of tools and techniques but of questioning attitudes, values and assumptions about the nature of man at work, the nature of superior-subordinate relationships, in behaviour patterns which are rooted in history and in sub-cultures. Change in these areas is likely to be slow and gradual, rather than obvious and dramatic. Many of the theories are essentially optimistic, ignoring fundamental conflicts of interest between employers and employed, and not recognizing the importance of collective bargaining as a countervailing power. As we point out later in our analysis of I.C.I.'s productivity deal (*see* Chapter 8), managers there were exposed to the thinking of the major behavioural scientists. The reaction varied from those who thought the ideas were unrealistic and poppycock, to ardent if somewhat naïve, enthusiasts. In between were those who were genuinely confused.

The enthusiasts often, and perplexedly, encountered a lukewarm response to some of their initiatives. When attempts were made to devolve more responsibility on the workforce as part of a job enrichment programme, it was put firmly back in the lap of supervision ('let them sign the clearance certificates for unsafe areas at work'). The unions depressingly showed much more interest in increased wages than in intrinsic job satisfaction.

Some cynics observed that the findings on motivational theory by people such as Herzberg were not vehicles for establishing a different relationship between managers and managed but only a more subtle form of managerial control which did nothing to alter the balance of power which was at the heart of the we/them interface.

Similarly, Chris Argyris's work in the field of sensitivity training, designed to develop improved interpersonal relations, and therefore increased openness, collaboration and trust, was regarded by some as a kind of brainwashing exercise, again doing nothing to disturb the distribution of power. They condemned what they saw as merely prescriptive remedies based on individual or group therapy, and overlooking the necessity for institutional or organizational change or even the role of technology as a determinant of workplace behaviour. Likert had warned managers that, when moving from a system of tight control to a system of participation, an initial response of apathy, resentment and even open hostility could be expected. If men have been conditioned for as long as they can remember to a reward system based exclusively on money (down to the most precise of work measurement standards, be it lifting a spanner, tightening a nut or carrying a bag of cement), and to a control system based largely on orders, it would be surprising if overnight they responded to a totally new set of expectations.

Increased participation is likely to be a lengthy and difficult task. Likert found that whenever the level of participation went appreciably beyond the skills, values and expectations of the people involved, they seemed to feel that it was not legitimate and they were unable to cope with it successfully. If anything, they became more insecure. Such findings have relevance to the ambitious attempts to involve the workforce in the whole process of industrial democracy, as we indicate later in Chapter 9.

Rarely is changed behaviour the function of a single variable.

Whilst the work of the behavioural scientists on management thinking has a recognized place, other changes had been taking place at the same time. Managers were just one of a whole group of people – parents, teachers, football referees, the church – who were witnessing a revolt against authority. Unions were becoming more organized and powerful and in some cases, more militant. Capitalism itself was coming under increasing scrutiny. A Conservative Prime Minister, Edward Heath, who at one stage was extolling the virtues of the managerial and executive class, a few years later, as a result of some conspicuous scandals in property speculation, asset-stripping, infighting and wheeler-dealing in certain takeovers and mergers, was moved to refer to 'the unacceptable face of capitalism'.

The increasing pollution of the environment, deriving from advanced technology, was producing a powerful lobby of conservationists. Managerial speeches soon became laced with phrases such as 'social responsibility'.

Managers felt increasingly under attack. They began to conceive of themselves as a professional class, similar to doctors and lawyers. They had formed an Institute of Industrial Administration as long ago as the 1920s. Whereas engineers had for a long time organized themselves in professional institutes, managers were, as a class, only a gradually emergent profession. But in 1974 the British Institute of Management devised a Code of Best Practice incorporating a Code of Conduct, which they urged their members to adopt as a basis of practice. Individual membership of the British Institute of Management with 50,000 members only involves a fraction of the United Kingdom's managers, though collective membership would marginally add to that number.

The Code does not, as yet, have the status of those required by the Medical or Bar Council nor does it have the same sanctions for disciplining erring members, but at least it is a public acknowledgement of a manager's explicit responsibilities not merely to the legal shareholders, but to his suppliers, customers, employees and the environment.

Although, as we indicated earlier, the manager initially was a very preferential employee, with far superior conditions of service – and many would argue still is – over time, many of these perks (pensions, profit sharing, holidays) have become available to the workforce as a whole. So the manager sees an erosion in fringe differentials. Even in terms of earning power there has been an erosion. This change in differential treatment could alter again in favour of the manager. The relevance of this matter is that the manager, particularly the middle manager, does not see a large gap between himself and the average employee. As Sir Frederick Catherwood, Chairman of the Council of the British Institute of Management, put it in an address in 1974 to a Belfast group of managers: 'There is not a difference of interest between managers and men, just a difference of responsibility'.

If this is so, where then does the conflict lie in the we/them divide? Is it structural or to do with values? In a given situation there may be an immediate clash of interest, the manager cutting costs in the pursuit of efficiency, the shop steward fearful of the possible consequences in terms of redundancy. The clear common concern in the survival of the enterprise which employs them both becomes obscured, one suspects, by divisions based on class and education which still persist in this country more than they do in Europe and the States.

THE ROLE OF THE SPECIALIST

Personnel and Industrial Relations Manager
We have used the term management rather loosely. We distinguished between the owner and the manager. It is necessary to be more explicit. Essentially, in the context of this book, management has meant primarily production management who, in the past, undertook all the responsibilities for both the product and for shop floor dealings with men and the unions. Increasingly with the growth of companies and the accompanying complexity of the organization, there has grown up a breed of managers with specific responsibilities for the personnel and industrial relations functions. Their growth and importance is a relatively recent phenomenon and no chapter on the role of management in industrial relations would be complete without some mention of their evolution and their role. In many companies their position has become highly influential. They have been the guiding minds behind many of the productivity deals and in the application of behavioural science theories. But it was not always so. In the early part of the century, so far as they existed at all, it was in a lowly welfare capacity.

Some of the more progressive employers, such as Rowntree and Cadbury, appointed welfare officers to look after the interests of their workers and to suggest improvements in working conditions. Unfortunately, other companies did not follow their example until forced to do so as a matter of expedience during the First World War. Masses of people who had never worked in factories before were recruited because of the manpower shortage caused by mobilization. Dilutees joined skilled workers in munitions factories, and women were employed in large numbers. Shop floor disputes proliferated as official union authority had been weakened owing to the industrial truce. In such circumstances, managers were only too glad to hand over the more detailed administrative and welfare problems to officers specifically appointed for this purpose. Unfortunately, few companies had any clear understanding of where these officers stood in relation to the management structure. Many felt that they were not part of management at all, but merely the providers of a service which was largely outside a typical manager's duties and responsibility.

Demand for such services fell between the wars. The manpower shortage, which had necessitated such appointments, ceased because of demobilization and inter-war depressions. The Second World War, however, brought similar manpower problems. In addition, shop stewards had been given a degree of protection in the exercise of their duties by the Essential Work Order, 1941. As employers could not dismiss shop stewards as easily as in the past they were required to deal with them to a greater extent. Companies turned once more to welfare officers to help them cope with the problems of recruitment, selection, training and welfare of employees. They also appointed 'labour officers' to aid them in dealings with shop stewards – sometimes one officer carried out both functions.

Post-war demand for these services did not cease, as had been the case between the wars, but instead increased owing to manpower shortages created by full employment. The efficient use of manpower was not the only reason for their retention. There was also the question of the increasing power of the shop floor and the shop steward movement. The expansion in demand for welfare and labour relations officers posed many significant questions. What was to be their role in the organization? Where did they stand in relation to other managers – were they even managers at all? What should their duties and responsibilities be? Confusion was evident in the terms employed to describe these new appointees – they have been variously entitled 'personnel officers', 'personnel managers', 'labour relations officers' and 'personnel administrators'.

The personnel specialist had great difficulty in establishing credibility for his function; a difficulty which often persists today.

> The constant worry of all personnel administrators is their inability to prove that they are making a contribution to the enterprise. . . . Their persistent complaint is that they lack status. . . . As personnel administration conceives the job of managing worker and work, it is partly a file-clerk's job and partly 'fire-fighting' to head off union trouble or to settle it.[13]

Line managers were quick to hand over their industrial relations problems to these specialists who, in turn, were glad to receive them as it meant – they hoped – an extension of their authority and an increase in status.

Personnel officers thereby inherited a mess which was not of their own making. Management, through lack of coherent industrial relations thinking and practice, had lost much of their former control over terms and conditions of employment. They had conceded to union and shop floor pressures over a period of years in order to maintain short-term production interests. Settlements were usually made on an *ad hoc* basis with little thought for future implications. Where formerly managers had sole authority to make decisions on such matters as dismissal, discipline, manning levels and redundancy, they now had to share this authority with unions and shop stewards. This is not a condemnation of joint regulation or collective bargaining but rather an expression of regret that these matters did not come about as a result of *planning* but only as a result of *concession* on the part of management. The resulting mass of union-management agreements, the growth of shop floor custom and practice and informal arrangements with shop stewards, left a bewildering situation for managers schooled in the principles of scientific management. The belated arrival of the personnel specialist was therefore a welcome relief for managers and supervisors.

The unhappy lot of the personnel officer was further exacerbated by confusion about his place in the management structure. This position was caused to some extent by the distinction between 'line' and 'staff' management. Line managers are those required to contribute directly to the achievement of company objectives. Staff managers provide advice and services to assist line management. The personnel specialist is regarded as staff. In theory, this meant that he should merely provide information and advice about problems concerning the workforce. In practice, line managers in general have transferred much of the responsibility for shop floor relations to the personnel department – mistakenly considering such matters to be the sole preserve of the personnel officer. But managers and supervisors have direct day-to-day contact with their workers and are therefore in the best position to deal with problems that arise – in the light of advice given by the personnel officer. This rarely happens, however, and usually the personnel officer is placed in the confusing position of having many aspects of line function while possessing only the authority of staff.

His position in the company may be further confused by the absence of a senior manager specializing in his area. Even by the mid-1960s many companies did not have a personnel director on the board. In some cases, personnel problems were handled by the directors of other functions, such as production, marketing and finance. Fortunately, there is a growing tendency to appoint more specialist personnel directors. The absence of clear personnel policies in many companies can lead to serious problems concerning the role of personnel specialists; the Donovan Commission observed:

> Many firms have no such policy, and perhaps no conception of it.... Many of the older generation of personnel managers see themselves simply as professional negotiators. Even if a personnel manager has the ability to devise an effective personnel policy, the director responsible for personnel (if there is one), or the board as a whole, may not want to listen to him. Many firms had acquired disorderly pay structures and unco-ordinated personnel practices before they appointed a personnel manager, and the burden of dealing with disputes and problems as they arise has absorbed his whole time and energy.[14]

The message from Donovan was loud and clear – all firms should have industrial relations policies, and responsibility should start at boardroom level.

The Department of Employment published the Industrial Relations Code of Practice in 1972. It was intended to give guidance on the promotion of good industrial relations and to help with questions of interpretation under the Industrial Relations Act, 1971. The Code is interesting because it was what the government considered to be good industrial relations practice. Before issuing the Code, the Department of Employment published a Consultative Document for the benefit of employers, unions and workers. It was intended to stimulate discussion about industrial relations. It stated, *inter alia*, that responsibility for good industrial relations lay with employers. Employer representatives countered by claiming that this was a *joint* responsibility to be shared by employers and unions. Due notice was taken of this objection and the Code of Practice stated: 'Good industrial relations are the joint responsibility of management and of employees and trade unions representing them. But the primary responsibility for their promotion rests with management.'[15]

This was, and remains, a major responsibility, and to assist management the Commission on Industrial Relations investigated the problem, publishing its findings in a Report entitled 'The Role of Management in Industrial Relations'.[16] It urged companies to establish industrial relations policies (where they did not already exist), and that such policies be initiated by boards of directors. It urged further that a particular director or senior manager be given sole responsibility for industrial relations. It recommended involving managers and employees in the formulation of policy – the principal aim being to get commitment from those who produced it in order to aid implementation. It stressed that industrial relations formed part of the line managers' responsibility: 'Since industrial relations are an integral part of company operations it follows that line managers are personally involved by virtue of their responsibility for the employees within their particular area'.[17] Personnel managers can then devote their time and talents to developing their proper role of providing specialist advice and service. The Report stated, of his standing in relation to other managers: 'The personnel manager is an integral part of the management team and, whatever his position in the hierarchy, should be consulted and be able to influence all decisions where there are human implications. His fundamental role is to make line managers more effective without diminishing their authority.'[18]

Indeed, some of the firms with the most successful industrial relations records are those where responsibility for industrial relations is placed unambiguously on the shoulders of the line manager. The specialist is there to advise him. His own behaviour, though, is the most important single factor.

PART II

7

Managing Conflict

SOURCES OF CONFLICT

It is a curious feature of conflict situations that when differences arise, conflict tends to increase and as a consequence people become very confused, participants as well as spectators, as to the real issues.

It is important for a manager in a conflict situation to diagnose accurately at what level the difference exists. Basically it can be at four levels – a difference about the information available to both parties, a difference about means, a difference about goals or a difference about values.

To resolve the conflict different action is required according to the level of difference. By far the easiest to resolve is conflict at the informational level. How often do we not find that both parties have 'got hold of the wrong end of the stick', and are not in possession of the full facts? This can be as true of domestic or political disputes as it is of management/labour ones. One of the problems in the Northern Ireland situation, for example, aggravated by the breakdown in communication through the separation of the two communities into ghettoes, is the prevalence of rumour, the distortion process that takes place, and the difficulty at getting at the facts. Was it two gunmen or three? Were there fifty stone-throwing youths or 500? Did the police or army precipitate the event or arrive after it had started?

So with union negotiations. In the mining dispute in December 1973, the miners talked of increases of only 7 per cent; the Government said that miners had been given increases of up to 13 per cent and 16 per cent, special cases to be accommodated within their counter-inflationary Stage Three policy. The important thing in conflict situations is to quickly establish common ground, to find areas of agreement. Usually at the informational level this is achieved by making more facts available. There has been increasing pressure

155

on companies to make more financial information available to their employees. Firms in the past have been reluctant to do this for fear that the unions would make exorbitant wage demands. A cold dose of the truth, showing that there is little or no profit to pay a dividend or to plough back into the company for future investment, can convince most trade unionists that the company is not in a position to meet high wage increases. If the company have had a highly profitable year, the unions will conversely be interested to know what share they may expect.

So often parties in dispute are arguing on the basis of different information available to them. The role of a conciliator or arbitrator is to increase the amount of common information. In a very competitive conflict situation, one sometimes sees information being hoarded, to be produced as weapons at strategic moments to 'beat' the other side. One has to assume that ultimately both parties have a common aim in working towards a compromise, to a mutually beneficial solution.

The next level of disagreement or difference is at the level of means or methods. Two parties may share a common goal such as the restoration of law and order in Northern Ireland or peace in the Middle East but they differ widely in the means by which they believe such goals may be achieved. So wide apart may be the differences in method advocated by extremists on both sides – for one side it could be the release of all internees and the disbanding of the R.U.C., for the other the restoration of Stormont and the 'B Specials' – that it is vital to test the reality of the common goal. Do they really want peace at any price, or are their real goals not common but different, such as victory? When firms commit themselves to a productivity bargain, do they and unions have in mind a new relationship or just a bargain?

Parties in dispute need to be very explicit indeed about their common goals. Conciliation, then, focuses the attention of both parties on their common goal, keeping it constantly in their mind as a means of uniting them. In industrial terms, the miners may have accepted the necessity of closing a pit. They may be arguing about redundancy arrangements or transfer to other coalfields.

When the dispute involves conflicting goals, such as a United Ireland or Union with Great Britain, conflict resolution becomes that much more difficult. The need here is to explore whether there are *any* common goals which both parties can commit themselves to e.g. that they both will attempt to achieve their ends through the use of peaceful and democratic means than by resorting to violence; that they do not wish to get their children drawn into the conflict; that the United Nations force would be an acceptable third party. In industry, management may wish to dismiss a shop steward; the unions may oppose this move. Both sides might share a common goal that they want to resolve the problem in such a way that it does not damage the cordial management/union relations that have prevailed until that time and therefore wish to press for arbitration as quickly as possible.

Finally, the most difficult and fruitless areas of conflict to resolve are those to do with values. These are deeply held beliefs about what is good and right. Some people believe, for example, that it pays to be kind to children; others hold that it is more important to be firm. Another may believe strongly in the business man's ethic, that one of the most important values is efficiency. Go to Africa, or even Southern Ireland, and the value that is cherished more is enjoyment, or time for a chat and a drink with a friend. Business can wait till tomorrow. Who is to say which is right? If efficiency, and pushing up the Gross National Product, means polluting the environment, per-haps the price one has to pay for an improved standard of living isn't worth it. In England the middle classes felt that cleanliness was next to godliness. For working classes, homeliness was higher on their list.

Values tend to be implicit rather than explicit, though sometimes they get expressed in industry in political terms. A Marxist looks for state control of the means of production and distribution, whereas a free enterprise advocate seeks the extension of the capitalist system. Disputes in industry are seldom argued in these terms, even by avowed communists. But values play a part in management/union behaviour to which too little attention is paid.[1]

Values are the things that move us, that make us what we are, that account for large portions of our behaviour. What is interesting in an industrial relations context is to see a discussion taking place superficially at one level, when the real issues are at a far deeper level.

Not long ago a shop steward was dismissed in a factory in an area of high unemployment where industry had been attracted by regional development grants. The dispute went to arbitration, and argument centred on whether the shop steward, in his capacity as operator, had performed the work required of him. The facts concerned such matters as whether the shop steward had been warned and so forth. But as the full story emerged, it became clear that what was really causing the friction (and another incident would have set it off if it hadn't been this) was the resentment which this shop steward felt towards the apparent patronizing attitude of both the firm and the general manager in bringing employment to the underprivileged. The general manager felt that gratitude for their investment would have been a more becoming response. He was full of the best intentions. He felt he had had to ensure abuse and insults and total lack of understanding.

The miners' strike in 1974, when it came, was not just about the actual sum of money demanded. Members were not balloted on this point. They were asked if they supported their Executive. Loyalty is a value particularly cherished by the mining community whose work situation compels a sharp interdependence on each other, so to be loyal to their Executive would rank very high in their priorities. Some miners could well have been confused. At a rational level, significant numbers might have said 'yes' to the particular pay offer of the National Coal Board, but their guts said 'no'.

This is part of the 'them and us' gap. It is present unacknowledged at so many management and union encounters. It is not a gap that is easy to close, but it is important at least to recognize its presence, to be aware of how it may be influencing the matter under dispute. When the climate is right, it is helpful for management and union to talk through their differences, to get to know each other at a personal level. Trying to do better for our children than we did ourselves seems to be a value shared by all social classes. Divorce, and bereavement and the birth of a child recognize no social boundaries. Managers and managed need occasionally to share their common humanity. The work situation does not provide many opportunities. But the 'them' and 'us' division is a subtle and complex one. Part of its tangled skein lies in the human and class relationships which have been with us a long time. There is more social mobility nowadays. Earnings have upset the old balance of staff and labour. Young well-qualified housemen in hospitals are less well paid than many manual workers. So there is less need for the division than there was in the past. It is something no nation can afford and something we need to talk through in a manner which is non-confronting.

Managing Conflict

Since the Second World War, particularly in Europe and the United States, there has grown up a new hybrid branch of the social sciences known as peace or conflict research.

Some of the relevant studies focus attention not on what the conflict is about but the manner in which it is handled. Blake and Mouton in their book *The Managerial Grid* examine different styles of management, in particular as they affect commitment, creativity and conflict.[2] The Grid has two axes, one concerned with solving the task, the other concerned with relationships. A manager with a high concern for task and a low concern for people's needs will meet conflict by trying to suppress it. At a meeting he will raise his voice and shout down the opposition. A manager with a high concern for people will meet conflict by 'soft soap'. He does not wish to hurt people's feelings. His strategy is to pour oil on troubled waters, to suggest that people are getting unnecessarily heated, that they are making mountains out of molehills, and if only everyone can get round the bar over a drink the problem will be seen in its true perspective. This strategy essentially represents suppression of the underlying causes of conflict. The suppression is through kindness not force.

When conflict arises, managers often settle for a middle position. If neither parties can obtain their goal except at the expense of the other, conflict is resolved by each side settling for half a loaf each. They have not obtained what they wanted, namely a whole loaf, but they have prevented the other party achieving its goal too. Stalemate is not totally satisfying, but neither is it dissatisfying. A compromise has been reached. By its nature compromise is temporary – a kind of holding operation. The real issues may still not have been examined, merely postponed for another day.

Some managers may have such a low regard for the task and for people's real needs that when conflict arises, they run for cover, adopting a strategy of avoidance. How often at meetings do not people stand on the touchline watching the main protagonists fight it out, by prudent silence remaining uncommitted, keeping their options open. When challenged to declare a view, their plea is for more time to consider the matter, perhaps the setting up of a working party, or answers which conflict (on the one hand this, on the other hand that).

The least frequently adopted style is that of honest confrontation of the underlying causes of conflict. The arbitration case previously mentioned would be a good example. At the superficial level, the debate was conducted the whole time as though it was a dispute about a work-study time and rating. The real issue, the smarting resentment of English patronage in bringing work to relieve unemployment together with its expectation of gratitude amongst a people who are proud, provincial and almost xenophobic, was never discussed. Had it been, it may not have been satisfactorily resolved, but at least both parties would have been made aware of what the true causes were.

Blake identified five predominant ways of managing conflict – Avoiding, Forcing, Compromising, Smoothing and Confronting. Experience tells us that we adopt all of these strategies and we would argue that what determines which one we use is the situation. Research has thrown up another more significant finding, namely that though the situation will govern the style that we use, all of us have a predominant style, one we instinctively use more often than the others regardless of the situation. So that those whose prime orientation is towards the accomplishment of the task will meet conflict situations by such habits, often operating at an unconscious level, as interrupting other people, insisting on the importance of what they are saying, shouting other people down. Other people, whose chief concern is for relationships, will quickly back down, withdraw, apologize.

Another important research finding is that not only do most people have a dominant style but they also have a back-up style to which they resort when the dominant style does not work. A common characteristic of people whose instinctive behaviour is to use force if they are challenged is to retreat into silence. 'If I can't get my way, I'll opt out.' 'Play football my way or I won't play at all.' Some, when challenged, may quickly seek middle ground.

These various ways of handling conflict may meet with corresponding behaviour by the other party. A forcing strategy may meet with a 'fight' response or an 'avoid' one (the latter being probable when a fight strategy is thought not likely to be successful). Again, people who remain silent during stormy meetings are frequently allowed by others to go on doing so. When someone tries the soft-soap approach, 'We're getting this matter out of perspective, let's go and have a drink', the chances are high that the other party collaborates and goes off for a drink, rather than sticking his ground and saying, 'I don't think a drink will solve anything. The main point of contention between us has nothing to do with mileage claims. What really gripes you is that I am authorized to sign claims and you are not'. Many of the differences which disturb people are not at the intellectual level but at the emotional level.

What has all this to do with industrial relations? Simply that it is important for managers and shop stewards to have an accurate assessment of their own conflict style of management. Not infrequently, they believe it to be other than it is. The style adopted will have a significant influence on the matter in dispute.

IMAGE EXCHANGE

A common tactic for helping people to obtain a better perception of themselves is to use an image exchange. This can be conducted at either an individual or group level. In industry, much of management/union behaviour is conducted in response to a stereotype of the other party. An image exchange often highlights this. A simple method is to take a group of managers, give them either some blank slips of paper or even some marked cards and ask them to select ten or so adjectives which most accurately describe them and lay them down on a table in rank order, picking that adjective first which is most characteristic of them. Ask shop stewards to carry out the same exercise. An exercise carried out by the authors in a large international company with middle managers and shop stewards, typical of many, showed the following response:

Managers' Self-Image	Shop Stewards' Self-Image
Hard-working	Sincere
Caring	Understanding
Consultative	Friendly
Forward-looking	Trusting
Trusting	Emotional
Decisive	Constructive
Honest	Rational
Cost-conscious	Democratic
Tough	United
Profit-conscious	Aggressive
Risk-taking	

The next part of the exercise is to invite one party to scrutinize the other party's list and check it for accuracy. If they do not accept what they see as their perception, they are asked to alter it. The process is then reversed. The managers are asked to comment on the shop stewards' self-image. A number of important developments take place. People do not like their self-images to be altered. When they are, it affects their objectivity in studying other people's self-images. If their own self-image has been badly mauled the element of revenge enters when they come to look at the other party's.

What happened to the images described above was as follows. The shop stewards' perception of the managers and the managers' of shop stewards showed some changes.

Shop Stewards' Perception of Managers	*Managers' Perception of Shop Stewards*
Cunning	Sincere
Anti-union	Aggressive
Cost-conscious	Mixed-up
Worried	Democratic
Dedicated	Trusting
Forward-looking	Emotional
Consultative	Friendly
Trusting	Understanding
Decisive	

There are a number of observations one could make on both of these lists, which provide an interesting commentary on the present state of British middle managers. The popular image of the manager is of the risk-taker, the entrepreneur, noted for his decisiveness. Many managers, particularly in large companies, find themselves so overwhelmed by constraints in the system that they settle for more modest virtues. Some supervisors, who were present on the occasion mentioned, threw out of the pack 'Risk-taking' and 'Tough' as not even meriting a place on the bottom of the list.

On another occasion a group of shop stewards were asked to list managerial traits. The list included the following adjectives:

Profit-conscious	Creative
Cost-conscious	Risk-taking
Demanding	Dogmatic

Devious	Obstinate
Non-communicative	Sly
Arrogant	Concerned for human
Inefficient	relationships

They were asked if any of these adjectives could be said to be applied to their own behaviour. In a moment of engaging and disarming honesty, they admitted that the following adjectives could be used of them: demanding, devious, arrogant, dogmatic, sly, obstinate.

It is interesting that none of these adjectives – unlike, for example, profit-conscious – relates in any way to what might be described as a manager's function. They represent human behaviour that could be applied to any situation. The response to the industrial relations situation is seen primarily in emotional not intellectual or objective terms, a fight between conflicting interests, where one expects the same behaviour from the other party as one uses oneself. The issue becomes not 'what's right' but 'who wins'.

Industrial Relations is a kind of game – who can outwit whom. The strategy is to play hard to get, not to be seen to give much away, keep the cards close to your chest. Shop stewards, particularly, expect management to play this way, they think them fools if they do not. They feel the cards are stacked in such a way that they have little choice themselves but to play this game, whether they like it or not. What really hurts is not that they should be outwitted (as there are certain rules governing the encounter) but whether they should be outwitted, with the loss of face that entails.

The final part of an Image Exchange is for both parties to sit down and provide evidence to support their description of themselves. It often transpires that actions which they took were misinterpreted and a significance attached to them out of all proportion, and possibly a communication blockage is revealed. The party which altered the self-image is also asked to produce evidence to support changes which they made. A better understanding of differences may emerge.

A variation of this technique designed to build support between two groups is to ask each group to list the positive features which they observe in the other group, together with the negative features. Lastly, to predict how the other group will have answered these questions.

These techniques have been tested in the field of management/

union relations. Their main purpose is clarification, to isolate the issues worth working on. The first part of the exercise is carried out in homogeneous groups (management and unions). The tendency of groups is to concentrate on the negative list, which rapidly fills up first. The positive features emerge more slowly and somewhat grudgingly. You must be careful of crediting the opposition with too many good points. The advantage of this method is that it is psychologically reassuring to know that the position is not all black, and occasionally one is surprised to discover that something about ourselves we had not taken very seriously is seen as positive by the other group. Having established the positive features, the groups then mix their membership to look at ways of reducing the negative features.

In negotiations, a valuable technique to adopt, particularly for an arbitration or conciliation, is to reverse the roles of management and union so that each party obtains a better understanding of the accuracy of the views of the other party. This is achieved by asking management merely to state, not argue, the union case to the satisfaction of the trade union; then asking the trade unions to state management's case to the satisfaction of management. This is rarely achieved without some interruption to the effect, 'No, that's not our case, we are not making that point.'

LABORATORY CONFRONTATION METHOD

What has been described up till now has been largely methodology, ways in which parties with conflicting interests can be brought together to resolve their conflict. The 'Laboratory Confrontation' procedure brings together in a controlled setting and for a specified period of time representatives of conflicting groups and enables them to negotiate the differences stemming from their relative positions so that they may join in a common approach to create the conditions and changes both groups can accept. This method assumes that adversary groups are mutually dependent on each other, and that neither group's position is of lesser value (neither group is wrong). The basic ingredient of the 'Laboratory Confrontation' is the creation of a new society, a society of equality of opportunity and fairness of treatment, to be shared by the two adversaries; the central ethos of the laboratory society is that both sides win; and the introduction of a third party facilitator enables the antagonist groups to enter into negotiations with comparative comfort.

There are a number of other ground rules such as: each group selects its own participants and has no right of veto over the selection of the other group; there should be an equal number of participants (ten is favoured); the individuals selected in the group will be considered to be opinion makers; the group should reflect a cross-section of the views of the group.

A final rule, which is somewhat question-begging, is that the groups will subscribe to the position that their difficulties with the other group may be resolved through the give and take of a frank and thorough dialogue between participants from both sides.

A very well developed model of this kind of technology is to be found in *Corporate Excellence Through Grid Organization and Development* by Blake and Mouton.[3] There is an analysis of a paternalistic firm with a shrinking profit margin faced with a walkout from a major international union. External factors were forcing management and union to co-operate, something that had not been actively sought in the past. A basic premise was to set aside the more immediate symptoms of friction and misunderstanding and examine the basic issues which underlay.

The objective of both groups, management and union working separately, was to develop a description of what they believed would constitute the soundest possible relationship between them; in other words to postulate an ideal situation. If joint agreement could be reached concerning behaviour characteristic of a sound relationship, the second step would be to develop a common understanding on the actual relationship between the two groups (i.e. what is characteristic of management's action and what is characteristic of union's action). If agreement could be reached on both of these, the final step would be to explore how the relationship could be changed from what it actually was today to what it might ideally be.

Management's description of an ideal relationship was one in which the union would have a better understanding of the economic situation. The union felt a basic condition of a sound relationship was one where management were fully informed on the contents of contract bargaining.

Initially, understanding, not agreement, was sought, of how the other group thought and felt and why they saw things the way they did. Exploring areas of disagreement were to be left till later. As a result of the exercise, management obtained a deeper insight into its paternalistic attitude, that the company knew what was good for employees, that they had been negligent in what they had communicated to them, that the settlement of grievances had been protracted. The unions, on reflection, felt themselves to be more sinned against than sinning. They acknowledged their lack of understanding about money but maintained management had given little information away. They felt handicapped by the impermanence of their positions, compared with management, subject as they were to election by their members. They had frequently reported waste to management who seemed unconcerned, despite their references to costs.

As so often, first-line supervisors turned out to be major causes of grievance, particularly in relation to delays in decision-making. Other causes of friction were highlighted and identified, but seen against the possibility of a fundamentally new relationship.

STRUCTURAL CONFLICT

This methodology is based on a number of assumptions which themselves are questionable. One is the recognition that co-existence is the main functional way in which groups can relate to each other. The issue is not whether conflict is good or bad but whether it is handled constructively or destructively.

The assumption is that conflict is a universal phenomenon that exists at all social levels and that human beings are rather bad at handling it. Incompetent handling produces polarization, escalation, misperception and the self-fulfilling prophecy. A thesis which states that conflict is universal in all societies and will become violent as a result of mismanagement overlooks the structural element of conflict. A particular social conflict may be directly related to a particular social order. The particular arrangement of social classes, or the uneven distribution of wealth and political power, may be vital matters in the conflict situation and no amount of laboratory confrontation or seeing the other man's point of view can overcome what may be a sense of deep social injustice.

One suspects that the belief that destructive handling of conflict leads to violence, whereas a constructive handling of it implies a peaceful outcome, is basically a political attitude as much as a behavioural science one. The suppression of violence is felt to be more important than social justice, or the radical changes in large economic and political structures which may be necessary to achieve social justice. Conflict researchers tend to believe that social justice can always be achieved by bargaining and reform processes, the evolutionary as opposed to the revolutionary process of history. They emphasize process aspects of conflict and ignore the substantive issues involved in the particular case. The oppressed or exploited may feel it better to die on their feet than live on their knees.

It is probably true to say that this thinking was influenced by the threat of a nuclear war. Anything was preferable to that, where everyone would be the loser and none the victor. Conflict situations can be described as win/win (when both parties gain); win/lose (when one party can only gain at the expense of the other); and lose/lose (when both parties lose) which is what a nuclear holocaust would be.

After the Second World War, increasing affluence, the nationalization of basic industry, full employment, a rising standard of living and generous social security benefits – compared with the deprivation and bitterness of the hungry thirties – encouraged people to believe that the ideologies dividing labour and capital were being softened in a world where all could share equally. J. K. Galbraith became the prophet of plenty and Harold Wilson in 1964 set out to remove inequality in the white heat of the technological revolution.

If equality is available to all, politics is reduced to a series of bargains to be struck between various marginal groups who for some reason have not obtained their rightful share of the new affluence. It was in this social atmosphere that conflict theory was developed. Conflicting groups can meet. All they need to shed are their misperceptions and prejudices. Any differences are psychological rather than economic.

The truth of the matter is, of course, that despite improved standards of living, there are glaring inequalities of wealth and power. Each society contains its own contradictions which arise from the distribution of money, of status and control. So conflict resolution is not just a matter of clearing away mistrust and misunderstanding replacing them with communication. It is also concerned with political matters such as the re-allocation of power.

The conflict in Ulster, for example, is not just about the misperceptions existing between Catholics and Protestants, but about the allocation of houses and jobs, the structure of the voting arrangements, the maintenance of one party in power. The lack of intermarriage, segregation in education, the tendency to move into ghettoes and the consequent breakdown of communication, certainly encouraged the creation of myths, fantasies and stereotypes about the other side. The Protestant's knowledge of Catholicism took little account of the changes in the Church brought about by Vatican II (admittedly fewer in Northern Ireland than in other parts of the United Kingdom). It would be insulting both parties though to say the disagreement was all a consequence of misunderstanding. It was also about a clash of political philosophies. Political philosophies ultimately rest on the use of force, either to defend a system (which is what the police and the army do) or to bring it down (which is what urban guerillas and revolutionaries attempt to do).

The structure of capitalist societies necessarily involves a basic division between workers who sell their labour and capitalists who dispose of it. For the system to work there must be a number of inequalities between the two groups of people. Unfortunately in Great Britain, this inequality is reflected in the educational system which turns out 75 per cent of the community at the age of sixteen, not highly literate (many averse to higher education) but with sufficient skills to work in factories. The other 25 per cent emerge from the grammar schools with more skills and either never work in factories or, if they do, join the managerial ranks. The situation is eased slightly because of some upward mobility from the ranks and because the monetary reward system is such that some factory workers can earn more money than some of the more highly educated 25 per cent.

This is a situation of potential conflict. It works because people, by and large, are prepared to accept it. If the conflict became overt, its resolution would not be as a result of getting managers and trade unionists together to clear up their misperceptions. Only structural alteration could solve the problem. Similarly, Alan Fox[4] would argue that only a structural alteration will bring about any fundamental change in the relationships between managers and managed.

He makes a distinction between social (or human) exchange and economic exchange. The relationships which exist between senior managers are those of social exchange, and are characterized by high trust and high discretion. Obligations are diffuse. There is reciprocity in the relationship but it is not something that is written down. In such a relationship goals tend to be shared.

In marked contrast, the relationships between management and unions are at the level of economic exchange. Characteristically this relationship involves low trust, low discretion and tight specification of roles. Labour is de-humanized, merely a commodity to be sold and bought. Features of economic exchange are bargaining, grudging concession, and wary mutual inspection. Power is crucial in such a relationship, if only in order to preserve balance. Negotiated collaboration is the only response to low trust situations. Trying to obtain trust through welfare schemes, Fox argues, has not brought any significant gains. Management's attempts to invoke high trust behaviour without structural changes required for the institutionalizing of high trust are likely to be self-defeating. This is a matter we shall pursue further in Chapter 9 on Industrial Democracy.

The relevance for conflict resolution is that there is an assumption by superiors that occupants of low discretion roles are likely to have goals that to some extent conflict with their own and therefore that bargaining is the only appropriate mode of resolution. The assumption among those in high discretion roles, on the other hand, is that goals will be shared. Threats, games and false positions would be regarded as inappropriate behaviour, the problem-solving mode being more acceptable.

INTER-GROUP BEHAVIOUR

Many studies have been carried out on groups whose members initially had no reason to distrust each other and who before their formation into groups might be thought to share a common interest. Physical separation seems very quickly to produce psychological separation and, without much external stimuli, each group perceives itself to be different from the other group, and not only different but superior. Most groups have a superiority complex.[5]

If conflict between the groups becomes more than superficial, certain traits begin to appear, regardless of the composition of groups. Two groups, each with a mixture of shop stewards and managers, for example, will behave similarly to unmixed groups when put into situations of even mild competition. In fact, the tendency of a group is to compete rather than collaborate with other groups. In many ways, competitive behaviour is more stable than collaboration. Collaborative behaviour is risky. It puts a high premium on trust. 'If we take this step, how will the other group behave? How will it perceive our gesture? Will it be understood? Will they take advantage of us?' These are the kinds of questions all groups ask of the other. If trusting behaviour looks weak it may not be understood quickly; it may even be misinterpreted.

An interesting experiment in competitive behaviour is to take two groups and ask them separately to perform a common task, which they are required to write up in the form of a report. Then pair off members from one group with members from another. The task, using the most objective criteria, is to decide which of the two group reports is the best. This should be done by the allocation of marks out of a hundred. The only stipulation built in is that the marks cannot be allocated on a 50-50 basis. In such conditions, objectivity tends to fly out of the window and the main pre-occupation, sometimes operating consciously but frequently at the sub-conscious level, is to win, to bring home the bacon to your own group.[6]

Physical separation makes communication difficult. Other phenomenon are noticed. Most groups need an enemy for internal cohesion and close ranks under external threat, so that group boundaries become difficult to penetrate. Understanding decreases, differences multiply and common ground disappears.

Groups gradually lose perspective on their own behaviour. Over time the other group is perceived as more evil. The other group's behaviour may frequently be seen as a function of the personality of one person in it. Group pressures on an individual to conform are particularly strong, the more so when he does not understand the issues under discussion. The price may be paid later. If a person is not committed to and involved in a group decision he may opt out when the situation becomes difficult. These pressures put group negotiators in a difficult position. They get caught in the hero/traitor trap. If they 'bring home the bacon' their position is enhanced. If, for the most rational of reasons, they concede to the other side, they may well be rejected and replaced. Success for a group, measured in selfish terms, strengthens the group in believing they were right and confirms their course of action for the future. 'We told you so' sums up the attitude.

If there is little trust between groups, and you have to know a group well and find their behaviour predictable before trust can occur, openness in communication about your own group's goals can be threatening. One of the problems needing to be resolved, where it is apparent that the only way groups can make progress is by co-opera-tion, not by competition, is 'Who starts trusting first?'. The trouble is that one violation of trust (which could be a mistake and totally unintended) spoils all credit. 'I told you so. I knew we couldn't trust them' is the sentiment, even if objectively and quantitatively other gestures were made which were positive. They are quickly forgotten.

If these behaviours can occur between groups with no history of antagonism to cloud the issues in dispute, it is not difficult to imagine the problems facing management and union with centuries of mistrust behind them, with all the differences of social class separating them, not to mention the structural conflict that may be present.

It is vitally important for managers and workers to be aware of all the forces operating in the situation, behavioural as well as structural, and to discern, if they can, what forces are prevalent at any one moment. It is not difficult to recall occasions when we have observed many of the above phenomena in inter-group situations.

Certain behavioural characteristics are discernible in situations where one party is victorious over the other. If this position has been obtained as a consequence of violation of trust, the winners feel victorious and gloating but these feelings are mingled with guilt and possibly fear of retaliation. The losers feel duped, foolish, rejected and angry. When both sides cheat, and lose, the prevalent feelings are frustration, disillusion, disgust, uncertainty and even stalemate. Successful collaborative behaviour produces emotions of friendliness, satisfaction and credibility. The formation of the Northern Ireland Executive in 1973 (of parties which previously were in quite fierce opposition but after hard bargaining evolved a collaborative solution) displayed quite astonishing euphoria. Morale was extraordinarily high, the atmosphere, amongst erstwhile opponents, highly supportive

The win/lose situation produces other characteristics. The winning group becomes more cohesive. The leadership is consolidated. There is a danger that they may become complacent and lose some of their fighting spirit. The losing group, on the other hand, may splinter. Scapegoating takes place. It may in the process learn more about itself. Its major pre-occupation may become defeating the other group rather than achieving its original objective.

In thinking about inter-group behaviour generally and then applying this understanding to management/union relations, one can see some of the inherent difficulties in introducing worker participation. Two management groups, production and maintenance, are set up ostensibly to collaborate. Even here one sees competitive behaviour, particularly if resources are scarce and in high demand. How much more so for groups who are structured for opposition.

The history of trade unions is of organizations set up in opposition to employers, to prevent the exploitation of their members. Militant trade unionists will argue that a worker's prime loyalty is to his union, which gives him protection, not his firm which gives him employment. A company will take a contrary view.

The truth is that the unions in their origins and development have been designed for opposition. So participation undermines their position as much as it does managers. Do they really wish, if pressed, to elect foremen? Are they prepared to carry the responsibility for poor decisions? Collaboration is as risky for them as it is for managers and requires a radical rethinking of their position. They may not desire some of the changes which worker participation calls for. Hugh Clegg pointed out some years ago: 'The trade union is industry's opposition, an opposition which can never become the government.'[7]

The subject is one on which a good deal has been written, and many ideas produced. In truth, some hard thinking is required to work out what it will actually involve, what changes in attitude and structure both sides will have to make. It is not just a matter of management relinquishing their prerogative. The unions may have to surrender some of their own cherished positions too.

8

Productivity Bargaining

People talk frequently about good industrial relations without being very specific in describing them. Are 'good' industrial relations a means to an end, such as profit or productivity (which are not ends anyway)? Or are good industrial relations something intrinsically worthwhile – good, just and moral? Or are they both? Or something else? Few people seem to have thought through this issue. For some the concept of Productivity Agreements appeared to offer a way forward. They were particularly popular during the sixties. With economic recession in the late 70s and various forms of wage restriction by Government, they may become fashionable again.

Some of the productivity agreements were a conscious effort to combine political pragmatism with an attempt to incorporate some of the findings of the behavioural scientists, the Elton Mayos, the McGregors, the Maslows and the Herzbergs. How to combine productivity with job enrichment and increased individual motivation was the trick. Yet who can say now that these Productivity Bargains were the great break-throughs they were heralded as at the time? Were they just old wine in new bottles (better packaged, of course)? It would be comforting to believe that productivity and profit were support systems for the quality of life.

The pragmatism behind Productivity Agreements stemmed from the fact that employers were becoming increasingly aware of foreign competition. Subjected as they were to economic pressure, they looked particularly at those costs which were more directly under their control, principally labour costs, and at how that labour was used.

The period was also marked for some of the time by the presence of the National Board for Prices and Incomes, and the general requirement for wage restraint, so that wage awards which could be attributed directly to increases in productivity were regarded more favourably.

As a consequence Productivity Bargains were frequently used as flags of convenience, rather than as a genuine attempt to work out a pattern of new relationships – useful to employers, unions and government alike as an excuse to pay out additional money in a time of credit squeeze and wage restraint. They became devices to help the country out of its recurrent economic crises.

Those concluded purely as a result of external pressures made no impact on the underlying industrial relations problems. Productivity bargains conceived in an atmosphere of mutual suspicion and hostility changed little. If the history of good productivity bargains has taught us one thing, it is that they are the culmination of a long, enduring effort to cultivate better management/labour understanding.

Aside from its function as an excuse to pay out more money, to get past Government legislation, why has productivity assumed such importance? What are some of the factors that inhibit productivity? Are they all union-inspired? Or is management to blame? Are productivity bargains the way ahead? What should be the characteristics of a productivity agreement?

The National Board for Prices and Incomes defined a productivity agreement as 'a settlement in which workers agree to make changes in working practices which themselves lead to more economical operation of a plant, a company or an industry. In return an employer agrees to increase pay, to improve fringe benefits, to raise the workers' status, or to make a combination of these improvements.'[1] In other words, there had to be a specific contribution to increased efficiency rather than a mere promise of intent.

A productivity agreement thus involves the concept of exchange. Both parties benefit. It is a process based on self-interest and mutual advantage. This is in contrast to traditional collective bargaining which more clearly reflects the existing power relationship between the two parties and the operation of the local labour market. When labour is tight and skills scarce the unions can exploit their strong bargaining position. The miners' strike of 1974 was a supreme example of a union with its foot on the economic jugular vein of the nation, obtaining a wage claim, unrelated to any norm other than their enormous bargaining power at the time. This is in stark contrast to the strike of post office workers in 1971, for example, who had to settle on the Government's terms.

In their book *A Behavioural Theory of Labour Negotiations*, an analysis of a social interaction system, Richard E. Walton and Robert B. McKersie identify four sets of activities in all labour negotiations:[2]

1. *Distributive Bargaining*, which essentially produces competitive behaviour, where one party can only win at the expense of the other.
2. *Integrative Bargaining*, where the stance of both parties favours problem-solving and co-operation to increase joint gain.
3. *Attitudinal Structuring*, which affects the basic relationships between social units.
4. *Intra-Organizational Bargaining*, which describes behaviour aimed at achieving consensus within one's own organization e.g. how far out in front can a shop steward afford to be without losing his basis of support.

Productivity bargaining has to do with the last three sets of activities. In the event, attitudes formed from the past, fears about the future, the tendency of groups (particularly those structured in a polar way) to compete – all mean that behaviour will shift from time to time to entrenched positions.

The N.B.P.I. (Report 23) laid down seven criteria for model productivity agreements:

1. It must be shown that the workers are making a direct contribution towards increased productivity by accepting more exacting work or a major change in working practices.
2. Forecasts of increased productivity must be derived by the application of proper work standards.
3. An accurate calculation of the gains and costs must show that the total cost per unit, taking into account the effect on capital, will be reduced.
4. An agreement covering part of a plant must bear the cost of consequential increases elsewhere in the plant, if any have to be granted.
5. The scheme should contain effective controls to ensure that the projected increase in productivity is achieved, and that payment is made only as productivity is increased or as changes in working practices take place.

6. There should be a clear benefit to the consumer in lower prices or in improved quality. In some instances, 'lower prices' may mean lower than they would have been if the undertaking can prove that factors outside its control would otherwise have led to higher prices.
7. In all cases negotiators must beware of setting extravagant levels of pay which would provoke resentment outside.

How successful were those firms which entered into productivity agreements in meeting these criteria? The evidence available to the Royal Commission on the success of productivity agreements in reducing costs showed a marked lack of specific detailed calculations, but many organizations still regarded themselves as well satisfied with the outcome of the agreements they had entered into.

As we will argue in more detail later, the benefits, in many cases, turned out to be different from those intended. Crudely buying out a restrictive practice proved not as important as management and union getting together round a table and trying to work out how the plant might be run more efficiently. Some firms, such as I.C.I., started out from the beginning to conduct a twin operation – to use productivity agreements on the one hand as a means of reducing unit costs, but also as an opportunity to create a new relationship for its workforce, inspired by some of the findings of the behavioural scientists.

A senior I.C.I. manager, introducing junior managers to the first I.C.I. Productivity Agreement, started with a quotation from Douglas McGregor's *The Professional Manager*:[3]

Perhaps the greatest disparity between objective reality and managerial perceptions of it is an under-estimation of the potentialities of human beings for contribution to organizational effectiveness. These potentialities are not merely for increased expenditure of effort on limited jobs, but for the exercise of ingenuity, creativity in problem-solving, acceptance of responsibility, leadership and the development of knowledge, skill and judgment. When opportunities are provided under appropriate conditions, managers are regularly astonished to discover how much more people contribute than they believed possible.

He added, 'This quotation epitomizes for me the ultimate purpose of M.U.P.S. (the I.C.I. Agreement) – to set people free to realize their responsibilities'. A far cry from the specific guidelines suggested by the National Board for Prices and Incomes and, as we show later in this chapter, not matched by a similar response from the unions, who seemed discouragingly pre-occupied with issues of redundancy, of yielding too much too soon, in allowing non-trades people to use tools, of committing themselves in writing, or anxious about what grades they would be on, and whether their jobs and grades would be protected when they got older, and what unions trademen's mates would be in.

Others saw Productivity Agreements as an attack on restrictive practices, the outcome of which was low productivity.

There was not much dispute about Britain's low productivity in the sixties, the table below shows.

Productivity in Metal and Engineering Industries

Number of men per job required to produce the same output

	Steel	Chemi-cals	Metal products	Elec-trical ma-chinery	Transport equip-ment	Non-electrical ma-chinery
United States	1	1	1	1	1	1
Great Britain	2·3	3·4	2·2	4·2	3·2	3·5
West Germany	1·7	2·6	3·2	3·8	2·4	3·2
Sweden	Figure not available	2·5	2·6	2·3	1·4	1·9
Italy	1·2	2·5	4·2	2·3	2·1	2·4
France	1·6	3·0	3·1	2·6	2·0	2·3

Source: *The Economist*, October, 1966.

An article printed in 1972 in the National Institute Economic Review entitled 'Labour Costs and International Competitiveness' reinforced the point:

There is of course no single explanation of the declining inter-national value of the pound. There can, however, be hardly any doubt that one highly important factor has been the failure (before 1971) to improve productivity at rates comparable with those achieved in most other major industrial countries. Between 1960 and 1970 estimated output per man/hour in manufacturing

177

industry increased in the U.K. by rather under 50 per cent. . . . But the corresponding rise in West Germany was about 70 per cent, in France 80 per cent and in Netherlands and Italy around 100 per cent, while in Japan it was close on 170 per cent.[4]

Wherein lie the causes of our low productivity? Primarily in our restrictive labour practices, which exist here on a far greater scale than anything to be found in the States. Certain craft jobs may call for as many as four or five trades; hence the unedifying spectacle of skilled workers waiting literally for hours before they can proceed on a job, lest they infringe on the work of another craft. No wonder Bill Allen, the Emerson engineer who helped pilot the famous Fawley Blue Book, called us 'Half-time Britain'.

Again, to quote Jock Haston speaking from his experience of training E.E.T.U. shop stewards, at the E.E.T.U. College, Esher.

Once we have explained to workers that if they work half-time they are paid for half-time, economics becomes an understandable subject. It is easy to grasp that it matters not how skilled we are as negotiators. It makes little difference how militant we are when we negotiate. We negotiate round a product. If it is a product of 20 hours' effective work in a 40-hour week, that's what we are paid for. Skilled workers, who wait literally hour after hour in one shipyard store, who wait for instructions, wait for tools, who wait for transport, where it has always been like that since they were apprentices, they grow up with a contempt for management. It's 'their' fault, they say. At least we are being paid whilst we hang around. We are being badly paid but we are in work, and when the ship goes out we might be out for a few weeks. When trade unions teach them it is an illusion that they are only paid for effective work, they will seek to put an end to this nonsense.

ORIGINS OF RESTRICTIVE PRACTICES

Whose fault is it? Is it 'their' fault, i.e. management's? The reasons are complex and go back into our industrial past as we indicated in earlier chapters. It is sometimes held that the unions themselves are solely responsible for the prevalence of restrictive practices, jealously defending their individual or group interest. Perhaps it would be more accurate to say that the unions maintain what management established in the first place.

Was it not Adam Smith who said:

> The improvement of the dexterity of the workman necessarily increases the quantity of the work he can perform; and the division of labour, by reducing every man's work to one simple operation and by making this operation the sole employment of his life necessarily increases very much the dexterity of the workman. . . .
>
> The advantage which is gained by saving the time commonly lost in passing from one sort of work to another is much greater than we should at first view be apt to imagine it. It is impossible to pass very quickly from one kind of work to another that is carried on in a different place and with quite different tools.[5]

Adam Smith preached this concept to employers. The universities taught it to the educated sections of the population. The syllabuses of the old Mechanics Institutes show the training of men in bands of skill – so generations of managers and workmen were brought up on this principle of specialization, so different from the medieval craftsmen whose skills embraced a wider range of job performance.

The situation was aggravated even more by some of the work of Frederick Taylor at Bethlehem Steel described in Chapter 6. Taylor thought that detailed analysis of a job could lead to a greater advance in efficiency than the increase in energy exerted. One of the many tasks he analysed was that of loading pig iron. The loading of pig iron involved seventy-five labourers loading an average of $12\frac{1}{2}$ tons of pig iron per day. Through his analysis, Taylor broke the job down into a series of minute logical steps. Then he selected the strongest man he could find, an enormous Dutchman, and offered him a dollar per day (a 60 per cent increase in wages) if he did exactly what he was told, no questions asked, no initiatives to be taken.[6]

Not unnaturally, the Dutchman was interested in this financial reward and, under careful supervision, was found to be capable of loading $47\frac{1}{2}$ tons per day. Incredibly, this performance was then used by Taylor and the management as a norm for all workers regardless of their physical capabilities. As a consequence all the men's wages were raised to 60 per cent and the company saved considerable money, but the workforce was reduced from 500 to 140.

Taylor believed, as did Adam Smith, in the concept of economic man and was determined to reduce inefficiency in industry through the application of scientific method. But, as we wish to stress in this book, a man at work is more than an economic animal. He is a participant in a social process, a process which encourages co-operation with his fellow worker.

It was fatuous to create a population of workers geared to the principle of specialization, especially when the spectre of unemployment was ever present, and expect them to be converted overnight to the principle of flexibility. The Bethlehem steel experience simply reinforced the workers' distrust of the employers, who had fallen in love with their new control technique and seemed only too anxious to use it regardless of the social consequences.

The concept of specialization, which does contain a core of truth, and the ensuing restrictive practices, is not, of course, confined solely to manual workers. The professional, whether engineer, doctor or lawyer, can be as fierce as any tradesman against the encroachment of what is regarded as his specialism.

Having preached *specialization* for so long, management must expect a considerable period of re-education to be needed to persuade a working population that flexibility should be a condition of their skill and working life.

Trade unionists, not unnaturally, played a defensive role in respect of productivity. If the worker was conceived by economist and engineer alike as little more than an instrument of production, upon whom less care and attention was lavished than the machinery and tools he operated, what incentive was there for him to think more broadly? Inevitably, his energies were taken up with survival and obtaining a more equitable distribution of the fair day's pay.

The trade unions became interested in productivity when they experienced the effects of the inability of many employers to maintain a stable and rising level of output, and so employment for their members. Under the leadership of that remarkable trade unionist, Walter Citrine, then General Secretary of the T.U.C., the Trades Union Congress of 1927 had the alternatives presented to them. He put before them the dilemma which has always plagued the movement. Were they a political force or a bargaining unit?

Three roads were open to them:

1. To declare it was not an aim of trade unions to increase the efficiency of industry but hasten its collapse.

2. To keep up the defensive struggle to maintain and improve existing standards, but to accept no responsibility to improve the existing organization of industry.

3. To participate actively in a concerted effort to raise industry to its highest efficiency by developing the most scientific methods of production, eliminating waste and harmful restrictive practices, removing causes of friction and avoidable conflict and promoting the largest possible output so as to provide a rising standard of life and continuously improving conditions of employment.

It was the third option that he invited the unions to choose, opening up a new era of collaboration between management and men. He received a ready response from the Brunner, Mond group of employers who saw the possibility of a new social contract. This was a call not just for an adequate pay packet, tolerable working conditions and stability of employment, but for a more co-operative working relationship. Considering that Citrine made his appeal in the year after the General Strike, it was a remarkable offer. Unfortunately, the depression which followed the strike made it impossible to realize. I.C.I. had to wait forty-five years before they were able to pioneer in 1972 their famous Weekly Staff Agreement, which embodied many of the ideas implicit in Citrine's offer – that a worker's responsibility should be enlarged, that he had informational rights, that a respect for his status as an individual would be more likely to yield identification with the enterprise.

The Trade Union attitude towards productivity and the maintenance of restrictive practices, then, has been governed by fear of change, fear of decline in status, fear of unemployment.

The Second World War, however, ushered in a period of full employment, a situation which, despite fluctuations, obtained till 1975. The end of the war also saw the emergence of a Labour Government which laid the foundations of our Welfare State.

First Attempts – Attacking Restrictive Practices
The early attempts at Productivity Agreements aimed at removing restrictive practices.

The term 'restrictive practice' has proved difficult to define but has generally been regarded as 'an arrangement under which labour is not used efficiently and which is not justifiable on social grounds'.

That definition begs a number of questions. Who is to decide what is 'efficient' and what is 'justifiable on social grounds'? Do employers decide what is 'efficient' and the unions what is 'socially acceptable'?[7]

In practice Productivity Agreements concentrated mainly on such matters as the removal of excessive overtime; relaxation of demarcation whether inter-craft or between craft and non-craft workers; the abandonment of 'mates'; increased flexibility of labour; reduction of manning; flexibility in hours of work; cutting down time-wasting practices such as tea-breaks; removal of output limitations imposed by workers; introduction of new equipment.

In return, they offered workers increased pay, improved hours of work, superior fringe benefits, enhanced promotion prospects or status, even greater security. Where overtime really was excessive and regular, it was difficult in some cases, even with an enlarged stable wage, to match 'take home' pay.

Even agreements which appeared on paper to be only about manning standards on machines or jobs or the reduction of overtime sometimes led to a recognition that wider change was inherent – a change in the attitude of the worker to his work. And that too meant a change by managers in the way they regarded and handled labour.

Esso's Productivity Agreement for its distribution workers, signed in January 1966, was known as the Esso New Deal, and pioneered by managers who had had experience of the Fawley Productivity Agreement and were imbued with the idea that nothing was impossible in the sphere of Trade Union negotiations.

THE BLUE BOOK

To Esso Petroleum, at their Fawley Refinery, must go the credit for introducing the first major productivity deal in 1960, enshrined in the famous Blue Book. The tendency with Fawley is to look at its outcomes. What is often ignored is the management thinking that preceded it. We have described earlier in this chapter the need for more flexible ways of operating if workers are to produce as much as their Common Market counterparts. There has to be no less a revolution in management flexibility.

The Assistant Refinery Manager, when asked what had made the Blue Book possible, replied 'the habit of discussion'.[8] Fawley was blessed with some talented employee relations staff. So good were they at their job that they tended to usurp line management's responsibilities. Line management were pre-occupied with the technical challenge of building the largest and newest refinery in the U.K., and more than content to let employee relations staff cope with the social and human problems thrown up by fast technical change. Any separation of the so-called personnel function from other aspects of management, however, is likely to lead to trouble. After all, the main function of management is organizing the work of others.

The 'habit of discussion' meant looking behind the institutional arrangements of industrial relations (the procedures, agreements and rules) at the human beings whose needs they were meant to serve. It was recognized that management had to win the consent of the managed, particularly in those decisions that affected them. Much of this was done through informal person-to-person consultation which achieves a number of purposes. It indicates management's readiness to examine the problems of its workforce. It even provides a relief from the frustration of much of the work situation.

One of the authors was working with Esso in 1959 and remembers some of its characteristics. There was a good deal of christian name familiarity at Fawley, which probably owed something to its American origins. But more conspicuous was the atmosphere of informality. It had fewer of the hierarchical trappings associated with firms of similar size – managers arrived at work at the same time as the men, there were common and shared and relatively modest canteen facilities, and fewer status symbols for managers. There were a number of joint management/union committees, chaired alternatively by a management and union representative, agreeing pay rates for changed jobs. There was a refreshing absence of any authoritarian spirit in the discussions.

Had not management created a favourable climate, the changes that were made might not have been so dramatic. The main changes achieved at Fawley were a reduction in overtime, the abolition and re-deployment of tradesmen's mates (through increasing the number of craftsmen and using auxiliary non-craft labour for specific tasks), the abolition of set tea-breaks, and some increased flexibility, in exchange for increased pay, the consolidation of pay grades and the abolition of the by now outmoded rating scheme.

Fawley's informality of management in some ways acted as a hindrance to flexibility. Many practices had been accepted as 'custom and practice' but when the unions were asked to reveal the extent of their concessions they insisted on a fair degree of exactitude. They were concerned more with the letter of the law, not the spirit. As one senior A.E.U. shop steward graphically put it: 'The men had agreed to do so much in the agreement and they were working to this. If management wanted to carry this further then they must present their proposals and expect to pay for them. What was this spirit being talked about? People were doing what had been agreed in the Blue Book'.[9] Words became critical; even more so their interpretation. The wording of the Maintenance and Construction Section had been that when Process Workers were trained to do the minor maintenance jobs 'they should be free to carry out this work whenever circumstances permit'. In the Process Section, an additional phrase had been added 'and when a Maintenance and Construction man is not easily available'. Again, inter-craft flexibility was limited to 'during shutdowns'.

Management's attempts to obtain greater flexibility whether at an inter-craft level or between craft and process worker, met with limited success. Nor was there much multi-craft supervision.

Even management's attempts to buy out the demarcation areas by raising the money was not a sufficient bait. The disappearance of craft differential meant more than money. Dilution meant a threat to the craftsmen's status, something money cannot easily compensate for. Yet as Allan Flanders points out in his book, *The Fawley Productivity Agreements*,[10] during a fourteen-hour shutdown in the latter part of 1962, when a 'work-to-rule' sanction had been imposed by the craft shop stewards, everyone co-operated to get the job finished and a good deal more flexibility was worked than the agreements provided, the difference being that it took place at the men's and not at management's discretion. Time and again, ownership and control in relation to the job are the key factors in negotiating change.

OTHER AGREEMENTS

Where Fawley paved the way, others followed. Prominent among them were the oil companies, Mobil at their Coryton Refinery, Esso at Milford Haven, Shell Chemicals at Carrington. In different ways, they were bold and imaginative attempts to buy out restrictive practices, such as the removal of mates, or the abolition of overtime, which had grown up like an insidious weed, and to substitute for it time off in lieu.

Shell went into battle under the slogan of 'Time, Tools and Ability'. Their agreement contained such clauses as:

The removal of all barriers to productivity where these take the form of unreasonable demarcations between groups of workers and the substitution of the general rule that considerations of time, tools and ability alone determine the extent of each man's job. This does not mean that, in the case of a craftsman, any man's basic craft skill will be disregarded or that considerations of productivity are to be subordinated to safety and commonsense.

Operators, in addition to their normal duties, will be able to perform certain plant maintenance tasks by themselves, and will also be able to work under the direction of craftsmen on tasks which involve a basic craft skill.

The company had already undertaken on 1 January 1966 to unify the existing arrangements for payments during sickness and operate a single comprehensive scheme, at the same time as improving the holiday entitlement for the majority of hourly-paid employees. Time recording was also discontinued. As management explained, the intention was to continue to use the basic skill which each man had and employ him to the full in doing work within his original trade or classification; and to lift only artificial and outmoded barriers which had prevented men from doing work they were fully competent to do, and only did not do because some rule, accepted routine or tradition, prevented them.

Security of employment was felt to be paramount, the need to feel secure being crucial to anyone who was being called upon to agree to the abandonment of practices basically designed to give security. But through a policy of voluntary retirement and avoiding recruiting, Carrington were able to meet an expanded capacity with 600 fewer employees. Workers received pay increases of up to 28 per cent. The company maintained that they had no option in view of the pressure on prices in a market exposed to international competition.

In 1963 a Shell international study team with knowledge of productivity at installations in the U.S.A. and elsewhere in the world had visited Carrington and reported that, according to the accepted standards in the prevailing industrial climate, Carrington was 20 per cent overmanned.

A distinctive feature of the Shell Petrochemicals Agreement was that, unlike Fawley, where management had drawn up a Blue Book containing a list of proposed institutional changes before they approached shop stewards, at Carrington management had invited a Joint Shop Stewards Committee to suggest ways in which traditional practices might be changed to produce higher efficiency. Their proposals differed from management's, particularly in the difficult area of interchangeability between crafts and between crafts and operators.

Two working parties from management and shop stewards were commissioned to produce a mutually acceptable draft agreement. They worked full-time. Word by word the agreement was built up, each clause being put to the relevant groups of men for approval.

At Coryton, Mobil's objective was to improve productivity by achieving a better performance in forty hours than had previously been achieved in forty-seven hours each week. In return the unions were given an assurance of no redundancy and maintenance of average earnings, which turned out to be a guaranteed salary of about 30/- per week (£1.50) above previous gross earnings. Some felt that the canker of recurrent overtime should be cut out of a working man's life. A vicious circle sets in. Unobtrusively, because of relatively low earnings, work is delayed so as to create overtime. Coryton produced a revolutionary proposal, not merely to reduce overtime since it can so easily spread again, but to root it out altogether and give time off in lieu.

The trade unions officials had a difficult task. The Esso Agreement at Fawley, the only yardstick available at the time, had been severely criticized among union officials for buying union birthrights too easily. The agreement covered such matters as mates being upgraded or transferred to process work, some reduction in manning and craft flexibility, mixed craft crews, craftsmen cleaning up after their jobs.

The management approach at Coryton, aided by Fred Oldfield, a consultant working with them, was very open. They did not present cut-and-dried solutions but indicated 'what they had in mind'.

Mobil were at pains to emphasize that productivity bargaining was not simply a process of buying out restrictive practices but harmonizing the objectives of the employer and employee, part of their philosophy of participative management. They wished to avoid what they regarded as the acute bargaining situation of Fawley.

What was significant about many of those early agreements was, paradoxically, that they were in capital not labour intensive industries – but also, that they were introduced in compact, self-contained units in companies with good industrial relations records. They were plant bargains; and in order to avoid repercussions many firms had to leave their Employers Associations.

How feasible was it to introduce a far-reaching productivity agreement in a large company with sites scattered all over the country? We examine in some detail how one such company, I.C.I., introduced its Productivity Agreement. In doing so we concentrate on the *process* as much as the result, for we believe there are fundamental lessons to be learned about industrial relations from a company which was endeavouring to establish a 'new social contract', not merely a shift in demarcation lines.

I.C.I. attempts at Productivity Bargaining – The Background

One of the most interesting experiments in Productivity Bargaining was that initiated by I.C.I. in late 1965 and not made operational until 1971. The I.C.I. endeavour is interesting for a number of reasons. Here was a company, which enjoyed a good record on industrial relations, acknowledged by union leaders, not strike-ridden as the motor-car industry was. Ever since its formation in 1926, it had taken an enlightened, if paternalistic, attitude towards its employees. As early as 1934 the company's chairman Lord Melchett (Sir Alfred Mond) had talked of all employees being on staff. His successor Lord Fleck in 1942 had argued for a personnel policy that was rational, not arbitrary. A staff grade scheme had been introduced in 1928. Other welfare schemes were being offered in the thirties, such as pensions and holidays with pay, at a time when dole queues were filling Britain's streets.

Hand in hand with these benefits went generous physical provision. A visitor to Billingham, for example, a large I.C.I. complex in the industrially depressed north-east, could not fail to be impressed by the range of social clubs, the playing fields for a variety of sports, a cinder running track and athletic stadium, a theatre and a rifle range, not to mention the most modern and comprehensive medical and dental facilities. Hospital and benefit schemes helped those who were sick. There was even a Retired Employees Summer Outing Scheme, which took ex-employees to the seaside for the day. Company housing, similar to that provided by Rowntree's and Cadbury's, had been built for employees. Apprentices not only enjoyed a well-equipped Training Centre and scheme but even company-sponsored and -owned Outward Bound facilities. Similar provision could be found on other large I.C.I. complexes.

Contemporary historians might argue that the style of management was old-fashioned and paternalistic. We have, as parents as well as managers, become accustomed to the revolution of rising expectations. Both children and workers regard yesterday's luxuries as today's necessities. Company loyalty and goodwill is a difficult thing to measure, but on Teesside I.C.I., through its enlightened approach during the grim 'thirties (where shop stewards could recall soup kitchens at the time when Harold Macmillan represented Stockton as their M.P.) had built up a bank of loyalty amongst its older workers which stood it in good stead in the post-war years. Changing social habits – the growth of night clubs, the modernization of Working Men's Clubs, with their capacity to engage top class comedians, the mobility provided by the car – have made company social provision somewhat redundant. Long-Service Award presentations, where employees receive more than a handshake, no longer have quite the same flavour as before. The growth of modern private estates and the real increase in spending power since the war have made company property, sited next to the factory, markedly less attractive.

I.C.I., too, was early to introduce a profit-sharing scheme for all employees. It had created a vast apparatus of consultation through largely, but not wholly, non-unionized Works Councils and Staff Committees. These Councils operated at Works and Divisional levels. Twice a year, at Scarborough and Blackpool, at considerable expense, a Central Council was convened, where for two days the chairman and the Main Board gave an account of their stewardship to delegates drawn from the divisions, and wined and dined together. Increasingly this twice yearly jamboree was seen by workers as an opportunity for a day out, a binge, two days' holiday at the company's expense. Managers regarded it as a distraction from the real problems of work. As one Personnel Director observed, 'I got an overwhelming impression of unreality as people made vast speeches before the whole Main Board discussing whether the qualifying period for Long-Service Awards should be reduced from thirty-seven-and-a-half years to thirty-five.'

The situation, though less lavish, was no different at Works level. Matters affecting terms and conditions of employment were outside the remit of Works Councils, so the discussions tended to be marginal to the real issues facing management and men. The system required an equal number of management and shop floor members. The shop floor side attracted the born committee men, those who loved being on their feet, shadow-boxing with the works manager about the lack of protective gloves or cold chips or late buses or damp changing lockers. Subordinate managers witnessed the proceedings mostly in silence except when called on by the works manager; the expressions on their faces generally registered extreme boredom. By the more militant of trade unionists, who contracted out, or if they were tradesmen insisted on their own Council, they were regarded with a mixture of contempt and mistrust. Many shop stewards felt that works councillors had preferential treatment, readier access to senior management's ear, were sometimes able to get grievances remedied more quickly. They felt that I.C.I. had set them up to avoid more direct confrontation with the unions, as a means of keeping unions at bay. Whilst this allegation has some justification in the matter of white collar staff, the charge is an unfair one as regards manual workers.

It is easy now to see the weaknesses of the Works Council Scheme, but at the time they were introduced, I.C.I., as in much else, was ahead of the field; and, judged by contemporary standards, it was an honest attempt at consultation and accepted as such by the workers. The company had set up its own Union Negotiating Procedures and, being large enough, was able to stand outside any nationally negotiated machinery, such as the Chemical Industries Association, and establish a company agreement with the twelve signatory unions. When it came to negotiating a Productivity Bargain, this independence potentially gave it an added advantage. As far back as 1926 there had been a Trade Union Advisory Council. The Brunner, Mond tradition had been to treat unions as serious organizations. In the late 'forties, under the influence of Russell Currie, Work Study Incentive Schemes had been introduced, and yielded substantial increases in productivity.

The picture is of a company which, by a number of standards, would be regarded as progressive: whether in its technology; its marketing strategies; its recruitment of able young engineers and scientists as W. J. Reader so brilliantly narrates in his work *Imperial Chemical Industries – A History*;[11] its advanced and humane welfare schemes; or its readiness to introduce more efficient ways of working.

Despite this record, comparative studies carried out with European and, more particularly, American counterparts showed I.C.I.

to be less productive. Teams were sent across the Atlantic. All came back with the same depressing figures, showing that it took twice the number of men to perform the same amount of work, particularly in maintenance work. Admittedly the wages of the Americans were about twice those of the British workers. There was in the U.S. a certain disenchantment with the Work Measured Incentive Schemes. It was found (a) they were too complicated and not readily understood by workers, (b) they were costly to administer, (c) they placed too much emphasis on quantity and not enough on quality, (d) that, in time, the original 'values' got out-of-date and out-of-hand because of creeping technical changes.

The abandonment of such schemes in the U.S. was felt by some observers not to be so damaging as relinquishing them in this country would be, because of a different attitude of the average American worker to work. As a matter of history, the United States has provided rich rewards to many who went there in search of opportunity and success. Stories of hard work and struggle leading to success are a constant theme of films and magazine stories. Many a young truck driver still encourages himself by thinking that some day he will be an executive, with a high income and an important position. His own Board is likely to comprise many who started at his own level. In consequence, he does not grudge the successful men their wealth or power, nor does he think it wrong for those who have struggled to the top to receive substantial incomes.

Moreover, the differences between the manual worker and the white-collar employee in social position, status and conditions of service have been less in America than in Britain. It has been common for the worker who showed merit to become a foreman and thence to reach the position of works manager and executive. As a consequence of increased job specialization, especially in those companies where a high degree of technical knowledge is necessary, this freedom of opportunity has been diminishing. Companies however still proclaim the principle of freedom of opportunity by recruiting university graduates as operatives or assistant foremen.

The other information that study teams brought back from their visits to the U.S. was the interest some of the leading companies were showing in the findings of the behavioural scientists, particularly those whose studies were in industry. People like Douglas MacGregor, Abraham Maslow, Rensis Likert, Fred Herzberg, Kurt Lewin and Chris Argyris,[12] to mention but a few of the leading figures, were in different ways focusing attention on such matters as human motivation and alienation from work.

In short, a picture was emerging of relatively high productivity, of disenchantment with work-measured incentive schemes, of narrower gaps between worker and white-collar employee, and a feeling that the behavioural scientists had something to offer.

The American studies served to reinforce some of management's own doubts, namely, that they were reacting to a wages structure that was becoming increasingly inappropriate. Work study was not felt to be suitable where judgement and thinking were required (and changing technology requires more thinking by key men, such as control room operators). Many work study times for maintenance were felt to be not worth the paper they were written on, and many of the times on the cards not capable of standing up to critical examination. Both management and unions, if it suited their purpose, connived at fiddling the scheme.

There was also recognition of other, more human, factors – the increasing social unacceptability of staff/shop floor divisions, that educational standards were rising so that people were less prepared to do dull jobs, that there was a new type of employee who compared a job in I.C.I. with jobs in other firms not, as in 1930, with no job at all.

The American studies showed there to be more restrictive practices adopted by the unions in Great Britain than in the U.S. There was the stimulus of increasing international competition. Other firms had negotiated productivity agreements of one kind or another. The moment was ripe for I.C.I. to make a move. There had been a half-hearted attempt, when the forty-two-hour week was reduced to forty hours, to wrest some productivity concessions from the unions, but as I.C.I. were relatively late in conceding forty hours, the unions saw little reason to give anything in return. Something more dramatic was required this time. The omens were favourable.

The First Attempt – Manpower Utilization and Payment Structure (M.U.P.S.)
The Donovan Commission had indicated the shift away from national bargaining to plant level. All I.C.I. agreements were at that time negotiated nationally, not on a site basis. So it seemed natural to hammer out the principles with the national officers of the unions, leaving the officers at local level to work out the details. In

the event, even the hammering out of principles proved more protracted and exhausting than was expected. National officers of unions had many calls on their time, so the discussions initially were intermittent, when they needed to be prolonged. They were carried out in secret. It was argued that starting at the shop floor level would involve enormous delay, as sites were so various in their technology.

The initial agreement, signed in October 1965, was for trial only. Three sites were selected, two in the north-east and one in the north-west, picked ostensibly because they provided a reasonable geographical spread and displayed a variety of working practices. Picked also, one suspects, because they represented areas where the unions were most strongly organized, the argument being if one could obtain an agreement in the north, the other sites in the midlands, the west and the south would readily fall into line. The reason for trials was to allow both parties to withdraw, if the outcome was felt to be unsatisfactory to either party, if management were not achieving the savings they hoped for, if unions felt the surrender of demarcation lines was too great. Optimistically, it was assumed the trial would take just over a year, by which time enough data would have been assembled to implement the agreement across the company.

The agreement got off to a bad start. Its title was verbose and unimaginative – Manpower Utilization and Payment Structure (M.U.P.S., as it was more popularly known – but even that had a leaden sound). It was hardly the title to inspire men to new action. Although the company made itself responsible for the simultaneous distribution to managers and shop stewards of a twenty-page, badly cyclostyled copy of the agreement – enough to discourage the most ardent reader – it had been agreed that the unions would make themselves responsible for communicating its contents to the labour force.

The initial reaction of the shop floor and local officials was not entirely surprising – namely that a deal had been concocted behind their backs. What did it all mean in practice, was the cry? Management was inhibited from supplying the answers. The local officials – or many of them – found they had other and more pressing engagements. They were not rushing forward to spell out in detail what the agreement might mean in the local situation. Some national officers travelled the country to do some explaining but did not meet with the most rapturous of welcomes. The Executive of the Amalgamated Engineering Union (as it was then called), on signing the agreement, went off for a six-weeks visit to the States. An unfortunate gap was created. An initial and cursory reading of the document encouraged some to proclaim it as a Charter for the Transport & General Workers Union, a slogan which did nothing to allay the fears of the A.E.U., which saw itself as the union with most to concede and the least to gain in return.

Meanwhile the company mounted a massive training programme to acquaint its managers with what the new agreement meant for them.

What were the initial proposals? There was the usual opening bromide, intentions wrapped up in semi-legal jargon, 'of achieving and maintaining the maximum efficiency in the company operations and in ensuring that the payment structure and conditions of employment are appropriate to the present-day industrial situation.' But what about the ways in which this would be achieved? The company were anxious not to do a 'Fawley Exercise', in which a set of demarcations would be bought out by higher remuneration, to be followed at some later stage by a further list of less restricting demarcations, which could be removed but only at a substantial price. The exercise was not to be viewed as a 'once-off' operation but was designed to create a flexible situation in which improvement could be continuous. To unions accustomed to very exact definitions, flexibility held the possibility of a slippery and downward slope.

The crucial proposals looked innocuous enough on paper.

(a) Production operatives with suitable training could use tools to carry out the less skilled craft tasks which form only a subsidiary part of their work.
(b) In appropriate circumstances tradesmen would be expected to operate plants.
(c) Tradesmen and general workers could be given general supervision by men of any background.
(d) Tradesmen could do work of other trades which forms a subsidiary part of the main job of their own trade, according to their availability at the time.
(e) Support work for tradesmen could be done by tradesmen, semi-skilled or general workers, as is appropriate in the circumstances.

In implementing these proposals certain factors were to be taken into consideration. A job should be looked at in its totality, and if it was largely craft work it would come within the craft sphere of influence. Similarly, if the job was predominantly general work it could come within the general worker sphere. Manning should aim to get the right man in the right job, ensuring that men of high skill should carry out as little mundane work consistent as with maximum efficiency. Method study and work measurement would continue to be used as means of establishing and maintaining correct manning levels at standard performance, and, of course, any necessary retraining would be carried out before changes in practices were allowed.

Discussing and arguing principles is one thing, particularly if it is done at national level, implementing them on the ground level is a totally different matter. That was to be the subject of local discussion and agreement on each trial site. The trial sites, unlike many of the 'model' sites visited in the States, were not green field sites but relatively small works sections within much larger industrial complexes, with considerable histories of custom and practice behind them.

Nor did the local union structure on the craft side, particularly with the A.E.U., facilitate autonomous decision-making. Two of the trial sites lay on either side of the river Tees. Billingham, an older site dating from the original merger that created I.C.I., had a different history of industrial relations from the newer, largely post-war industrial estate of Wilton, which had developed no comparable relations with the community. Because of local union structure at district committee level, Billingham found it difficult to go it alone or out of step with Wilton, where discussions were difficult and protracted.

Men on the shop floor were much more concerned with practice than principles. No new era had dawned for them. The more immediate issues were 'How much am I going to get paid?' and 'What am I going to have to do differently?' The twenty-two Job Appraisement categories for the general worker and four merit grades for the tradesmen were to be telescoped into eight Job Grades and expressed as an annual salary, which would be paid weekly. Potentially the salary structure was more rational, providing opportunities for the highly-skilled leading control room operator to receive a reward comparable to his craftsman colleague. Although in theory it is

194

sensible for 'men of high skill to carry out as little mundane work as is consistent with maximum efficiency', what happens in practice if men, not of high skill but average skill, e.g. fitters, spend most of their day doing mundane craft work, such as packing pump glands? Even in modern chemical plants, such highly skilled work as scraping bearings or lining up turbines forms a relatively small part of the total amount of fitting to be done. So the engineering fitter may have to look for job enrichment from other trades, such as the electricians. Not unnaturally, they took their stand on the matter of safety. Only a time-served electrician was qualified to maintain high-voltage equipment. Maybe the fitter could remove tail-ends from motors. Although changing electric light bulbs could hardly be described as highly skilled work, what were the company going to do with Joe who had spent the last four years doing virtually nothing else, or with the fitter whose job it was to insert the valves into the tops of ammonia cylinders? Another problem area was, of course, the proposal to allow craftsmen (and general workers) to do more work unsupervised. The possible reduction in supervision through developing higher calibre operators and tradesmen did nothing for the anxiety of assistant foremen, who played little part in discussions of the new jobs that would arise, despite reassurances from the company. As Ernest Schumacher has remarked in his book *Small is Beautiful*, being as large and complex as I.C.I. is uncomfortable.

Apart from some of the anxieties mentioned above, other more traditional fears asserted themselves. How could a craft union deny the principle that all tradesmen were equal? Common observation would not lend support to that principle. The official union response was not that certain men are better than others at skilled work but that management always give the most skilled jobs to the same favoured group of fitters and so do not allow the others to develop their proper potential. The other principle that needed to be defended was that no process worker should be paid more than a craftsman. Equally, the general workers were as keen to lift themselves from their humble status and show that the top jobs they were required to do demanded as much, if not more, skill as the run-of-the-mill fitter, albeit of a different kind and associated perhaps with the operations of a particular plant. For example, it was felt that fitters might do some elementary slinging, but the élite of the Transport and General Workers Union, the riggers, who regarded their work as conferring almost craft status, were in no mood to see their jobs compromised.

The Boilermakers, who had craft substructures within their own ranks, felt they would have made sufficient concessions to productivity if they achieved some blurring of these lines, without the need for further flexibilities with regard to other craft unions.

The company's aspirations, consistent with the mood of society as a whole – to diminish the differentials between shop floor and staff by providing comparable conditions of employment, and, at the same time, to provide more rewarding jobs with less supervision and the abolition of the work study incentive scheme as the sole means of obtaining work from people – were responded to at a different level by the unions. It was not the security of the annual salary they responded to, or the more stable conditions of employment represented by longer notice for dismissal, or payment for sickness absence, but the greater personal insecurity of the unknown, the jostle for their rightful place on the new job scale. What were they giving away? What control were they surrendering? Would the enlarged job be all that different? Were they really on staff conditions as they queued to clock in (a measure subsequently abolished)? Who was going to do the assessing for the new jobs? Were the unions to have a hand in it?

Prior to the Productivity Scheme the company had been integrating its process and maintenance management and supervision into a single production group at plant level with separate support groups on a works basis for major maintenance and services. The new flexibilities required from operators and tradesmen under the Productivity Agreement seemed a logical extension of this integration. But logic plays a relatively small part in human behaviour so it may seem better to hold on to what you have got. Management were caught up in the classic dilemma: to achieve change; do you try and change attitude first and hope practice will follow or do you make structural changes which themselves lead to new attitudes?

The changing of attitude and practice turned out to be a much slower process than the company had anticipated. It was hoped that the trial sites would have completed their studies in something over a year. In the event, they were protracted and continually delayed. At times the unions refused to sit round the same table together, and one union even imposed a ban on discussion.

A massive training programme for managers was launched to familiarize them with the company's thinking, its evolving personnel policy, what had led them to launch their Productivity Agreement, what assumptions it was based on (some of which many managers were reluctant to accept). The programmes had both an informational and behavioural content. It was in the context of M.U.P.S. that many managers first heard about Herzburg and job enrichment, about Theory X and Theory Y management, and that they looked at emotional resistance to change. There was some recognition that exhortation was not the best means of obtaining acceptance for a new way of operating. Courses were arranged not merely to convey to shop floor the realities of international competition but to encourage managers to examine M.U.P.S. from the point of view of each category of man likely to be affected by it, to identify those aspects which were likely to appeal and those which were likely to prove obstacles, to look at what man-management means in the absence of direct financial incentives.

First Trials
During 1967, as the trial sites became deadlocked, there was increasing pressure from other parts of the country for the Agreement to go ahead elsewhere. Initially the national officers of the unions agreed to a number of additional sites. They finally agreed that, if local agreement could be obtained, any site could go ahead. It is interesting with hindsight to speculate whether the company and unions were wise to choose the areas they did, the north-east and north-west, with their bitter experiences of unemployment and depression. As it happened it was places like Stowmarket, in Suffolk, and Gloucester – rural areas and relatively small-sized, compact units of around 2000 employees, free of the harrowing experiences of the 'thirties – which were the first to implement the Agreement. It could of course be argued that the technology involved – paints and fibres – was newer and that management attitudes were correspondingly more enlightened.

A lesson to be learnt is that industrial relations differ widely even throughout the same company. When joint teams of management and unions, from successful sites, visited the north-east, the trade unionists saw them as management men, ready to surrender things that would not have been conceded in the north.

Another more painful lesson is that change is a slow process. The I.C.I. plant at Gloucester obtained final agreement for trials on 1 January 1968, over two years after the agreement had been issued in October 1965. Although not initially designated a trial site, it had diligently and comprehensively set about preparing its managers, supervisors and workers.

Gloucester is interesting in a number of ways.[13] It made a serious attempt to involve its foremen at all stages in the discussions and dealt with process and maintenance together, encouraging them to lead discussions with their work groups to explain M.U.P.S. It arranged for management to talk personally to foremen about their problems under M.U.P.S. It kept the discussions confined to small groups. Working Parties were set up under the independent chairmanship of the Training Manager from which production managers were excluded as a matter of policy, so that shop stewards were able to discuss new job descriptions untrammelled by management interference – and, left on their own, came up with sensible improvements in working. Before Gloucester was declared a trial site they had abolished clocking first for shift and then day workers, gestures which indicated management's goodwill. They had managed, on separate occasions, to hold large meetings of all workers to keep them informed about progress. A problem which occurred at Billingham, and which can easily happen when a small group of men get together to tackle a common task, is that group cohesion starts to take place. Management reveal a willingness to be more open to upward influence, to share problems, to talk more candidly. A spirit of give and take develops. In such circumstances, shop stewards can all too easily distance themselves from the men they represent and become too busy in discussions with managers to have time to attend to the day-to-day problems of their members.

But Gloucester was not without its problems. Industrial relations take place in a wider context than a particular plant. The interest which the shop floor were showing in the advantages M.U.P.S. held out for them were shattered by two events, a recession in nylon production which led to lay-offs and, in July 1966, the Government-imposed Wages Freeze. Discussions on M.U.P.S. were temporarily discontinued. Towards the end of 1967 the local A.E.U. became cool towards the agreement, partly influenced by outside pressures, such as a national meeting held on Teesside at which a resolution was passed that all craftsmen should be in the same grade and that it should be the top one on the scale; the Transport and General Workers Union seriously considered pressing the company for a separate agreement should the craft unions not agree. Fortunately, this did not happen, and the agreement for trials commenced on 1

January 1968. As a consequence many people wanted to see where the success lay. Perhaps part of an answer could be found in the fact that shop stewards and operatives played a major role in explaining the ideas of M.U.P.S. to visitors.

Meanwhile even as late as mid-1968 progress at one of the original trial sites at Billingham was held up because the mass of A.E.U. members on Teesside had become opposed to M.U.P.S. in principle, not because the men or their stewards on the trial site were opposed to it. Indeed they had showed a willingness from the beginning to enter into meaningful discussions with management and had already made substantial progress before the union ban on discussion. The union ban was partly a request for more money (highly attractive original salaries were being slowly eroded by a rise in the cost of living and wage rates paid at a local refinery). It also arose out of a feeling that the craftsmen should be the most highly paid workers and that the company had acted deviously in including a top grade and then saying it only applied to special people like planners and technicians. There was also a request from all shop floor representatives at Billingham for a guarantee of no redundancy as a result of M.U.P.S., a difficult pledge to give because of the possibility of plant closures necessitated by changing technology.

Weekly Staff Agreement (W.S.A.)
Although some of the smaller sites had managed to implement a M.U.P.S. trial, the resistance of the larger conurbations, particularly in the north, forced the company and the unions to think again.

In June 1969, they launched a revised agreement, this more happily and simply entitled Weekly Staff Agreement (W.S.A.), which enshrined the main principles of the earlier agreement, but recognized more directly the need for local circumstances to determine the particular shape the agreement would take on different sites. At the same time guidelines for joint investigation methods were issued.

The main differences between W.S.A. and M.U.P.S. was that the new scheme omitted the more specific and contentious examples of 'utilization of manpower' as stated in the original agreement. So that, in M.U.P.S., 'Production operators with suitable training can use tools to carry out the less skilled craft tasks', gave way in W.S.A. to, 'The underlying intention is not to make substantial changes in the general allocation of work between craft and non-craft employees but to eliminate wasteful practices wherever they occur'. This took account of tradesmen's anxieties and softened the impact. The magic words in the new agreement were 'some flexibility'.

> Some flexibility between craft and non-craft employees to assist in the continuous working of plants. Such flexibilities will be introduced by agreement between local managers and workplace representatives of the Signatory Unions concerned. They will not involve the more highly skilled part of the craftsman's jobs or the use of tools other than those necessary for simple operations.

The Agreement, for the rest, dealt in generalities about the need for working more efficiently and providing more satisfying and rewarding jobs; and for management and unions to understand each other's point of view.

The unions wrested from management two important concessions not present in the original agreement, namely, that there would be no enforced redundancy and reductions would be achieved by normal turnover or other locally agreed means; that Weekly Staff employees should undertake to join an appropriate Signatory Union, and this would be a condition of their employment.

This released the log-jam and the problem then became how to prepare all the necessary job descriptions and arrange for all the job assessment teams to visit the various works, so that they could qualify for the new rates of pay. What size should be the unit for transfer to the new agreement? A section? A plant? A works? A site? The unions, after so much procrastination, were clamant for approval. There was some pressure to cut corners, but the need to analyse demarcation or flexibility in detail inevitably slowed down the process. Another interesting phenomenon could be observed: a certain pairing between management and workers, who presented beautifully bound job descriptions, and ran through mock presentations – all for the benefit of the assessment panels, who for their part felt these competitive and laborious presentations merely slowed down the proceedings.

But an important feature of the new W.S.A. was that management and unions started by consulting their members – no more secret deals – and when a draft agreement had been reached it was circulated to everyone in the company and a further round of consultations ensued. W.S.A. more accurately reflected what Donovan had commented on, namely the movement of power away from the centre to the plant. It was owned rather more personally by management and men. It represented a recognition of a change in the distribution of power in I.C.I.

By the end of 1970 90 per cent of the company's 60,000 weekly staff were covered by the new agreement, with some pockets of the recalcitrant north to be accommodated. Even the new agreement saw some hard bargaining. Intensive efforts were mounted to bring together all employees from a plant, shop floor, shop stewards, supervisors and managers.

The setting of these meetings helped. One useful pattern evolved. A small joint working party of management and shop stewards set up the event. The meetings were held off-site, all were dressed alike, 'not me in my mucky overalls talking to a well-dressed manager', as one shop steward observed. Someone from the central training staff acted as an informal chairman. Shop stewards would make it their responsibility to introduce the sessions, and explain the purpose of the day. Numbers were limited to twenty to twenty-four, at a time, the audience representing craft and non-craft.

Such an atmosphere allowed people, sometimes for the first time in their lives, to air their anxieties in public, and candidly, across the craft/general worker interface. There was reassurance from process workers that they had no desire to rush in and do tradesmen's jobs. What they wanted was the right to nip up a gland or change a bulb or a control room chart in the middle of the night, rather than wait two hours for the shift fitter or electrician to come. There was a good deal of friendly banter – 'I don't know, Charlie, you have more tools in that cabin of yours than the shift fitter. If they called in all the tools from process they could kit out the factory'. There was overt recognition that these flexibilities existed already, particularly on night shift, indeed much wider ones than were hoped for from the agreement. They were based however on older and more fundamental man-to-man relationships which transcended union divisions. Particular process workers would benefit from enormous trust by their craftsmen colleagues. Where tradesmen were chary was in committing these flexibilities to paper – like signing away their birthright. It was all right having an informal understanding with Tom that he could undertake minor maintenance work. Extending this provision to cover Dick, Harry and Jack was a different matter. It was a matter of trying to obtain night-time arrangements during the day.

The new word was not 'giving away work' which suggested final renunciation – and tradesmen found it difficult to see how process workers could get higher grades unless they gave them some of their work – but 'work sharing'. The effect was the same but a different connotation was felt. Allowing someone to do maintenance work when it was sensible and the specialists required were not available, where it would help the job along and save downtime, or when the person doing it is connected with the job and not pulled out of the control room – provisions such as these removed the tradesmen's fear of takeover.

There was blunt speaking between men and shop stewards, and managers obtained a better understanding of some of the pressures shop stewards were subjected to from the shop floor. Some shop stewards showed a fine grasp and understanding of the agreement which somehow they had failed to communicate to the shop floor.

Shop floor workers were perplexed by the relatively low management profile. The new agreement had placed more onus on the men to decide what should go into a job, what a good performance would look like. Tradition had accustomed them to expect these initiatives from managers.

Managers, too, recognized the shift in power that was taking place. 'I'm on the way out as a manager, my kind. It comes naturally to me to give orders, the newer managers don't think like that.'

The 'historic' us/them divide reared its head from time to time. Current managers might interpret job descriptions and flexibility wording in ways mutually acceptable to management and union, but what about future managers? Previous experience had suggested that on other occasions new managers twisted things to their advantage. Such are the realities which lie behind the principles when management and men engage in dialogue.

If there were difficulties for tradesmen there were even greater difficulties for foremen and particularly assistant foremen. When chargehands on the process side had been elevated to assistant foremen and staff, unlike their craft colleagues, many had surrendered their union membership and felt vulnerable as a result. As M.U.P.S. and W.S.A. meant demanning, even if this was to be achieved by natural wastage or deployment, there was a good deal of uncertainty in the ranks of supervisors as to their jobs. Were they to be put back to the tools? Given golden handshakes? Fobbed off with the prospect of new and challenging jobs – collecting data, developing new systems, training operators for new responsibilities, helping with the installation of the new system? The main criticism would be that they were kept in the dark, but until new job descriptions for the shop floor had been agreed, it was difficult to be precise.

The company went ahead, relying largely on loyalties engendered in years of faith brought about by fair treatment.

Such Agreements, giving the shop floor conditions of employment comparable with staff – reflecting the movement of society as a whole – and raising their salaries substantially, not unnaturally produced a reaction from staff. Many were concerned not with clocking or holidays or notice, but with the fact that the shop floor had received much in money and had given relatively little. If a fitter's reward for productivity was to obtain £3 a week more for conceding the right of a process worker to do some elementary fitting jobs under certain conditions, the laboratory technician was prompted to think of what more productive ways of working he might offer the company for a similar reward. So emerged a Staff Development Programme which was not just a crude attempt to widen the differentials once more. It showed that industrial relations involves a network of complex arrangements between different groups in the company. To pioneer an agreement at shop floor level without reference to the rest of the system is to invite disaster.

Agreements on paper do not change deeply ingrained attitudes overnight. One rather naïve senior manager asked a group of shop stewards, 'Well, I would like to know from you what does it feel like now that you are on staff. How will it be different?' He was met by blank incomprehension. It was difficult to know what the manager had in mind. Perhaps a set of stereotypes, that staff were responsible people who ungrudgingly worked overtime, had a different attitude to their work. (Stereotypes of staff tend to emphasize the positive aspects, not that they may take an hour and a half over their lunch break. Fiddling expense accounts, not unknown, is no different from fiddling a work study scheme.)

We have tried to narrate the story as it happened, highlighting the main difficulties encountered. Are there any lessons to be learned? Did it represent a major break-through in industrial relations or just a tinkering about with the system?

The first lesson is that deals done at the top behind closed doors – however well-intentioned, and union leaders acknowledged the company's intentions to establish a new social contract – are **no** longer admissible. The company over-estimated the union response. It was as though they anticipated a generous and reasoned response to the New Deal fitting for a company that had by most accounts treated its employees generously. Perhaps there was a certain arrogance implied in this assumption. I.C.I. recruited first-class chemical engineers. Their planning was usually sound. They were acknowledged to be first-class builders of chemical plants. Yet in 1969 they had to rethink their Productivity Agreement, for which in 1965 they had allowed a twelve to eighteen months trial.

If the unions, particularly the craft and the A.E.U., showed more resistance than expected, managers were at times bemused. What was this participative management line that was being sold? Did they really believe in it? Many technically trained and oriented managers and foremen were initially extremely sceptical, and some remain so. Could they manage and supervise without benefit of a bonus scheme? Was there to be no monitoring of performance? To remove supervision and bonus scheme and replace them with a different assessment at first sight seemed to jeopardize the very trust you were trying to establish. As management were becoming accustomed to having their own performance assessed through such methods as 'Management by Objectives', it was not unreasonable to develop some similar mutual target-setting criteria for shop floor.

As the discussions and delays became more protracted and union 'intransigence' stood in the way, some of the idealism of the New Deal faded. There was even a mood, 'If the unions don't want it, let's forget about it, and carry on as we have been doing. By the time it is in we will have saved nothing'. The arithmetic in the end became very difficult to work out, though I.C.I.'s profits remain healthy and significant demanning took place. The company had effectively introduced a completely new payment structure. As we argue in our chapter on worker participation, perhaps the exercise should be judged as a landmark in a new relationship between managers and managed – not the finished article, but a few steps forward, seven years of struggle as management explained to men and men explained to management their problems and perspectives. It amounts to a fundamental change in a complex of activities and relationships that have deep roots.

A few cautionary comments for those who follow in their path might include the following. Comparisons with American firms' labour forces (though not their profitability) can do much to antagonize. Workers (and managers) must first be persuaded to recognize the need for change. Building up trust and allaying fears is an important part of the process. This can best be achieved by involvement of all in small discussion groups. Small plants stand a better chance than large sites, and infinite patience is needed to grapple with, not just a job description, but the suspicions and fears arising from years of mistrust. The evidence suggests there is no short cut.

Fred Oldfield, who played a significant role in the Mobil Agreement at Coryton, used to pose a few simple but relevant questions, which all those intending to introduce a productivity agreement might ponder. They act as a kind of checklist.

1. *What are management (or unions) essentially looking for – a victory or a new relationship?* One is to do with money and can be easily negotiated; the other is much more complex, a journey into the unknown.
2. *Is management offering a package which means 'power over' or 'power with'?* Is there a genuine attempt to share, not just the hand-out at the end of the day, but the thinking at the beginning of it? This requires a revolution in both management and union thinking. Unions have to decide whether their wish is to operate exclusively as a power bloc or sometimes as a problem-solving group.
3. *Both sides should work* TO *an agreement not* FROM *it.* The latter suggests it is someone else's work. All one can do is react to it. The relevant question is 'How shall *we* do it?' For managers who have been paid to do the thinking, it requires an ability to listen; for unions it means taking initiatives. Ownership is critical. It must be joint.

Productivity agreements offer a useful vehicle for workers' participation. New relationships may be forged between top union leaders and the C.B.I. over beer and sandwiches at No. 10 Downing Street, but the ones that matter are those worked out at the factory floor between managers and men, learning from each other in the accomplishment of common tasks. Union attempts to go it alone (at Upper Clyde or the Scottish *Daily News* or Meriden) have not up till now been very fruitful. They serve only to demonstrate the importance of complementarity and interdependence – workers need the skills of managers as managers do of workers.

Finally, it is impossible to exaggerate the importance of the personalities involved in the bargaining process. Relationships occur between people rather than organizations. Successful productivity agreements have resulted from the dedication and commitment of shop stewards and managers over a period of time.

DECLINE IN PRODUCTIVITY AGREEMENTS

As we argued at the beginning of this chapter, productivity agreements have been inspired by a number of motives, perhaps the most common being the wish to overcome the difficulties imposed by a Government wage freeze. For those who were wanting not much more than an opportunity to 'do a deal', or even for those who were seeking merely a buy-out of restrictive practices, the collapse of the Government's Statutory Incomes Policy in 1969 and the eventual demise of the National Board for Prices and Incomes, removed the inducement for Productivity Bargains. Other considerations apply to those firms who were seeking a rather more fundamental change in traditional relationships, such as I.C.I.

When unions involved in Productivity Bargaining saw their colleagues in other firms obtaining substantial increases in wages based on the 'straight' wage claim and relying on the more traditional methods, they were strengthened in their resolve not to give away more than they needed. Firms committed to organizational restructuring as part of their productivity deals had to apply what they assessed to be reasonable cost-of-living and other increases at the same time as they were negotiating flexibilities of working.

Productivity bargaining had its greatest vogue in the 'sixties. A decline came in the early 'seventies. By July 1970 Incomes Data reported (Report No. 95 July 1970 p. 27): 'The old incomes policy bar to more than one increase within twelve months had been smashed'. Productivity bargaining, if it is achieving organizational change, as we have observed, is a protracted and intricate affair. If interim union claims, occasioned by rises in the cost of living or scarcity of labour, become so frequent, even the buy-out type of agreement finds it difficult to cope with such simultaneous pressures.

'Smashed' the Incomes Policy may have been, and external pressures may have forced the unions to revert to more traditional methods of bargaining. But it would be unduly cynical to say that all those hours in which management cultivated the 'habit of discussion' and developed the skills of listening, in which shop stewards undertook new and daunting responsibilities and engaged in a common and different kind of dialogue, were wasted – that these new practices were smashed, and management and union reverted to their former positions and perceptions.

Productivity bargaining resulted in a reappraisal of traditional notions of managerial prerogative. Management authority was redefined and legitimized. It allowed industrial relations to take on a wider perspective.

Perhaps management thought a new era had dawned, that in future they would not need to yield to wage claims not based on quantifiable increases in productivity. They found they did. But productivity agreements exposed both managements and unions to the 'wind of change', after which things would never be quite the same.

A change of government in 1970 introduced a different dynamic. The Conservative Government's attempt to control industrial relations through their Industrial Relations Act, with its inevitable emphasis on legal restraint, had little in common with the new concepts of man and power and organizational values. Those firms with good industrial relations records and in the middle of negotiations of new deals with their workforce found themselves, in the first instance, embarrassed by the legislation.

One effect of productivity bargaining, reflected by the Donovan Commission, was that it had the effect of formalizing collective bargaining at plant level. This had major implications for those firms who traditionally negotiated at national level, and who referred to headquarters for advice on particular problems which they felt might have repercussions elsewhere in the company. Productivity bargaining may have had the effect of bringing both sides together for the joint solution of problems of mutual importance but unions more than management welcomed their new-found autonomy.

One of the problems facing management, when the workforce continues to press for increases in wages, is to keep alive the collaborative atmosphere of the discussions characterizing productivity bargaining. Although agreements may be designed as open-ended, management's scope for further improvements through subsequent negotiations is limited. Perhaps we should look upon productivity agreements as events which formally may only be repeated once or twice in the same production unit and are unlikely to evolve into a standard means by which management and the workforce combine to secure change to the benefit of both sides.

The experience of negotiating them can create a new climate in which more traditional forms of bargaining can take place. I.C.I. took seven long years to see their agreement through from start to finish. Despite the frustrations, attitudes were changed or modified. But pressure of time, combined with rapidly increasing inflation, is likely to mean a return to traditional bargaining.

The inability of individual companies to protect their achievements from erosion by hostile factors in the external labour market is a serious handicap to the long term prospects for productivity bargaining.

9

Industrial Democracy

We have referred earlier to the difficulty both unions and management have in breaking out of old moulds and forming new relationships. Power sharing and worker participation have become popular slogans, meaning different things to different people. For some it is an argument about representation on the Board, for others an extension of the area of control which a worker may exercise over his immediate job environment. The subject was given an added urgency as a consequence of the fifth directive of the E.E.C. Commission, issued in September 1972, which called for the establishment of co-determination in all member states. Its aim was not only to secure, preferably through legal provision, a two-tier system of formal authority within a firm but also to guarantee to workers the rights of representation on the senior tier, and so participate in the decision-making process at that level. An early proposal, put forward in June 1970, had called for a separation of the management functions from those of supervision and control in all enterprises within the community. Europe and Israel offer a variety of interesting attempts to tackle the problem.

Yugoslavia

Yugoslavia was one of the first countries to introduce industrial democracy in a manner which paradoxically ran counter to traditional Communist theory, with its emphasis on central direction. The Party exercised its control of industry locally through workers' councils elected from within the industry itself. This organization was seen as an instrument of economic efficiency, rather than social control; in other words a means by which a backward country could become industrialized.

The 'Fundamental Law on the Management of State Economic

209

Enterprises and Higher Associations in Working Collectives' was passed in 1950 in an attempt to overcome the main causes of the failure of the country's first five-year plan – namely over-centralization and lack of worker involvement.

Under this law the management of industry is carried out by a Workers' Council, a Management Board and a Director. The Workers' Council is elected from everyone employed in the working unit and is the major policy-making body of the firm. The Council is responsible for agreeing wage rates, production targets, for the distribution of excess profits, whether in the form of a bonus to workers and, if so, the allocation.

The Management Board is elected from employees directly, not from the Council, and is responsible for how the policy decisions should be put into action. Like the Council members, the Board members are elected for two years. Because they have to take operational decisions they meet fairly frequently, but when not attending meetings they continue with their normal employment.

The Director was originally appointed by the state, but since 1950 has been appointed, after examination and interview, by a special commission of the people's commune and the Workers' Council. He can be dismissed only with the agreement of both bodies. He is responsible for the day-to-day operation of the works and appoints the necessary supervisory and technical staff. Although he and his staff are the only professional management within the unit, he is in no way responsible for policy, and, while he advises the Board and the Council, he is ultimately responsible to the Community and Council and can be dismissed by them. The Yugoslavian system of industrial government is not dissimilar to the English system of local government, the Director playing a similar role to that of the Town Clerk or the Chief Education Officer.

Although the economy of the country is subject to central direction, the Yugoslavian system of industrial democracy confers on the worker the right to decide the policy under which he lives, the right to receive certain information, the right to pass an opinion. The interesting aspect is that the original motive was industrial efficiency, not political philosophy. The system, in the event, produced consistent economic growth of 13–16 per cent and a marked increase in the quality of goods produced. It could be argued that such results were easier to achieve in a rural than an industrial country and that the system of industrial democracy is easier to operate in relatively small economic units. Yugoslavian industrial democracy has yet to face the problems of a large-scale industrial economy.

The Yugoslavian system has helped to produce a better-educated, more industrialized society, which is well-informed as to its industry and fully aware of the consequences of decisions made by the individual for the well-being of the enterprise. Decisions have ranged from wage rates to long-term technical and financial problems. It is interesting to note that in some cases when the Workers' Councils have acted in an autocratic manner and imposed their status on others, production has fallen.

Attempts to establish local worker control have been made in other East European countries, notably Poland, but there has been nothing to match the success of Yugoslavia. In Poland, Workers' Councils dealt only with labour matters and not with general policy. They had something in common with British productivity councils. The benefits attributed to them concerned such matters as lower absenteeism and better quality control.

ISRAEL

A unique and unusual form of industrial democracy is represented by the Israeli Kibbutz, the declared aim of which is to provide a system of corporate ownership and corporate distribution of profit, to the benefit of those who live in the community. This is a very demanding form of society. No wages are paid. If a person leaves the Kibbutz he leaves with nothing, however much he may have put in. The Management is in the hands of a committee selected by the whole Kibbutz, but policy will be decided by the general assembly of the whole Kibbutz. Decision-making is a public activity made in the presence of the Kibbutz community.

As in Yugoslavia, the economic units are relatively small, though some Kibbutzim have yearly investment programmes of over £200,000 per annum. A recent study showed that whereas the annual value of the output per man in private industry in Israel averaged £3,500, the figure for equivalent Kibbutz industries was £4,400.

The distinctive features are a total commitment to the concept of industrial equality and a sense of complete ownership of the enterprise. The rewards in 'Herzberg' terms are not money but achievement, recognition and a respect based on success. It is in every way the most complete expression of industrial democracy in the world, and its strength lies in the individual's complete commitment to the way of life it requires, with its emphasis on the moral value of labour, and its ability to solve some complex industrial problems through involvement.

In any study of industrial democracy, however, it is to the highly industrialized societies of Germany, Holland, and Scandinavia that most attention is usually directed. West Germany particularly is held out as the exemplar. It should be recognized that industrial democracy is not dissimilar to political democracy. It takes its character from the environment. It has historical antecedents. Whilst it is helpful therefore to look at the experiments of other countries to see what can be learnt and adapted to our own situation, wholesale transplant, as with heart surgery, is likely to produce rejection.

Since the German experiment is one to which the T.U.C. gives some attention, it may repay analysis here. German industrial law specifies that joint-stock companies employing more than 500 workers must have three administrative bodies – the General Assembly of Shareholders, the Supervisory Board, which is appointed by the General Assembly, and the Board of Management, which is appointed by the existing management from within the company. The Supervisory Board's function is to lay down broad lines of policy and to supervise the activity of the Board of Management.

In contrast to the British trade union movement, the German trade unions number fewer than twenty and are organized on an industrial basis so that one union will cater for all grades of employees within the industry. In Britain we have as many unions in the motor car industry as there are in the whole of German industry. Their organization is strongest at national level and their main function is to negotiate national agreements with the employers. Although local trade union organizations exist, their functions within an industrial plant are mainly carried out by the Works Council – this would not be possible without industrial unions – and whilst the vast majority of Works Councillors are strong unionists, the union has a very small formal negotiating and consultative role to play at local level, and tends to operate within the framework of the Works Councils.

The origins of Germany's industrial democracy are not without significance, since they owe more to political than industrial history.

Industrial Democracy, or Co-Determination as it was more popularly known, was introduced after the Second World War by the Allied Control Commission, more as a means of filling a power vacuum which existed in German industry than as part of a well-ordered plan for worker participation. The Allies were anxious to prevent the German industrialists from re-establishing their powerful pre-war position. There was the need to repair the ravages of the bombing and to obtain industrial stability. There was a need to gain the confidence of the German trade unions, 'to recognise the rights of the workers', if only to limit the possible advances of Communism. The principle of industrial democracy embraced all these objectives, and, at the same time, re-established a practice which had developed under the Weimar Republic, but which had been suppressed by the Nazis, namely that of Works Councils which had been made compulsory for the whole of German industry by a law passed in 1920.

Consequently, the allies re-established Works Councils throughout German industry and set up Co-Determination Commissions comprised of labour leaders, industrialists and civil servants, to manage the introduction of Co-Determination into the Mining industry. Gradually the powers of the Works Councils were widened.

It is fair to say that the industrialists, resentful of the limitations Works Councils placed on their power, were opposed to them. When the Federal Republic was established in 1949, the Christian Democratic Party, which came to power, limited the spread of Co-Determination by legalizing the system and resisting trade union pressure to extend it. It is interesting now to reflect that the principles and structure were laid down twenty-five years ago but the concept has not been extended. This says something about managerial prerogative, to which we shall refer later in this chapter.

The 1951 Act on Co-Determination offered full Co-Determination but applied only to the coal mining and later the iron and steel industry. Under this law the Supervisory Board of a Company was made up of equal numbers of shareholders' representatives and employee representatives, the latter being nominated by the trade unions after consultation with the appropriate Works Council. One independent member is elected to the Board by the representatives of both the shareholders and workers in order to ensure a majority in case of block voting.

The 1952 Act on Co-Determination, which covered the remaining industries, only offered partial Co-Determination, since workers' representatives on these supervisory boards were at the level of one in three.

Provision is also made for the employee representatives to appoint the member of the Management Board who will be responsible for Personnel, the Arbeitsdirektor. This is the only occasion on which a member of the Management Board is appointed from below and means that in effect the Personnel Director is dependent upon the trade unions for his position. It is this provision which has caused most resentment amongst German industrialists.

The law covering ordinary Co-Determination, although it firmly established Co-Determination at local level through the Works Council machinery, severely curtailed the power that workers' representatives could exercise over the Management Board. This was achieved in a number of ways. Employees were only entitled to one-third of the positions on the Supervisory Board and these had to be elected directly by the employees, a measure designed to limit the power of the unions. Nor were the workers' representatives empowered to appoint anyone to the Management Board.

The law of 1952 also defined the responsibilities of Works Councils. Broadly, the Works Councils were to represent the Workers' interests in dealing with management and were bound *by law* to co-operate with management for the promotion of their mutual interests. The law required management to meet with the Works Council at least once a month and required the Works Council to hold quarterly meetings with all employees at which the Council reported its activities and at which a representative of the employers could be required to report on the firm's policies. The firm and the Works Council were also required to establish a small Economic Committee which discussed economic problems and enabled the Works Council to be kept informed of the firm's economic position.

The Works Councils generally have authority to act in the following fields:

1. The interpretation of national agreements and their application to local situations. (The Council itself has no power to take industrial action against an employer although individuals as union members can encourage the union to initiate such action.)
2. The administration of company-owned welfare schemes.
3. Deciding local conditions of employment e.g. shift systems, starting and stopping times.

214

4. It must be consulted on any major decision regarding the hiring and firing of personnel. (In practice this means that its agreement is required before a firm can go ahead.)
5. It must be consulted about training arrangements.

The responsibility for welfare is a significant one since it means that the Works Council can determine, in joint consultation with the employers, considerable fringe benefits, including such matters as pensions. They can also investigate all queries relating to wages.

The Works Councils have various sub-committees with well-defined limits. They are drawn from all employees. The law does, in fact, prescribe that the offices of Chairman and Vice-Chairman of the Council must be split between shop floor and a salaried employee. Arguably salaried staff are prone to take a longer term view than those on the shop floor, whose needs tend to be more immediate and short-term. As they are in the minority, in a clash of interest shop floor views would prevail.

In theory, then, the German worker and his representatives have the right to be involved in the formulation of policy, the supervision of the operation of his company, the negotiation of his local conditions of employment and the operation of fringe benefits, the right to be kept informed about the economic progress of his firm and the right to have a consultative system. In those cases where full co-determination operates, he has the right to appoint the person responsible for formulating personnel policies. In comparison, the rights of British workers rarely go beyond the right to negotiate and the right to consult.

It is difficult to assess the benefits of industrial democracy in Germany. Supervisory Boards and Works Councils up till now have operated within conditions of a boom economy, not a declining one. There has been the 'surplus' labour of 3 million transient workers, drawn from such deprived countries as Turkey and Spain. Some positive gains can be pointed to. Works Councils have generally been effective in their operation of fringe benefits and have helped to create a responsible attitude towards them amongst workers. The quarterly meetings with employees doubtless play an important part in keeping people informed about the firm, and the Works Councils have been effective communicators. They are not seen as mouthpieces of management.

On the other hand, there is no apparent advantage in having local wage negotiations carried out by a Works Council as opposed to local trade union officials, although the fact that the Works Councils are well informed on the firm's economic position could make it easier to reach agreement.

The most controversial aspect is employee representation on the Supervisory Board, and management, in their own way, have become as skilled as trade unions in concealing, or tailoring, the information that finds its way to the Supervisory Board. Employers still see employee representation as an unnecessary limitation on their power. The unions regard it as a necessary part of industrial democracy.

It must be accepted that its benefits include a well-informed industrial community and a more egalitarian managerial climate which, in view of Germany's tradition of authority and social order, might not have occurred without it. Professor Fogarty in a recent report maintains that there has been a steady erosion of traditional management prerogatives and an extension of the field of matters for collective bargaining, accompanied by a corresponding sense of responsibility on the part of trade unionists.

FRANCE

The pattern in France has been of a much more diluted version of workers' control. By law, organizations employing more than fifty people are required to set up Works Councils. Membership must include representatives of the employer and employees, and where employees belong to a trade union their representatives must be given the right to sit on a Works Council. Staff employees are also entitled to be represented on the Council.

As in Germany, Works Councils are elected from the body of the employees in general, not on a union basis, and hold office for a period of two years. Their role is much more restricted than that of German Works Councils. Their decision-making capacity is restricted to such matters as safety, welfare and medical arrangements. The Council, for example, appoints the Works Medical Officer. The finance for the welfare schemes is provided, after consultation, by the company.

On economic matters, they have no decision-making powers, but have the right to be consulted about the economic situation of the firm. They are entitled to see in advance all financial documents which are sent to shareholders and to submit their views to shareholders on the management of the company.

In joint-stock companies, the Works Council has the right to nominate two members, one representing wage earners and one salaried staff, to attend meetings of the governing body of the firm. Their role, however, is purely consultative. Such measures require consent by management. Directors can, and do, meet informally to take key decisions. The system can only work properly where all parties are committed to it.

Neither employers nor unions seem much interested in extending participation beyond the level of the management of welfare schemes. One needs to look at the composition of French trade unions, particularly the communist-dominated ones, and at the political situation in France. The Communist unions are not interested in systems designed to operate the capitalist economy more efficiently, and have been unwilling to educate their members to be capable of understanding the complex economic factors which influence a firm. It is easier for unions to appeal to their members' more immediate interests, namely their concern about wages.

The French unions highlighted a problem which we will refer to when we come to consider the T.U.C.'s attitude to industrial democracy. Should Works Councils be considered as possible instruments of social change (and so of political power), for opposing or subverting capitalism, or should they be regarded, as in Yugoslavia, as a means of achieving greater industrial efficiency?

Faced with the possibility of structural disruption, French management has been careful to keep information about the firm's policy and economic position to a minimum, and allow their employees to channel their energies into the administration of welfare schemes.

Modest though they may be, the workers' rights of industrial democracy in France are wider than they are in England and are backed by law. They can *decide* matters which affect their immediate environment, such as working conditions and safety. They also have rights of information and consultation, even though they may not have been able to take full advantage of them. It is significant that this legislation has been introduced as a means of establishing social control, not in order to increase industrial efficiency, which may be one of the reasons why the system has failed in France.

More recent developments have concerned not involvement and participation in the decision-making process but participation in the sharing of profit. In 1967 profit-sharing was made obligatory in all types of enterprise employing more than 100 people, on the grounds that it would stimulate interest in the creation of profit and lead to a more equitable distribution of the wealth a firm creates. The profits which accrue to employees cannot be distributed for five years, during which time they should be invested either in the company or in national development projects. The aim is to maintain industrial growth and strengthen the employee's interest in the firm. It does have the merit of concentrating more on the question of industrial efficiency than social control.

SCANDINAVIA

Industrial democratic systems in Scandinavia were some time based on voluntarily agreed Works Councils. However, legislation in Parliament has recently altered this. The Norwegian Parliament has enacted laws requiring all companies over 200 employees to establish Supervisory Boards, with one-third of all members to be elected directly by the employees. The 'assembly', as it is known, elects the management and controls its major investment decisions. The Norwegian model differs from the German and Dutch ones in that it explicitly recognizes trade union machinery. It allows trade unionists to be appointed to the Board of Management as well as the Supervisory Boards. The Swedish system of industrial democracy, introduced in May 1973, provides for the election of two employee representatives to the unitary Board of Management of the company, with powers to vote on all decisions except collective agreements. Elections are solely through trade union machinery. The Danish scheme, embodied in the Companies Act 1974 requiring election to boards of companies employing more than fifty workers, on the other hand makes no provision for election through trade union machinery. All three countries have also been experimenting with a more 'grass roots' industrial democracy, namely the establishment of autonomous work groups.

HOLLAND

Works Councils in companies of over 100 employees have been in existence since the 1950s. They are mainly consultative bodies with rights of co-decision on issues such as profit-sharing, working hours, safety and pensions. In companies with a two-tier board system the

Works Councils have the same rights as management and the share-holders to nominate candidates to the supervisory board, but the nominees may not be employees or trade union officials involved in negotiation with the organization. Works Councils do have substantial veto powers over co-opting members to boards.

The T.U.C. in its studies of European systems, found widespread disappointment with the way in which Works Councils have operated. In Germany, the Works Council machinery was regarded as an alternative to the development of trade union activity at company and plant level and to a significant degree inhibited this development. The German unions now control 70 per cent of employee membership of Works Councils (although Works Council and trade union machinery and office holding are still rigidly separated).

UNITED KINGDOM

The United Kingdom has also seen a number of formal attempts at establishing industrial democracy, notably Glacier Metal and the John Lewis Partnership, although the British Steel Corporation and the Fairfields Shipbuilding Company provide other interesting examples.

The Glacier Metal system, which has been in operation for twenty-five years, establishes the right of the worker, through Works Council machinery, to decide on such matters as shift systems, starting and stopping, and welfare. The Works Council also has authority in the field of wages and salaries policy. All negotiated changes in wage rates must be approved by the Council before they are put into effect. This means that staff representatives are able to assess the effects of shop floor increases on differentials before agreeing to them, and *vice versa*. In addition any wage claim must be approved by the Works Council before it goes higher in the Company.

The Works Council has the right to be consulted on all matters affecting the well-being of employees. This means in effect that management is bound to notify and discuss any proposed new policy which will directly affect employees, such as proposed changes in pension funds or its policy for supervisory manning

The Works Council is an elected body which meets at least once a month. It is comprised of three grades of employees, senior management, first-line management and weekly paid staff. The places are allocated in proportion to the number of employees in the various grades, but there is a built-in check in the system against domination by a particular group, since the Council must unanimously agree before a proposal can be put into effect, which provides groups with the right of veto.

The weekly paid staff are elected to the Works Council via a system of Shop Committees. The workers elect the Shop Committees and the Shop Committees elect the workers' representatives on the Works Council. Elections to the Works Council are on the basis of individual ability not union representation, although in practice the elections generally result in all unions being represented on the Works Councils. The shop floor representatives who have been elected to the Works Council automatically become shop stewards and are empowered by the union to negotiate on their behalf. Only union members can vote and be elected.

Once the Council has taken a policy decision it is legally binding on all employees. This provision is written into the Contract of Employment and has the effect of preventing the work of the Council being destroyed by unofficial action on the shop floor. Because of the necessity of reaching a consensus, the Council can take a long time over difficult decisions.

The value of the Council is that it does provide a mechanism for working through problems before rather than after policies have been decided, and gives employees a good deal of control over their immediate working conditions and in ensuring that decisions once reached are enforceable until they are changed. It ensures that employees are protected from unilateral management decisions, that the Managing Director is open to employee questioning for his actions. The Glacier constitution grants rights to employees in addition to those of shareholders.

An interesting feature of the Glacier Metal system was that it arose out of dissatisfaction over the existing Works Council machinery, which was similar to that still employed by many firms, namely consultative talking shops concerned chiefly with trivia.

Another example of industrial democracy is the John Lewis Partnership, which runs department stores, supermarkets, factories and farms and employs 20,000 'partners', as they are called. All equity capital is held in trust on behalf of all who work in the business. So management manage on behalf of the managed and not on behalf of shareholders. The Chairman and the directors are managers, not owners, except in so far as they are co-owners with the other 20,000. The stated objectives are to run a successful business and to develop an experiment in industrial democracy.

The organization has a Central Council of 140 members, of whom at least four-fifths are elected by secret ballot annually by partners. Branch Councils are represented on the Central Council. Its members elect by secret ballot five of the twelve directors of the board of John Lewis Partnership Ltd (the holding company) and also three trustees. There are appropriate sub-committees which make representation to Branch Councils, but which also make provision for direct access to the Board.

Their professed aim is that partners shall share gain, knowledge and power. After the costs of business have been met, plus a sum for future development of the business, the rest goes (not to shareholders) but as a cash bonus to the 20,000 partners, in proportion to their pay. The fact that the sharing of gain is absolute makes discussion on expenditure realistic. If pensions or holidays are increased this will be at the expense of the bonus. Knowledge is shared through the provision of ample information through Central Council and branch meetings and house journals which give details of weekly sales or futute developments. In every trading branch there is a weekly communication session at which each department manager talks to his team about their job. There is a training department, who endeavour to ensure that each employee (or partner) knows as much as possible about his area of business and about the Partnership generally. The sharing of power comes from the capacity to spend money, on pensions, life assurance, subsidized meals, supplementary sick pay, longer holidays or discount on goods purchased. The constitution provides that councils can spend an amount, equal to 1 per cent of the payroll, as they please. Much of this power relates to fringe benefits.

The Council can make recommendations on many matters affecting the conduct of the business. There is a committee of the central council for the review of pay and allowances; it reviews in turn each group of pay rates, and considers whether they are fully competitive. If they do not think they are, they can recommend changes. The Council debates such matters as whether their shops should open for five days or six days a week. Although their power is only to recommend not decide, great weight is given to their recommendations.

MANAGERIAL PREROGATIVE

What is the essence of the problem? Why have managers become so interested in it? The process is a subtle one and may be illustrated by the story of a Personnel Manager of a large man-made fibres firm who on the occasion of his retirement felt the need to give some advice to a group of young managers about 'The challenge of the future'. He remarked that he had joined the Indian Army in the 1930s. In his Punjabi regiment he was accustomed to unquestioning obedience. After the war he had joined industry. His earlier years were marked by a labour force that in some ways seemed as acquiescent as his Indian Sepoys. He told his audience that things would never be the same again, that managers nowadays had to negotiate *everything*. That he was getting out, so to speak, whilst the going was good. What he was really describing was an erosion of what might be termed 'managerial prerogative'.

Business, so the argument goes, is about making decisions, about taking risks. The difference between obtaining an order or losing one can be a matter of minutes; judgement needs to be swift and firm. Despite all the apparatus of decision-making techniques and computers, managers still back their hunches. There may be something wrong with the technical mix of a product, a heat exchanger may be working imperfectly. The situations call for immediate action. The good manager thrives in an environment where he is called upon to make these quick decisions. That is what management is all about. That is why the manager chose the career rather than become a civil servant or a teacher. It is not that he set his mind on becoming an autocrat. He does not see himself in this role.

What it does mean is that personal decision-making becomes a habit; hence the importance of delegation, fixing responsibility, authorizing budgets. Too much consultation can create delay and inefficiency and in some cases accidents.

David McClelland has shown us that man has a number of needs – needs for achievement, needs for affiliation and needs for control and influence (or, as some would say, power).[1] In some people, one set of needs is more prominent than others. Social workers and nurses have stronger needs to affiliate. In fact, when the Salmon Report provided a career structure for nurses and gave them posts which were more management-oriented than patient-oriented, many of them experienced internal conflict. They had a better monetary reward structure but psychologically a less satisfying job. Academics have a strong need to achieve, to carry out research, for example, in controlled conditions, uncomplicated by human intervention. Increasingly in universities and polytechnics, they are being asked to manage large, complex educational enterprises, where their knowledge of biology or physics is of little avail.

These needs operate mostly at a sub-conscious level. It is only when academics achieve high office and find themselves having to make decisions about the price of meals in halls of residence or the allocation of car-parking space that they realize, with mixed feelings, that the job is not as satisfying as they imagined it would be.

Managers, on the other hand, whether they realize it or not, are motivated more strongly by needs to control and influence situations. Those who find their way most quickly to the top of organizations, rather than remain as engineers solving technical problems, are those whose power needs are the most strongly developed. That is not to say that good managers do not consult – they do – but to observe that really to share power is to lose something that is important to them. One can see this even where unions are not involved in the process.

We saw in Chapter 4 how Douglas McGregor identified two management styles, Theory X and Theory Y.[2] Theory Y management, based upon the individual's own motivation, was participative. Theory X, based upon the external reward system of threat and bribe, was based on control. Delegation, for a person who has important needs to control situations, is difficult and demanding. Many people imagine they do it when they do not. They ask a subordinate to carry out some task but build in various checks and report procedures, or intervene at the first sign of things going wrong, so that it is delegation in name only. Management by objectives has frequently failed as a method of management, not because of the paperwork involved, but because unconsciously the manager is reluctant to yield control.

The point is made at some length because this element of behaviour does influence industrial relations. This is very different from saying that managers are autocratic or domineering. They may be extremely reasonable. Having strongly developed needs for controlling situations is not something to be ashamed of but something to recognize in oneself and others. Nor is this need to be found exclusively amongst those who reach positions of leadership in industry. It is just as commonly found amongst those who occupy top positions in the unions, or amongst the more militant shop stewards. They get their satisfaction not from a fine piece of craftsmanship, but from influencing the situation a certain way.

Power-sharing calls for a fundamental change of attitude. The common parlance would be 'joint consultation'. Any discussion about participation immediately raises the question 'participation in what?' Very little has been done to involve the worker in the design and programme of his own hourly work or in the solution of operational problems. Whatever may be the economic structure of society (nationalized industry or free enterprise), individuals performing different tasks in the same organic system have to learn to work together.

The idea of worker participation is an attractive one and, although current recently, has been known for a long time. The Emperor Justinian fifteen hundred years ago declared that, 'Matters concerning all should be agreed by all'. Unfortunately, the degree of control over their daily tasks gained by the workman at his bench or the clerk at his files has been mostly achieved by industrial action, or the threat of it, not as a result of reasoned debate between managers and shop floor, putting aside their individual interest in pursuit of a common goal.

JOINT CONSULTATION

On the political front much has been achieved. Trade unions are equal partners with industry on many government bodies and industrial training boards. One can very easily become dazzled at the formal appearance of participation. Elaborate committee structures, with local, regional and national hierarchies, have been established by some enterprises for 'consulting the workers'. The annual gathering, at some seaside resort, is an impressive ritual, celebrated with lobster and foreign wine, amidst platitudes of general concern. One sees in nationalized industries those who once represented the workers at the negotiating table being offered commanding positions as worker-directors on the corporations set up to manage those industries. Some firms allow their employees to benefit from a profit-sharing scheme.

These gestures are beside the point. When the day comes, and over the last few years there have been any number of them, when workers refuse to carry out the instructions of another (and the National Union of Mineworkers is perhaps a good example), it is of little immediate use to invoke such ideas as nationalization, profit-sharing or worker-directors.

The coal industry makes an interesting example of an organization which changed its political face in the first flush of enthusiasm which followed the election of a Labour Government in 1945. Numerous consultative committees were established as a consequence of the Act of nationalization. They turned out to be a vast labyrinth of organized frustration. This was largely because the idea of joint consultation meant many different things to the extraordinary collusion of interests that nationalization was intended to be. The miners saw in it the promise of a new say in how life in the industry might be lived. The former managers probably had very mixed feelings, having been involved in the struggle to keep the industry in private hands. The paid staff on the Board, former miner officials, also had mixed feelings, caught as they were between what they understood to be their responsibilities to the Board, on the one hand, and their loyalty to their former workmates on the other. The failure of joint consultation to match the promise attached to it in the heady days of the new post-war era should act as a warning against similar euphoria with regard to ideas of joint consultation now stemming from Europe. The traditions in the mining industry were not those of Cadbury's or Unilever or I.C.I. It was difficult to achieve overnight a spirit of co-operation among those who for over a century had been sworn enemies, not only avoiding co-operation but openly despising it. Perhaps the lessons are that participation should not be attempted in conditions of crisis, where people feel threatened or resentful, but when they feel secure and relaxed. Nor can one impose the will to harmony by Acts of Parliament. Twenty-five years later, the Conservatives, in their famous Industrial Relations Act, had recourse to legislation for a rather different purpose, and with results equally unsuccessful.

PARTICIPATION IN WHAT?

Participation can be nurtured and encouraged only when the parties involved wish it to be. Those who are looking for peace and harmony should first identify the common ground. When management and unions are drawn up in opposing ranks they tend to see the different rather than the shared goals. Co-operation is something that has to be painfully learnt.

It is important for managers to display convincingly their own sincerely felt need for support. On those few occasions, when joint consultation has centred on the work rather than, say, the canteen conditions, it has foundered because the management have been unable to suppress their superior technical knowledge. Sometimes they openly display it, with references to research and computerization. Such an attitude inhibits any useful discussion. When two parties enter into a discussion it is to be hoped that both parties learn. One of the authors well remembers some genuine attempts by management to involve workers in the solution of design and operational problems. Well-meaning young graduates came, armed with slide rules and nimble minds, and overrode the objections of the workers who explained why the shutes would not work, or the gates close properly. The young managers blinded them with equations and technical know-how. The workers shrugged their shoulders and soldiered on. The equipment still did not work properly, despite modifications made by managers. 'They won't listen to us, will they?' was the reaction of the men. For those who worship technical expertise above all else, the disaster of Aberfan should stand as a salutary warning. The expert's judgement triumphed over the hunches of the locals.

The capacity to listen and accept upward influence is not easily acquired, as we have seen already. Management may well argue that they waste too many hours listening to talk about non-essentials. Much of the shop stewards' behaviour has become as institutionalized as the meetings he attends. In some ways, he can be very unrepresentative of the men. His role can also become stereotyped.

Sometimes one has to break away completely from the environment to establish new communication patterns. One such occasion one of the authors recalls is when a group of about thirty managers, supervisors and shop floor workers (shop stewards and operators), all drawn from one works, spent a week away at a hotel.

There was no planned agenda other than to examine how communications in the works could be improved. For most of the time discussion was carried out in three unstructured groups. It did not centre on media of discussion, factory notice boards and the like. Surprisingly to outsiders, the discussion was mostly about work.

Why had management replaced this machine with that one which caused more dust and bit into the rock slower and destroyed cutting heads more frequently? Did they know that the men had made their own guards? Was it not a more costly and wasteful process? Hadn't they thought of using two machines abreast instead of one? Questions and suggestions were showered on management. An eavesdropper might have been forgiven for thinking that a motor-cycle scrambling club was throwing out suggestions as to how they could all tune up their machines better for the next event. The discussion was animated, vigorous, critical, heated. It was an interesting refutation of the allegation that the last thing an employee is interested in is his work. There is the paradox that in today's industry he is alienated from it, and yet it is one of the ways in which he is, theoretically at least, allowed to achieve his dignity, a point to which we will return later.

The other main feature of the discussion was the candour with which managers and workforce spoke. It was a revelation to managers. They had never imagined that the workforce could be so job-centred and knowledgeable. Shop stewards and managers drew together in their humanity. They discovered what one might call trivial and irrelevant things in common: that a manager and a shop steward both had handicapped children, that their wives were asthmatic, that they were worried about how their children were doing at school. Shop stewards discovered that what they had taken for aloofness in a certain manager's behaviour was in fact shyness, which did not fit into their stereotype of the confident manager. There was surprisingly little back-slapping at the bar, which was characteristic of the casual relationships between managers and managed, betrayed at the long service presentations in the firm's social club. The week was expensive, the bridge built fragile and subject to erosion in the back-at-the-plant situation. But it showed what was possible and broke down some popular myths. Given sufficient commitment by both sides (and labour turnover and management mobility make the exercise difficult and in need of renewal), there was a basis for more profitable discussions on the plant.

The essence of participation is that it is a means of reducing the gap between those who hold power and those who do not, that it can be initiated by either superior or subordinate to debate an issue introduced for the first time by either.

Professor Revans in an interesting paper on Worker Participation,[3] submitted to the T.U.C. and based on his experience in a wide range of industries and occupations (coal-mining, chemical industry, hospitals), argues that the core of the problem of unrest, of the challenge to authority of the gap between managers and managed, lies in the matter of 'precedence'. 'What right have you, or anyone else for that matter, to give me orders?' is a question more and more frequently being asked, not only on the factory floor, but in the home and the school.

That question is asked less to the extent that workers are brought into the decision-making process, particularly in areas of direct concern to their work. Company policy is not the prime area over which workers wish to exercise control.

A genuinely fruitful discussion of the needs of subordinates is not to be confused with the make-believe and back-slapping of the old hands from the personnel department, running grievance shops for shop stewards. Lunching trade union leaders on fried scampi and white wine may have been the annual climax of the national consultative process for some organizations, and no doubt it was beneficial for the catering trade in the off-season. But such exhibitions are not to be confused with genuine participation.

The exercise of precedence can be felt just as starkly in the hospital ward as the coal mine. To the extent that the consultant allows the power gap to be diminished, by respecting the opinions of his ward sisters, so do the junior nurses feel their training to be more effective and so do the patients show benefit. A good information system is one where there is the opportunity of upward, as well as downward, challenge to what is being asked for.

Participation can take place at a number of levels, not just between managers and shop floor. As we argue elsewhere, it is rare for a manager to take a foreman into his confidence or allow himself to be influenced by him. Yet studies have shown a high correlation between a foreman's personal satisfaction with his work and his perception of the information system by which he is served.

Some managers feel it to be a confession of weakness to ask others how a job might be performed. There persists the feeling 'I'm paid to manage. This is what is expected of me'. A survey carried out in a large chemical firm, initiated by managers, attempted amongst other things to discover what foremen felt about managers. Managers were asked to predict what they thought the foreman's ratings would be. In the event, it turned out that the foremen had a far higher opinion of management than managers had assumed them to have. Supervisors learnt much about their own roles, particularly in helping the managers to appreciate how little they understood the feelings of their own assistants.

The more closely the shop floor are involved in exercises of participation, the more necessary it is that the exercises should be active and practical. If the consultation remains verbal and abstract, it is likely to inhibit the possible interest of people who, by virtue of their education, may regard words as the tools the boss class use to fool them. To invite a worker's views on conglomerate investment or marginal analysis or pricing policy is another way of playing the old hierarchical game. The critical questions must be 'Can the men contribute?', and the flipside to the record 'Will the managers listen?'

A programme of action should be related to the needs and motivations of those it concerns. Although shop floor could not be expected to make a contribution to pricing policy, not being in possession of the information upon which a sensible decision could be based, given an opportunity to organize their own local work group differently, a group of workers would regard it as failure if they could suggest no improvement. In participation as in all other forms of human action, a successful outcome demands relevant information, sufficient desire and appropriate skill. 'Who knows? Who cares? Who can?' are the three questions that effective action invariably demands.

Participation is likely to be effective if a number of conditions obtain. Managers need to demonstrate their awareness of the crisis in authority now pervading Western culture. They need to recognize that the amount of authority they can exercise over their subordinates is the amount that their subordinates allow them to, not the amount the manager's boss has conferred on him. Information must become more freely available. The White Paper on Company Law Reform (1973) emphasizes this. 'The more people can see what is actually happening the less likely they are to harbour general suspicions. Openness in company affairs is the first principle in securing responsible behaviour'.

Participation should not be seen as a last resort when all else has failed. Nor as something to be produced during times of crisis. One of the positive lessons learned when firms were thrown back on to a three-day week because of the miners' strike of 1974 is the amount of co-operation managers received from the trade unions. Employees were asked to vote on the best use of fuel and how work could be organized differently to maintain output and wages.

The crisis brought managers and managed together and threw into sharp relief problems which a five-day week had blurred. Senior managers were heard to utter 'It's not fair that managers should be paid for five days and manual workers only for three'. The single status issue was raised again. Why should there be differences in holidays, sick pay, canteen facilities, and, more important, job security? There are already considerable differences in pay between the secretary and the factory cleaner, the driver and the personnel manager. So participation is about sharing the bad with the good.

Participation is more likely to succeed when the parties share operational knowledge of the topic under discussion and when they perceive the opportunity of exercising influence. That means it must be rooted in the local situation.

Whether participation would reach a point when shop floor select their own foreman is a debatable question, but such suggestions have been made from time to time, particularly as the shop steward is seen to wield more power than the foremen in many plants.

THE TRADE UNION VIEW

The trade unions and organizations of managers or employers such as the B.I.M. or C.B.I., as might be expected, take a much more mechanical and instrumental view of worker participation and industrial democracy. The trade unions, as evidenced by the 1974 Interim Report of the T.U.C., see industrial democracy more in terms of social control than managing the enterprise more efficiently at an operational level.[4] They go to the heart of the problem by pointing out that, in law, management's sole responsibility is to the shareholders. The only limitation is in such matters as safety, hygiene, pollution and redundancy provisions. The hope is for company law to be changed making provision for much wider disclosure of information to all employees, but existing company law only requires disclosure to shareholders. The full implementation of the disclosure requirements of the Employment Protection Act, the Industry Act, and the Health and Safety at Work Act, is likely to alter the traditional relationship between shareholders and management. Putting worker directors on the Board in no way alters that legal obligation. The unions are seeking 'information agreements' through which workpeople can be provided with the information necessary for a better understanding of the relationships between pay, profits, efficiency and future prospects.

The traditional British trade union attitude, like the French, towards participation in the management of private industry, has been that of opposition. The basic conflict of interest between the workers and owners of capital and their agents (the managers) has made discussion of management decisions meaningless. The argument has been that the job of the trade unions (that was how they arose) was simply and solely to negotiate terms and conditions of employment and not to usurp the function of management. Neither should they be collaborating in a system of industrial power and wealth of which they disapproved. The unions took a somewhat different attitude to nationalized industry, and participated in the process of management in the public sector. Profit-sharing schemes they have regarded as a charade providing no control over managerial decisions, e.g. I.C.I. shares are non-voting and seen by the workers as just an annual bonus. The T.U.C.'s evidence to the Donovan Commission showed a more flexible approach: it went on to argue that the fundamental conflict of interest was not necessarily an overriding obstacle to participation, and that there should be trade union representation at several levels of an enterprise.

Their policy is to seek changes in Company Law, so that management boards of companies are not exclusively responsible to shareholders, and the law should recognize the equal importance of the workpeople by fifty-fifty representation on the Supervisory Boards of companies. They come out clearly against achieving this through an extension of the Works Council system, so popular on the continent. They see collective bargaining as the central method of joint regulation in industry (and the public services). Because the structure of company level bargaining is frequently multi-union (again unlike Germany or Sweden with their industrial unions), it is difficult to fit into any geographically based union branch and officer structure. The unions have a vested interest in maintaining their own status quo. Industrial democracy on a continental model would require more changes in their structure than they wish to contemplate.

They recognise, however, the shift away from National Agreements, which only establish a minimum union rate to be improved at plant and company level, although the bulk of the public sector is still largely tied to central agreement in such matters as wages and hours. The logic is that if workpeople can negotiate important additions to pay at the local level, they can become involved in a wider range of decision-making.

The T.U.C. report rules out productivity agreements as useful examples of worker participation. The union view is that management regarded them as one-off jobs rather than as a continuous process involving an extension of joint regulation over the work organization. Although they did embrace some areas of joint control, the 'buy-out' element of restrictive trade union practices involved a surrender of unilateral trade union control. Nor have the unions been impressed by the various job enrichment programmes, which they regard as essentially manipulative, subtle attempts to control workers increasingly alienated from their jobs by the nature of their work. These exercises have usually been not joint affairs but management inspired, though aided by the stimulus of the social scientists.

The trade union attitude to representation in the public sector has understandably been different. Trade union representation on the boards of the nationalized industries in the early days was based on the view that it was not in the best interests of the workpeople of the industry to have as their direct representatives members of the controlling board who would be committed to its joint decisions. The Minister responsible appointed trade unionists with special knowledge of the industry but not as representatives. Provisions of this kind were made in the 1969 Post Office Act and in the 1967 Iron and Steel Act, precluding the appointment to the relevant board a trade union member who was engaged in trade union activities in the industry concerned. On public boards the members with a trade union background are in almost all cases still from unions with no membership within the Board's employees. The 1944 T.U.C. document considered that trade unions should maintain their complete independence. The T.U.C. evidence to Donovan, however, adopted a more flexible approach.

Recommendations accordingly were made in 1972 by the various T.U.C. committees that appointment of trade unionists from unions within the industry should be made to the boards of the new authorities in the Civil Aviation field, the Regional Health Authorities and the Regional Water Authorities. The T.U.C. insisted that responsibility for appointment be operated through the T.U.C. The Government have not accepted the recommendations for Civil

Aviation and Water Authorities, but asked for trade unionists from outside the industry, who are supposed to represent the wider interests of the community. The same arguments obtain for teachers. Teaching unions are not normally represented on Education Committees, nor are the non-teaching unions involved in the education service.

BRITISH STEEL CORPORATION

The main innovation in worker participation was the Worker-Director scheme of the British Steel Corporation. This has no legislative backing, since the 1967 Iron and Steel Act did not include any provision for worker participation. The scheme involved the appointment of up to three Worker-Directors to Divisional Board of the British Steel Corporation. On appointment the Worker-Directors originally had to relinquish all trade union offices. The main objectives of the scheme were to enable a shop-floor view to be brought to the boards, to involve employees in policy making, and to provide a symbol of a new departure in management/union relations. The Trade Unions, reviewing the scheme in 1972, voiced a number of objections. The District Boards were only advisory to the Divisional Managing Director. There was a lack of contact between Worker-Directors and trade union machinery both at branch union and national level. Worker-Directors lacked representative character.

In 1972 the B.S.C. Board and the T.U.C. Steel Committee modified the original scheme. A new selection procedure allowed for a greater involvement of trade union members and the T.U.C. Steel Committee. Employee directors were given the right to hold and continue to hold union office, and allowed to take an active part in joint consultative meetings. Even now the final decision on appointments still remains with the Chairman of the British Steel Corporation.

The nomination of members by the T.U.C. Steel Committee helped to overcome the problem of elections and the question of balance of inter-union interests.

INDUSTRIAL EFFICIENCY OR SOCIAL CONTROL

The trade union attitude towards industrial democracy therefore is based on a number of concepts – the right of workpeople collectively to a greater control over their work situation, that collective bargaining should be seen as the major means of achieving it, and that it should be based on trade union machinery. As the T.U.C. report so aptly puts it, 'to extend the area of joint control and limit unilateral managerial prerogatives, using the present structure of collective bargaining machinery to bring into the field of negotiations matters which are currently outside collective agreements'. Matters which would be so covered include recruitment, training, deployment, manning, speed of work, discipline, redundancy and dismissals, minimum earnings guarantees, pension rights, sick and industrial injury pay and other fringe benefits.

In order to make sensible decisions, legislative provision would need to be made for 'information rights' for *individual workers*. Items listed by the T.U.C. include:

All information circulated to shareholders.

A job specification including responsibilities, management structure, and health and other possible hazards.

Employment prospects, including promotion opportunities and plans to contract or expand the workforce.

Access to their personal file and to an explanation by the employer on its content.

Workers' representatives should be entitled to additional information as follows:

Manpower: Number of employees by job descriptions; rates of turnover; statistics on short-time working, absenteeism; sickness and accident, recruitment, training, redeployment, promotion, redundancy, dismissal and a breakdown of non-wage income costs.

Earnings: Averages and distributions by appropriate occupations and work groups of earnings and hours including, where necessary, information on make-up of pay showing piecework earnings.

Sources of Revenue: Sales turnover by main activities; pricing policy; income from investments and overseas earnings.

Costs: Production costs; distribution and sales costs; administrative and overhead costs; costs of materials and machinery; costs of management and supervision.

Directors' Remuneration including country of payment.

Profits before and after tax; grants and subsidies; distributions and retentions.

Performance Indicators: Unit costs; output per man; return on capital employed.
Worth of Company: Details of growth and up-to-date value of fixed assets; growth and realizable value of trade investments.
Details of new enterprises and locations, prospective close-downs, mergers and takeovers.

The T.U.C. document says modestly 'it would be necessary for trade unions to reconsider their training programmes'. Reconsider is hardly the word. Revolutionize would be more appropriate. A massive education programme would be required and begs a number of important questions which the T.U.C. does not address itself to, such as the motivation of workers, apart from their capacity, to assimilate and process all this information. What they argue for loud and clear is the need for a *de facto* sharing of managerial prerogative, which is part of a world-wide process in which people are claiming power for themselves. The question we asked earlier still needs answering, 'Participation in what?' For most workers hardly participation in the shopping list the T.U.C. provides, but rather over their work which gives them ownership and dignity. That is not to say that some degree of consultation over the wider issues which affect whether they will have a job to perform is not also vitally important. It is a matter of scale.

In terms of structure there is an obvious clash between how the T.U.C. see the matter and how the employers see it. The T.U.C. see no future in worker-directors who behave just like other directors. They have no time for the European Works Councils or anything independent of trade unions, regardless of the fact that a considerable portion of the workforce is not unionized. Worker-directors must be directly responsible to their constituents in the firm. Appointments to supervisory boards are only acceptable when made through trade union machinery. The responsibility of worker representatives would be to trade union members employed in the firm rather than to the general assembly or shareholder.

They favour the creation of Supervisory Boards, but with powers in excess of those prevailing on the continent. They are looking for an extension of U.K. company law over decisions made by the Annual General Meeting of Shareholders as well as those of the Management Board. The Management Boards of companies employing more than 200 people should be divided into Supervisory Boards and

Management Boards. The Supervisory Board should be the supreme body of the company, able to overrule both Board of Management and A.G.M. decisions. Workers' representatives, appointed through trade union machinery, should occupy one-half of the places on the Supervisory Board. Nor should workers' representatives be obliged to relinquish union office. Even more audacious, they argue that E.E.C. proposals for harmonization would have to be adapted, in particular to provide for 50 per cent board membership and to be based on Trade Union machinery.

The T.U.C. attitude to control in the nationalized industry boards is that they are in effect supervisory boards. The main alteration they propose would be to ensure that trade union membership was brought up to 50 per cent. Not all of the trade unionists need to be drawn from within the industry; some could represent wider community and public interests.

THE MANAGEMENT VIEW

Employers' organizations and management, impelled by a number of forces, apart from the fifth Directive of the European Commission, have increasingly felt the need to provide for wider involvement of the workforce in the affairs of industry. Working Parties of such bodies as the Confederation of British Industry and the British Institute of Management have made submissions to the Government.[5] Increasingly British management are becoming aware of their professional and social responsibilities and are endeavouring to draw up for managers a code of conduct similar to those the more established professions submit themselves to.

The relevant C.B.I. report in its opening statement, commits itself, unashamedly, by 'reiterating our belief in the private enterprise system and in the profit motive that sustains it'. Change, if it is to come, can best come by self-reform, not legislation (a cry not different from that of the unions, who prefer social contracts to legislation), 'private enterprise should be encouraged to get on with its own job and not be subjected to legal coercion'. Substitute 'free collective bargaining' for 'private enterprise' and you have the union case perfectly stated. The assumption behind management and unions' statement is 'trust us, we can put our houses in order'.

The C.B.I. sees a need for wider participation in the decision-making process but this is to be obtained by greater disclosure of information and by improving the consultative machinery at *plant* level, not by 'some form of co-determination in legal form'. The legal responsibility of the board is to manage the company efficiently in the interests of the shareholders. The nearest employees are to being represented on the board is through an executive director responsible for personnel policy, who could also act as chairman of a company works council. He would not however be a delegate of the council. He would merely be its spokesman, representing its views to the board, and the board's views to the council. The two-tier or supervisory boards are rejected as 'not offering an acceptable solution to British practice'. 'To suggest that the establishment of a supervisory board, meeting at infrequent intervals and remote from the day-to-day affairs of the company, could effect any substantial improvement in this area is unconvincing. The existence of a supervisory board must take away from the members of the management board that feeling of ultimate and total responsibility which should be the most compelling influence towards effective management,' – such sentiments sum up the employers' view. The separation of function, as in West Germany, where a supervisory body has responsibility without power and a management board has power without responsibility, is felt to be unsatisfactory, offending against the unitary system of company administration in which important decisions emerge from continuous consultation at many levels rather than from independent conclusions reached at separate points in the structure.

The company's interests in the widest sense of the word are felt to be best protected by the appointment of non-executive directors who would provide the necessary independence and objectivity, but as many of them in practice would be executive directors of other boards, some people might feel this to be an insufficient safeguard. The C.B.I. recommend that the chairman of the Board should be appointed for a period not to exceed five years (preferably three), and look for a clearer distinction between his responsibilities as chairman and those as chief executive.

The British Institute of Management go further and suggest that the functions of chief executive and chairman should be separated. The chairman would be independent and elected directly by the shareholders for a two- or three-year period of office. Shareholders' interests would be protected by having an independent chairman and independent non-executive directors. Employees' interests would be protected by the co-option of two directors acceptable to the Board and the employees. The extension of the Works Council system, notable for its breadth of participation, lateral as well as vertical, is also advocated, together with greater disclosure of information.

There is a wide gulf therefore between the revolutionary proposals of the T.U.C. and the modest suggestions for employee participation put forward by employer and management organizations. These differences reflect a fundamental difference of opinion on whose job is it to manage. Employers' proposals savour of concessions – always the language of those in power; the trade unions think in terms of rights. The employers show more awareness of their responsibilities to creditors, suppliers and customers than is evidenced in the T.U.C. proposals. Managers tend to believe it is all a matter of professional conduct, and would like to see the adoption of a corporate Code of Conduct, which they feel most enlightened companies already operate. There is an undercurrent of awareness of the 'unacceptable face of capitalism' and the need to introduce some reforms, lest the free market economy be thought to run counter to social needs and the public interest.

Thus attitudes towards industrial democracy become polarized: it is seen by the unions as a means of social control and by management as a means of industrial efficiency. That is a matter that is best debated in the political arena. In the day-to-day encounter, management and workforce need to come together as a means of learning from each other. As we argued earlier, for the great mass of the workforce a willingness on the part of managers to listen and to accept upward influence, would be a greater step forward towards worker participation than heated debate about the nature of membership of Supervisory Boards.

The T.U.C. case underestimates the difficulties and responsibilities of management. Under the arrangement they propose, serious conflict at Board level could take place, most likely at a doctrinaire level. Compromise solutions are likely because of the clash of interest, solutions which may not be in the best long-term interests of the firm. There is no guarantee that the representation of workers' representatives on Management or Supervisory Boards will make management decisions any more acceptable to the rank and file, unless there is some system of control, e.g. that the Board's decisions should be binding on all employees as is the case to some extent in Glacier Metal. It is difficult to see this concept being acceptable to either the trade unions or management. It is, for example, very different from the idea that wages and conditions agreements should be made enforceable by law.

Can a worker's representative on the Board satisfactorily perform two roles, that of negotiator and representative of the workforce and that of managerial adviser seeking to ensure the introduction of the most efficient policies? There will be times when these roles are not compatible. Some trade unionists would prefer the more traditional role of advising and informing and consulting managers about attitudes and views they need to take into account when framing their policies. Management can accept or reject them. The unions can negotiate if management reject. The T.U.C. rather summarily dismiss the difficulties of representation on Supervisory Boards created by the prevalence of multi-unions.

Democracy is found to operate best at grass-roots level, and companies who do not have effective channels of joint consultation already are unlikely to achieve it by the introduction of workers' representatives at Board level. The least effective part of the German system is the involvement of workers at Board level, the most success-ful at plant and works level. Industrial democracy, like political democracy, must grow naturally; it cannot be imposed and regulated from above. It is important to involve as large a number of people as possible. With every sign that the centre of power in many unions is moving away from full-time officials towards local organizations, there are greater arguments for practising democracy first at the local plant level, involving workers much more in such things as starting and finishing times, overtime arrangements, the way the work might be done differently, the training of workers – matters about which workers can feel confident in speaking. The next stage might be for managers to submit an annual report to workers and be questioned by them on their management of the firm.

The evidence seems to be that industrial democracy has worked best when it has been seen as a means of improving industrial efficiency rather than when it has been used as an instrument of social control. The experience of the changes in the Fred Olsen Company at Millwall seem to bear this out. The docks were notorious, before decasualization in 1967, for bitter industrial relations. As one of the employees of the Olsen Company remarked, 'getting a job each day was like being herded in a slave market with a labour master selecting the men he required'. The establishment of the new terminal at Millwall with its modern mechanical equipment (a capital invest-ment programme of £1½ million) provided the stimulus for doing something different. Employees were invited to participate in the new venture. Works committees were established to deal with various matters, such as an Equipment Committee, which was to assess the right type of equipment necessary to do a given job. Part of the company's purchasing arrangements with suppliers involves the use of machines for a trial period. Numerous ideas to improve work efficiency have flowed from these discussion groups. The workers claimed they were not seeking worker control but some measure of joint policy-making and a share in the decision-making.

The absence of social amenities, previously a characteristic of the dock world, has been replaced by amenities at Millwall which are open to all; no reserved places in the restaurant or car park, no special status symbols. The result of all these changes has been that many of the old barriers between 'them' and 'us' have been flattened, with a corresponding increase in mutual trust.

But although, as one of the Olsen employees remarked, 'no management can manage without the full consent of its labour force', not all workpeople wish to involve themselves in management. The level of attendance at trade union branch meetings throughout the country (around 5 per cent of its members on average) suggests that most workers have better things to do with their time than participate in the running of their own union. Glacier Metal find that attendance at many of their committees is small. Consent to be governed is the crucial aspect of this relationship. Trust is present in a way it is not in the management of many companies. It is only managers who can create this trust, not governments, and it can only be done at the place of work.

AUTONOMOUS WORK-GROUPS

Much has also been made of the value of autonomous work-groups. Even in the Scandinavian countries, where they have been pioneered with such enthusiasm, the motivation to do so was not an unalloyed and unprompted management desire to make boring jobs more interesting for their workers. It has invariably been introduced to counter problems of recruitment, absenteeism and turnover. One might remark that some of the fancy sociological terms being invoked in this context may turn out on examination to have some fairly mundane commercial meanings. Where group working takes place the benefits for companies greatly exceed those gained by the workers. Since much of the available literature is management-biased it could give the impression to the outside observer that each scheme was introduced solely for the well-being of the employees. Before Britain's managers embrace autonomous work-groups as the answer to many of their problems they need to be aware of a number of features. One is the predominance in most of the work-group schemes of unskilled and semi-skilled female employees. On a number of occasions (shades of Elton Mayo!), they commenced with a redecoration of the work area based on the suggestions of the employees involved in the experiment. Secondly, Volvo and Saab – two of the best-known companies involved – have not been impervious to exploiting the publicity value of their schemes, even to the extent of trying to attract overseas visitors. By giving the impression (possibly a fair one) that vehicles from their plants are built with loving care, craftsmanship and pride, they have been able to gain considerable commercial advantage in a ruthlessly competitive market. However, one should not dismiss schemes which do relieve boredom and monotony even when the benefits are mainly by-products of management's attempts to solve their own problems.

Another feature which requires further examination is the changing role of the foreman in the light of group working. One of the most disquieting developments has been the various attempts to combine the roles of foreman and chargehand and even foreman and shop steward.

Although, as we have argued earlier, workers are likely to contribute more effectively at work when they can exercise some influence, unions may well resist work-groups if they suspect management's intentions. Although they are designed to stimulate a sense of purpose and make work more interesting, the increased responsibility can lead to unacceptable increases in stress and workload on the workers concerned. Some workers are resistant to even enlightened management attempts to improve their lot. Their view is that factory life may be barely tolerable but it is inevitable. They look for fulfilment in their lives not at work but when they get away from it. It is a tenable view.

In a curious way work-groups – particularly when they are successful – lessen the power of collective shop floor action, since they provide more production flexibility and less disruption. There is less product loss caused by absenteeism when the group tends to cover for an absent member.

So work groups give management greater control, despite claims of increasing worker influence.

CONCLUSIONS

This pattern across the world varies enormously. Yugoslavia has developed perhaps one of the most complete forms of industrial democracy. The paradox is that it should take place in a country which does not enjoy what would be regarded by Western standards as full political democracy. Some of the 'new left' in Yugoslavia still feel that there is a long way to go, particularly in the narrowing of the monetary differentials between the director and the unskilled worker, and point to the much smaller differentials obtaining between maximum and minimum salaries in China. The forms of industrial democracy thus range from profit-sharing/co-partnership schemes to works councils (whether based on union structures or not), to representation at board level, to participation at lower levels of work.

The Labour Party has stated its own position on such expedients as co-partnership in its Green Paper on 'The Community and the Company'.[6]

Various proposals are currently being put forward to make employees of a company 'members' of it in law (e.g. the 'Gower Committee' of the Industrial Society). Shareholders are referred to by company law as 'members'; but the proposals usually would limit the power of employee 'members' (e.g. to certain rights to information and the like). We do not believe that support should be given to this approach. The whole concept of a 'member' is an antiquated one, bequeathed to company law by the old law of partnership. In all but the small domestic companies the average shareholder is not a 'member' but an investor. Rights given by company law to 'members' would largely be inappropriate for employees.

The same result can, of course, be achieved by distributing shares to employees; but experience of such schemes suggests that they do not materially affect the distribution of power within the company. Even schemes to make employees 'partners' have not done so (see the report on John Lewis Partnership by Flanders,

Pomeranz and Woodward, *Experiment in Industrial Democracy* 1968). Most serious of all, such proposals ignore the functions of trade unions and collective bargaining, and by establishing alternative channels which can be used to by-pass trade union machinery, can create new sources of tension within the enterprise.

Profit-sharing arrangements can often be little more than ineffectual bonus incentives, being insufficiently related to individual and work-group efforts. Works Councils flourish best in times of full employment and economic prosperity; but in fiercer times they can be severely put to the test. The same is true of board-level representation, and one wonders whether legal enforcement will materially alter the situation.

Autonomous work-groups only marginally affect the authority and power structure of the firm. They present considerable dangers unless introduced via union channels as a natural extension of the collective bargaining process. The unions not unnaturally see collective bargaining as a more effective check on unilateral management decision-making than the A.G.M.

So we return to our central thesis – namely managers' need to re-examine their attitudes to managerial prerogative. Managements' own ideologies hinder this examination. They see themselves as non-propertied and having jettisoned traditional ownership concepts. The legitimacy of their managerial authority now rests on their image of being technically proficient and highly professional, indispensable to the efficient functioning of British industry. A fully-fledged system of workers' participation threatens that image. Perhaps, without damage to the important role they play, managers need to learn to be more vulnerable.

10

The Balance of Power

One way of looking at the history of management/union relations is as a battle for power between two groups with apparently conflicting interests. Trade unionism is the collective activity of wage earners in protecting and improving the conditions of their working lives. The laws of demand and supply condition the employee's attitude. He is forced on to the labour market because he can only subsist by selling his labour. Because he owns nothing but his labour, he is inevitably concerned about the instability of his position. Occupational class, in many respects, is irrelevant. All employees are obviously not in the same market situation; some are better off than others in such matters as monthly salary (as opposed to weekly wage), three months' notice (as opposed to one week's), greater job security and better working conditions. But the University teacher, for example, is as concerned about the threat to his security and standard of living as the hospital worker. He still has to sell his labour in order to subsist, although he may be operating from a more favoured market position.

One interesting phenomenon, which reinforces the point, has been the rapid growth in white-collar workers and the increased militancy of staff. Many companies had discouraged them from joining unions, persuading them that they could do better as a result of individual contracts.

The following table shows the spectacular increase in the membership of some non-manual unions between the period 1950 and 1964.[1]

Since 1964 growth has been on an astronomical scale. In 1974 the membership of N.A.L.G.O. was over half a million, whilst A.S.T.M.S. had reached 280,000 and N.U.B.E. 100,000. White-collar workers have traditionally been concerned about the differentials amongst themselves, i.e. people of like occupations and with comparable qualifications. A University teacher will be concerned with rates paid in the Civil Service. Polytechnic teachers, who feel that their best interests are unlikely to be served by membership of the N.A.T.F.H.E., have been exploring association with university teachers or the idea of founding a breakaway union. There is nothing new in this process, namely that the prime determinants of the actions of all employees are those actions involved in having to sell their labour in order to survive.

Name of Union	Total membership at end of 1950	Total membership at end of 1964	Percentage increase
National and Local Government Officers Association	197,056	338,322	71·7
Draughtsmen's and Allied Technicians Association	45,039	65,893	46·3
Clerical and Administrative Workers Union	33,150	79,177	138·9
National Union of Bank Employees	29,622	56,224	89·8
Association of Supervisory Staffs, Executives and Technicians	11,723	35,588	203·6

What is a more recent phenomenon is that white-collar workers not only compare their relative position with those of their own kind, but with the narrowing of the differentials between them and the blue-collar or manual workers. Most of their privileges, such as pensions, superior holiday entitlement and sickness benefit, and no clocking, have been steadily eroded. The blurring of the arbitrary distinction between staff and shop floor is likely to increase so, in the end, money will be an important determining factor (although some people forced to work in dangerous or deplorable working conditions, such as the miners, may be specially compensated).

It is interesting to observe that teachers who feel their standard of living, comparatively speaking, has been reduced, have resorted to the more militant tactics of the non-manual workers. Their attitude towards membership of the T.U.C. has changed. At one time it would have been considered unprofessional to belong to the T.U.C. Unions such as the National Association of Schoolmasters and the National Union of Teachers feel no such compunction nowadays. Although the British Medical Association, many of whose members became employees of the government as a consequence of the National Health Service, have behaved in a typically trade union manner when their conditions of work were threatened, they have not as yet succumbed to T.U.C. membership. The methods of collective action adopted by white-collar workers in protecting their interests may differ, but the intention is the same.

One is witnessing an inexorable spread of trade unionism and at the same time finding it increasingly difficult to distinguish manual from non-manual workers in their response to the problems which arise from selling their labour power in a free market.

Employers, on the other hand, own the means of production. It is their responsibility to manage the enterprise. Labour, however, is only one of the many costs they incur in the total process of manufacturing or providing a service. There are such matters as the price of raw materials, equipment and machinery, depreciation costs, the need to re-invest, to mention but a few. It matters little whether the enterprise is a state monopoly or a private one. Nationalized industries also have to compete in world markets and sell their final product at a price people are prepared to pay. If private employers wish to keep the price of labour down because it is a determinant of profit, public employers have an equal interest in keeping wages pegged at a tolerable rate in order to remain efficient. Because employees have to sell their labour in order to survive, the price of their labour is an essential subsistence matter, to be preserved at all costs, and even increased to meet people's expectations of a rising standard of living. Because of these conflicting pressures, there can never be a permanent agreement over the price of that labour.

It will vary according to a number of factors. When employees compete for jobs during periods of unemployment, wages can be depressed. When there is a shortage of skilled labour, it is employers who are competing and wages correspondingly rise.

Since the Second World War, until the recession in world trade and the Labour Government's anti-inflation measures in 1975 and 1976 the level of unemployment, on the whole, has been relatively low. Moreover the Welfare State legislation of the Labour Government of 1945 meant that social security provision was such as to remove the harsh social features of the 'thirties. Also during the 'seventies a new term crept into management terminology – 'social responsibility'. This was a term intended to cover not merely the need to conserve scarce resources or avoid the pollution of the environment, but an increased awareness of the total system in which an enterprise operates. Social responsibility raised the question whether managers' ultimate loyalties to shareholders (who 'owned' the business) were paramount or whether they were co-equal with a number of other responsibilities, to customers, to suppliers, and, perhaps even more, to employees. Were employees a commodity, like machines or raw materials, or did they too have an 'ownership' in the enterprise?

In an address to the C.I.O.S. World Management Congress in 1972 Sir Frederick Catherwood said:

> Competition is now inadequate as a philosophic basis for the market economy. It is also totally inadequate in legitimising management's authority. This is the other crisis faced by managements. Just as they need all the authority they can muster, the right of management to manage has been called in question. On what basis have managers the right to manage? The basis is that they can compete in the open market. It is on the necessity to live in a competitive world that the manager ultimately justifies his decision to dismiss a third of the workforce, to limit increases in wages and to change the method of work. But the social impact of the decisions cannot be swept aside any longer with the simple declaration 'management must manage'. The decisions made in the boardroom are now a matter of social concern and people outside the boardroom want to debate them. . . . So perhaps the most vital part of any management code would be the obligation to make the best use of resources under your control. The great professions after all, were not driven on by hope of gain. They were driven on by their professional code.

Many workers articulated their 'right to work', even when management had abandoned their enterprises as unprofitable. One thinks of such demonstrations as those accompanying the closure at the Upper Clyde Shipbuilders; the attempts of the Triumph workers at Meriden to take over the running of the factory; or the ex-workers of the *Scottish Daily Express* to run their own paper. Even on occasions less dramatic, the Government has intervened with public money (with Rolls Royce, for example, or by subsidizing of Concorde, or more spectacularly with British Leyland and Chrysler) in order to maintain employment.

It is pertinent therefore to ask 'Where does the balance of power lie?' Historically, it has always rested with employers. They raised the money to build the factories, they hired the labour to run them and paid the wages. When they were no longer profitable, they closed them and dispensed with the workforce. Ownership today is far more complex. It is no longer the archetypal 'small capitalists' who run British industry. The capital stock of many firms is made up of investments by Insurance Companies, or by other companies and even trade unions investing their funds in order to provide for the pension rights of their workers. Closing down a newspaper shop or a factory employing thirty people, where the outlay on equipment may be relatively small, may in certain conditions make obvious economic sense. But closing down a company representing millions of pounds worth of capital assets is not such a simple decision to reach.

Industry has been so concerned with the economies of size, building vast multi-million pound single stream ammonia or ethylene plants, or has so integrated its processes, as in the motor car industry, that it only requires a handful of workers to throw the whole system into disarray. What is an extra three pence an hour – such a modest claim – compared with the costs that would be incurred by loss of production? If profitability has been finely calculated, where a new plant being commissioned on time is critical, demands by contractors for abnormal conditions payments can prove irresistible. Or if, once a plant is commissioned, down-time is critical, it only requires a determined maintenance crew to demand a tough price for their labour during planned shut-downs, for management to capitulate. 'It is going to be expensive to pay them and will set up inequalities elsewhere and subject us to increased pressures but it will, in all likelihood, be cheaper to pay than to hold out', tends to be management's thinking. As one manager put it, in describing management/ union negotiations in the chemical industry, 'management's posture in face of union pressure is one of strategic withdrawal'.

Ask many managers for their opinion and they would endorse the above remark. They would complain that it is not only by withdrawing their labour – in conditions of relatively full employment – or setting conditions under which they will or will not do this or that job, that the unions demonstrate their stronghold on management decision-making. They would tell you it is the unions who determine how many instrument artificers should be in the A.U.E.W. or E.E.T.P.U. – which would affect how they worked – or which loaders should carry the bags which earned the high bonus payments. In their more pessimistic moments, they would proclaim that 'managerial prerogative' was as empty and ornamental as the 'royal prerogative'. 'The chief shop steward decides what happens round here', is a comment one hears. There are a few cases, usually where the person concerned has important power needs to be met, where a senior shop steward does wield unusual influence as a disruptive force. But ask any man on the shop floor or the average shop steward, 'Who calls the shots round here? Who has most influence on your work, your pay, your future?' and he invariably points towards the manager's office.

THE EDUCATIONAL GAP

The difference is perceived at a number of levels. The average man on the shop floor feels disadvantaged in a number of ways. The manager is usually drawn from a different social class and has had a superior education. It is idle to pretend that the class and educational gulf to which Britain is victim does not penetrate the ranks of industry. This is a point we develop in our concluding chapter.

If in some firms – and it is not true of all – innate distinctions are reinforced by special privileges, such as superior dining-room facilities, special accommodation in executive suites, reserved places in the company car park, and keys to some exclusive toilet, then the feeling of social distance between managers and managed grows stronger. If managers may come in at different times and retire at a pension two-thirds of final pay, whilst shop floor clock in, and, no matter how long their service, pocket not a penny of company money, the gap between the 'haves' and 'have nots' appears even wider.

Despite the introduction of comprehensive schools into our educational system; despite the increasing numbers enjoying higher education at different levels; and despite the increased spending on such things as foreign holidays, out-of-town restaurants, colour television and cars amongst manual workers, compared with those in occupations which were regarded as middle-class preserves – despite all these changes, the class structure is still much more evident in the U.K. than it is on the continent, particularly in such countries as Holland and Scandinavia. There, the distinctions are becoming increasingly blurred, so that it is no longer meaningful to refer to the 'working classes'. They would not be recognizable as a coherent social grouping. Divisions within the work situation are not reinforced in the same way by divisions outside the gates as they are in the United Kingdom.

A survey by Dorothy Wedderburn of Imperial College in 1970 into terms and conditions in over 400 manufacturing firms, both large and small, revealed quite surprising disparities. She found that in every respect – holidays, working hours, sick pay, pensions, time off with pay for personal reasons, discipline generally – manual workers were far worse off than their non-manual counterparts. Nearly half the firms had no scheme at all for paying their manual workers when they were off sick. (Figures revealed by the Department of Health and Social Security in 1974 showed that only 49 per cent of the roughly 24 million working population were covered by private pension schemes to supplement the benefit paid by the State.) The Wedderburn survey showed that 33 per cent of firms gave no pension coverage to their operatives, compared to 4 per cent for managers. Nearly half the manual workers' schemes had a pension calculated as a fixed sum per year of membership, whereas three-quarters of the non-manual workers enjoyed pensions based on final salary or on salary in the last years of service.

Pensions, with rare exceptions, are administered by trustees generally appointed by management. Rather late in the day the T.U.C. has argued for increased rights for workers in relation to the management of pension funds. On the whole, though, the unions have not used their alleged monopoly power to campaign for equal pay, pensions, industrial safety or redundancy through the traditional means of collective bargaining. Rather it has been Government intervention, both Labour and Conservative, through legislation that has obliged employers to introduce parity in these matters.

In the Wedderburn sample, 98 per cent of the firms made their manual workers clock in, as compared with 52 per cent of white collar workers and 6 per cent of senior managers, (with automatic pay deductions for lateness). Since 1970 many firms have abolished clocking.

Another distinction, rarely discussed but inherent in many of the problems arising in industrial relations, is in expectations about work. For managers it is a career and there is a totally respectable science known as 'management development' to ensure that progress is orderly. Even at the crude level of pay the Wedderburn Survey showed that in nearly 90 per cent of the firms not only were there greater chances of promotion for white-collar workers and managers but they had the possibility of a yearly pay rise compared with 20 per cent of manual workers. For workers, at the most, there is something known as 'retraining'.

The concept of career simply doesn't apply in the context of industrial manual work. The assumption is that work is unpleasant or boring or both. For managers, time is a scarce resource, for workers an empty residue. For them, work means a lifetime of waiting at machines where attendance is necessary but full attention is not. The only benefit of machine-age technology is that it is possible to day-dream a working life away, what one could describe as a 'non-career' situation with little personal control over time or physical movement.

Such differences cannot help but influence the whole climate in which discussion concerning a disputed work differential payment takes place. Although these forces colour the dialogue, they are rarely if ever matters for discussion themselves. It is therefore a fair question to ask where the real conflict does lie. Is it in the disputed differential or in a system which does not itself seem fair? Social mobility and educational opportunity have if anything brought the issue into the home. What is the average manual worker to think when he sees his secretary daughter from the outset of her working life enjoy a higher status than he has, let alone the benefits bestowed on his banking clerk son (including mortgages at 2 per cent interest and pensions of two-thirds of final salary)?

Another important area to which relatively little attention has been paid is language, a function partly of our educational system. It is not so much a matter of accent, although that plays some part. It is more a matter of vocabulary. It is common to hear the word 'mili-tant' used to describe the behaviour of shop stewards. One rarely hears of militant managers. It is a mistake to assume that the differ-ence is one of breeding or self-control. One of the answers is to be found in the gap in the speech patterns between salaried and wage-earning staff. With some exceptions, the former have a fuller vocabu-lary to draw upon and are correspondingly more articulate and so more self-assured. The latter suffer frequently from an impoverished vocabulary. Their speech contains many more clichés. Noise (or militancy) becomes a weapon to oppose verbal fluency. Television interviews between shop floor representatives and managers (or, as in the case of Ulster, army officers and citizens from the Falls Road or the Shankill) merely serve to highlight the gap. It is a well-known psychological phenomenon that people with strong emotions, but a limited capacity to articulate them, find an outlet in behaviour that is more aggressive and violent. 'Cash on the table' not only reflects an over-simplified solution to a problem but at times perhaps the boun-daries of vocabulary.

One wonders to what extent managers fully understand the situation. Full-time trade union officials frequently despair at the reluctance with which shop stewards commit matters to letter but prefer the telephone or backs of cigarette packages. The written inadequacy is even worse than the spoken. One of the authors, who has been closely involved with shop steward and supervisory training, has detected again and again the mistaken sense of shame that many men in positions of authority feel at their inability to spell and punctuate.

Managers frequently refer to communication as being at the root of their problems. Its dimensions are not fully appreciated. It is not just a matter of setting up adequate machinery but, without talking down to workers, communicating to them in a manner which they understand and in such a way that they can take effective action. The foremen are verbally on a closer wavelength to the men than are the managers who often sweep them aside, feeling they can do the job more clearly and comprehensively. But what they make up in comprehensiveness, they lose in authenticity. Lack of recognition of a language barrier makes management's professed objectivity sound like callousness by the time it reaches the shop floor.

Again, who is entitled to give orders? 'Would you please ask Mr so-and-so, the chief shop steward, to come up to my room, now, Miss Jones?' breathes the manager over the intercom. The shop steward cannot with the same ease pick up the phone and summon a manager. Or the manager has been asked to discipline a worker for absence or bad time-keeping. The worker shuffles uneasily into the carpeted office, cap in hand, wearing dungarees, nails soiled from work. 'Have you the file on Mr Smith, Miss Jones?' Miss Jones extracts from a capacious filing cabinet Mr Smith's record of absences over the last five years. To Mr Smith the contest is unequal. Power is perceived as lying with the carefully collected information, the superior literary and oral skills of the manager, his power of dismissal. Far from being a power bloc, the union appears as a last ditch defence. Thank God that the shop steward is there, banging the table on his behalf, urging sympathetic consideration of his case or threatening to bring out the men. The company's profit and loss account is not high on his agenda. He would neither know nor care very much, if the manager was being warned by his superiors that his costs must be reduced. So, one finds the paradox at an individual level of both parties feeling that real power rests with the other side.

DIFFERENCES OF POWER AT NATIONAL LEVEL

One could argue that the picture is very much clearer at national level, that it is obvious there whose foot is on the jugular vein. The London commuter, the housewife without electricity, the city coal merchant, will tell you that it is the unions who decide the size of the national deficit in the balance of payments. Some utterances by the more politically motivated union leaders who use their position to get a whole range of controversial political as well as industrial matters discussed at union conferences, lend colour to this view. Certainly the unions represent an important power bloc, and the more astute union leaders know how to exploit that position, but a closer analysis would suggest that the picture is oversimplified.

Although unions arose in opposition to some of the effects of capitalism, it is not possible for them to operate within the system as permanent bodies without taking on some of the characteristics of the system itself. 'Workers of the world unite' makes a good slogan. The fact is that the trade union movement is as competitive as the capitalist system, unions competing with each other over wages, policies, members and even jobs. Motions at the Trades Union Congress frequently call for greater unity and rationalization of the movement. Such appeals fall on deaf ears. Union mergers that do take place are determined less as a result of fraternal affection than cold pragmatism, such as the decreasing ability of the smaller unions to provide a comprehensive service to their members. So the movement as a whole, far from being monolithic, is fragmented. Union leaders accept that amalgamations are desirable for furthering unity – the prime union ethic – but they consistently reject moves to alter the shape of the trade union movement to give it a more rational basis.

Unions also operate within the political, democratic and legal framework of the country. They do not stand outside these influences and values. As we have argued earlier, private property has enjoyed a special protection under English law, more so than the person. 'An Englishman's home is his castle' enshrines many attitudes. Sir Anthony Eden, when Prime Minister, looked forward to a property-owning democracy. The owners of the means of production could be said to be a property-owning class. It has even, if only at a sub-conscious level, been the values of this ruling group which tend to prevail in society and certainly the ones the national press reflect. So when their interests are being attacked, public opinion is mobilized. Press accounts of industrial disputes invariably refer to the militancy of the unions, rarely to the incompetence of managers.

Strikes most seriously threaten employer interests, as we saw in Chapter 3, and as V. L. Allen argues in his book *Militant Trade Unionism*[2]:

> Strikes take place within a hostile environment even though they are a common everyday phenomenon. They are conventionally described as industrially subversive, irresponsible, unfair, against the interests of the community, contrary to the workers' own best interests, wasteful of resources, unduly aggressive, inconsistent with democracy and, in any event, unnecessary. The morality which assesses strikes in these terms acts on employees so that they approach strike action with serious inhibitions. Union officials are particularly prone to the anti-strike environmental influences because they are frequently made out to be responsible for the behaviour of their members. Once they are committed to a strike case, union officials tend to become defensive, apologetic and concerned about taking avoiding action. When they are actually engaged in a strike they are frequently motivated by a desire to end it quickly, irrespective of the merits of the issue.

V. L. Allen provides an interesting illustration in his analysis of a strike threatened by the National Union of Railwaymen in 1966 after the Prices and Incomes Board had reported that the N.U.R. were not entitled to a wage increase.[3] The General Secretary of the Union cautioned his executive very seriously about deciding on a strike, as negotiations were not totally closed. But the matter was taken out of the hands of the British Railways Board when the union executive met the Minister for Economic Affairs, the Minister of Labour and the Minister of Transport, who explained the difficulties of negotiating under duress and urged the union to call off the strike. The union executive refused. The Chairman of the British Railways Board had meanwhile sent a letter to the executive, describing the strike as an 'act of self-destruction', appealing to the union to call off the strike so that they could 'help me to help you'. The press weighed in for good measure. The *Guardian* reported that 'the union will forfeit all public sympathy if it now condemns Mr Raymond (the Board's Chairman) without a hearing', while *The Times* thought the

Executive would most probably accept the advice 'to give a public impression of reasonableness'.

By this time the affair was taking on some of the drama of a cliffhanger. The Executive were summoned once more to the presence of the Minister of Economic Affairs, whose exhortations were persuasive enough to the extent that the Executive divided by eleven votes to eleven over continuing the strike. The Railways Board produced their 'final' offer, which the unions rejected.

Negotiations, over the last week before the strike, worked themselves to a climax in further meetings with the Ministers of Labour, Transport and Economic Affairs who underlined the grave danger of a strike 'to the union, to the Government, and to the country', and threatened to withdraw all concessions. As on previous occasions, and as was to happen subsequently, the grand finale was beer and sandwiches at 10 Downing Street for the Executive, in the presence of the Prime Minister. In the early hours of the morning, whether fuddled by beer, fatigued by the protracted negotiations, beguiled by the Prime Minister or ashamed of their suggested lack of patriotism, the Executive called off the strike by thirteen votes to ten, without any firm material concessions being made to the railwaymen.

Perhaps their case initially was not a good one, perhaps the timing was bad, perhaps they should have chosen a work to rule. The point is that when unions call national official strikes, it is not easy for them to 'go it alone'. All kinds of other pressures are brought to bear and extraneous to the issue in dispute – appeals to reason, to patriotism, to think of others – deflating the resolve of all but the most ardent. This possibly explains why the majority of strikes which take place are unofficial ones, where people simply walk off the job for a shift before the pressures of socialization which accompany official strikes can take effect.

The threatened N.U.R. strike was in 1966. It can equally be argued that to settle negotiations for a single industry over the table at 10 Downing Street, whether the outcome is a favourable or unfavourable one for the unions, represents a real shift in the balance of power. The unions could be said to have arrived, not merely the unions in the nationalized industries. The National Union of Seamen, whose employers are drawn from the private sector, were also treated to beer and sandwiches at No. 10. The top treatment on strike issues, on the whole, has been with those unions involved in nationalized industries, though meetings of a more general kind have taken place in No. 10 between members of the C.B.I. and T.U.C. Since 1966 some of these unions, conspicuously the National Union of Mineworkers in 1972 and 1974, have bargained from a position of considerable power; in 1974 they successfully exploited the situation created by the action of the Middle East rulers in quadrupling the price of oil and depriving countries of it who were favouring the Israeli cause.

THE NATIONAL INTEREST

If a union's prime interest is to protect and improve the living standards of its members, then even appeals to the national interest are likely to take second place. Ted Hill, the former leader of the Boilermakers' Society, was frank enough to acknowledge this and once declared publicly that his function was to protect the narrow, sectional interests of his members. He was upbraided as irresponsible, unpatriotic, partisan and a threat to the nation's survival.[4] It is the Government, of course, which determines the national interest. The Government's role has changed from being concerned only with defence, or ensuring that minimum standards of health and safety are maintained, to being custodians of anything and everything which affects the national interest. Employers have largely been successful in identifying their own sectional interests with national ones. Trade unions have experienced much greater difficulty in demonstrating that their interests have positive national implications. Convention, however, demands that trade union leaders should be statesmanlike, and so in the main they are, modifying their own aims and methods to support what is put forward as the national interest. The T.U.C. accepted from a Labour Government a Prices and Incomes Board in 1965 despite considerable opposition from within the trade union movement, because of the balance of payments crisis which the nation was facing. They rejected the Conservative Government's Industrial Relations Bill in 1971, but the appeal to the General Council of the T.U.C. had not been couched in terms of its contribution directly to the national interest. On the other hand, the Labour Government's £6 limit, as part of its anti-inflation policy in 1975, was supported by the unions – even the Mineworkers – as their contribution to upholding the 'social contract'.

The argument begs the question of what is in the national interest. Is it anything the Government considers to be important at a particular time, such as the Channel Tunnel or a third London Airport at Maplin Sands or spending extravagant amounts of money on supersonic airliners? Is achieving a successful balance of payments position desired primarily because of the government's wish to maintain a satisfactory level of employment and high wages or is it because it wishes to maintain the country's role as an international banker? Perhaps one flows from the other. It would be nice to see it explicitly stated.

The history of government intervention has not always been a happy one for the unions. All governments tend to consider that their own survival is in the national interest and so identify their own political interests with those of the nation.

As V. L. Allen observes:[5]

> Throughout trade union history much political attention has been given to strikes because these have unequivocally disturbed the interests of both employers and governments. When it was presumed that strikes had an insurrectional quality the governments intervened by using troops and police in their coercive roles. Troops were sometimes used as strike-breakers but most frequently they were used to act as the protectors of strike-breakers or to move essential foodstuffs in a strictly controlled manner. Inevitably on such occasions the interests of employers were protected but the government invariably acted as though it were performing some public function, referring to the need to preserve public order, individual rights or essential supplies. ... At the slightest sign that their industrial behaviour is being seriously provocative most union leaders recoil, for they have no desire even to appear to be challenging the constitutional position of the government.

The behaviour and declared utterances of the Yorkshire miner's leader, Arthur Scargill, during 1974 and 1975 are a conspicuous exception to the general rule.

Union action is thus tempered and limited by the values of the system society upholds. Strong amongst British values is a reverence for Parliamentary democracy. V. L. Allen recalls the Parliamentary Debate before the General Strike in May 1926 when Mr J. H. Thomas, M.P., the leader of the National Union of Railwaymen, said: 'I know the Government's position. I have never disguised that in a challenge to the Constitution, God help us unless the

Government won' (Hansard, Vol. 195, May 3, 1926). A similar indication of where the trade union movement stood occurred during the strike of the London busmen in 1958, when the executive of the Transport and General Workers Union appealed to the General Council of the T.U.C. to support an extension of the strike. The General Council replied that 'an extension of the strike, which would bring the unions concerned into direct conflict with the Government, would end in a failure which would be disastrous for the whole Trade Union Movement'.[6] As doughty a defender of the rights of the workers as Michael Foot, when Secretary of State for Employment, found himself obliged to put national interest first – namely defence of the Government's £6 limit in 1975 – in resisting the claims of the junior hospital doctors.

The history of industrial relations shows that the power of the national interest has asserted itself more strongly when supplies of essential services have been disrupted, when unions have been strong and well-organized and able to exploit their market advantage to get higher wages. These have been times when the union actions have had economic consequences as a result of their effect on costs and prices. In the past there has been noticeably less government intervention during periods of unemployment, though the picture has changed since the war with massive injections of public money to regions of high unemployment such as the North East or Northern Ireland.

What is undoubtedly true is that, as society becomes more complex, the principle of voluntarism, two power blocs arguing it out in polar fashion, with the Government adopting a policy of non-interference, ceases to apply. If one has to think in terms of power blocs, it is necessary to consider three parties: the Government, the employers and the unions.

There is a limit to the effect of Government intervention, however. Incomes policy can only monitor national agreements. This is of limited effect since if you cannot control take-home pay you have failed to control the most significant element.

ECONOMIC OR SOCIOLOGICAL INTERPRETATION

Any analysis of industrial relations as a balance of power inevitably draws one into the political arena. Is strike action a behavioural phenomenon, as some social scientists argue, a protest against a particular system of authority? Or is it endemic to capitalism, a protest against the economic power of the employers with their needs for profit; something which persists despite significant improvements in living standards for employees, and something which is spreading across all manner of social barriers, and not an aberration of a temporary nature, which a little social engineering will eventually bring under control? Those who see the issue as a straightforward economic power struggle find their solution in transferring the means of production and distribution out of the hands of capitalists into public ownership. The social scientists' analysis rests on the assumption that all participants in industry have a common purpose – that they are collaborators in the production process. Implicitly assumed is an organic unity. They ignore the possibility of permanent disunity accepted by the Marxists, but study management activities from the point of view of a system, in necessary equilibrium. They therefore look for an improvement in industrial relations, not in structural terms but through better personnel management, a greater share in the decision-making process, more abundant welfare provision, removing demarcations between staff and shop floor, more efficient communication, and job enrichment exercises.

If the company opens its accounts fully to its workers, it is assumed that workers will be more tolerant, less aggressive, more willing to co-operate with management. The Marxists would argue that this might be only the beginning of trouble, for employees would then discover for the first time in intelligible language the precise wages, salaries and profit structure of the firm.

The Marxist interpretation, however, takes little account of what happens in those many cases where the profit motive is absent. Local government workers, teachers, hospital employees and civil servants are all in one way or another employees of state enterprises. Even in organizations which are fully state controlled and where the profit motive is not dominant, there will always be a conflict of interest between management and managed over what can be paid out as wages. The subsistence needs of employees will always act as a permanent pressure to increase the selling price of labour and the costs needs of employers act as a permanent pressure to keep wages within acceptable limits. Even in 'socialist' countries like Poland and East Germany, strikes and demonstrations have taken place over wage levels.

Government influence, through subsidy or nationalization or

majority shareholding in private companies, is increasing rather than diminishing. One inclines therefore more to the social science interpretation, that there is a necessary interdependence between managers and managed, which transcends matters such as profit orientation; that there is obviously an inherent conflict in such a situation, but what is critical is the manner in which it is handled. In a few cases there may be gross inequity which only structural alteration will cure. Perhaps Jim Conway, formerly Secretary of the A.U.E.W., expressed it best, when he drafted the crucial words under which the Industrial Society campaigns in industrial relations: 'the willing acceptance by managers and trade unionists of the essential role of the other'. Clearly the roles are different. The trade unions cannot become the management of industry nor can management do the union job.

POWER ON THE LOCAL LEVEL

Further curbs on union power are the sometimes protracted and clumsy democratic procedures, which union rule books force members to follow before decisions can be arrived at. A large centrally organized union will have a hierarchy of procedures through which some decisions will have to be processed. Rules are extraordinarily difficult to change. As a consequence they are often slavishly followed, even when totally inappropriate. Part of the movement of power away from the centre to the shop floor has been induced by the inability of the unions to respond quickly or effectively enough.

It is at the shop floor interface that manager and worker meet and, as the power has moved there, for better or for worse, it is there that industrial relations will deteriorate or improve. Experience and research confirm that where leadership and understanding of workers' needs are strongly in evidence, industrial unrest is low.

An interesting analysis of the quality of leadership and its correlation with productivity, sickness, accidents and even voting patterns in strike ballots is to be found in Professor R. W. Revans' illuminating and meticulously documented study of the fourteen collieries of the midland coalfield which comprised the Barnsley seam.[7] This seam is as homogeneous in depth and thickness as any in the coal industry. The pits had been sunk at the same time, employed comparable labour forces of about 2,000 miners, working under similar conditions both underground and on the surface.

After nationalization, six of the pits were administered by the Yorkshire Division, the remaining eight by the East Midlands Division. The East Midlands Division came under the dynamic and sympathetic leadership of Sir Hubert Houldsworth who entertained a simple belief that, in the ultimate, it was only coal miners who could get coal up the shaft, and that management were more dependent on miners than miners on management. As Professor Revans puts it:

> It was this simplicity of vision that took him into every colliery manager's office and into every miner's lodge in his division, always ready to discover what, if anything, he might do to help those in the coal industry to identify and solve their problems on their own. . . . He kept all central bureaucracy to a minimum and continually experimented with forms of delegation and involvement unknown in other fields.

The comparisons between the six pits of the Yorkshire Division and the eight of the East Midlands Division, over a period of ten years, showed that, by most of the indices of industrial relations, the East Midlands was consistently superior. The range is a wide one including the annual average rate of compensable accidents (and accidents occur more frequently where workers perceive work situations to be intolerable); tonnages of coal lost per miner in dispute; wage cost per ton; the strike ballots for peace in 1972 and 1974, where the East Midlands division cast relatively more votes for peace than did their fellow trade unionists.

Professor Revans' thesis is that these conditions emanated from the different styles of leadership adopted by the two Divisional Chairmen. In contrast to Sir Hubert Houldsworth was Sir Noel Holmes, an ex-major general. As Professor Revans puts it:

> Sir Noel Holmes was a courteous and courageous gentleman unlikely to lose his head in any emergency, but he embarked on his new duties borne down by a preposterous and crippling infirmity. The commanding presence, the personal gallantry, so exactly calculated to strike terror into the hearts of the King's enemies, could never but have aroused among those mettlesome Yorkshiremen at best an allergic indifference and at worst a contemptuous hostility. His power was lost before the man himself was known, gone with the echoes of his military rank when first they rolled

across the grey and wasted valleys of the Pennines. But it was the soldierly appointment of a traditional general staff, issuing detailed and continuous instructions to his field commanders, that brought the inevitable calamity: in pursuit of their masterful and imperative policies this battery of expert advisers gratuitously aroused the professional defiance of their own colliery managers. Whereas tradition had drawn the indelible line of battle between the miners and their local managers, it was the immemorial triumph of that first Yorkshire administration to drive its own officers to fight beside their men and against the centralizing forces. Nationalization in Yorkshire was powerless to reduce accidents, to avert disputes and powerless to win more coal for the same wages because it had lost the allegiance of its colliery managers at the outset.

The message is that managers and managed will always be tempted to exploit their market advantage in given situations. Whether the dialogue between them is pursued with acrimony and bitterness in an atmosphere of suspicion and mistrust, based on resentment of privileged positions, will depend on the nature of the day-to-day encounters between managers and managed on which, unlike the national economy, it is possible to exercise a great deal of influence.

The view is echoed by Mark Young, for ten years one of the National Officers of the E.E.T.P.U., a former member of the Communist Party and an outstanding union thinker on industrial relations:

The formal relations must not be mistaken for the informal, nor should we be under any illusions which is the most important. Seaside conferences are remote from the workshop or boardrooms of Britain. We can possibly afford a phoney, polemical, doctrinaire war at the top so long as the bottom proceeds along a modest, sober and constructive course and establishes a civilized system of industrial relations where it is possible to identify and agree a joint interest and disagree rationally where our interests clash. . . . They (the government, unions or employers' associations) have an important role and influence but in my view it's a secondary role. Whilst no one can completely insulate themselves from the climate these associations create and promote, the real quality of relations are those you create yourself in the industry you are responsible for.

Good industrial relations at plant level will reduce the number of domestic disputes. They can have little effect on non-domestic disputes, where different forces are at work. The shift of union leadership to the left in the '70s brought the unions into more open confrontation with the Government. Even Government influence is of little avail if a union is powerful enough, either in numbers or because its members occupy a critical role in the economy of the country, and is determined to assert its will. The classic example in recent times was the unmitigated opposition of the A.U.E.W. to the Conservative Government's Industrial Relations Act, and particularly its refusal to recognize the Industrial Relations Court. The union suffered a number of fines for contempt of court, in pursuit of its uncompromising and largely political campaign – political rather than industrial, in that its actions were directed against the Government rather than the employers of its members, although it was the employers and public who were made to suffer as a consequence.

But the union action demonstrated that there has been a shift of power at the national level, particularly where powerful unions are led by left-wing militants who are prepared to use their position 'to change society'. (With attendance at branch meetings at little more than 5 per cent, democracy within unions is a tender plant, and voting for union leaders a microscopic proportion of total union membership).

Hugh Scanlon, the leader of the A.U.E.W., took a less reverent view of Parliamentary institutions than J. H. Thomas, and was prepared to urge his union to enforce a stoppage of components for aircraft for the Chilean Air Force and to 'black' war materials as a protest against the military junta which overthrew President Allende. This political dimension of union behaviour has nothing to do with, and is disruptive of, the day-to-day relations shop stewards and managers are trying to build up in the workplace.

11

The Need for Change

Our argument throughout the book has been that the causes of conflict are multifarious, some rooted deep in our history and culture. It is unlikely therefore that any one 'solution' will bring a new dawn. Continental models with totally different histories are also unlikely to be applicable without adaptation.

It is a mistake, in fact, to think in terms of solutions or panaceas. Conflict is inherent in the structure of industrial relations. The best we can do is to be more fully aware of the various factors which contribute to its dynamic, and to strive for improvements. Some of these improvements must be at a governmental or societal level and are only marginally within our influence; others are more immediately to hand in the day-to-day encounters between managers and managed.

Even improvements can only take place if there is a reasonable consensus as to the nature of our plight, if indeed we are looking at the same set of facts and not living in a world that used to be or seeing it as we would like it to be – and these are real dangers for a nation that as an island is cut off from the mainstream of activities on the continent, and that recently enjoyed the prestige and power of an empire.

LOW PRODUCTIVITY

Our chapter on productivity bargaining included a table showing the economic performance of the U.K. compared with our major competitors. Since then, the figures have got worse rather than improved, almost regardless of indicator or industry chosen.

For example, figures published in the December 1975 issue of *Management Today* showed that 'In 1973 British Leyland produced 5·9 vehicles per man, against 8·3 for Ford U.K., 10·1 for Ford

Germany, 11·6 for Volkswagen and 14·6 (two-and-a-half times as many) for Renault. Man-hours lost by disputes, both internal and external, more than doubled between British Leyland's 1969–70 financial year and 1973–74.' This comparison is reinforced by labour productivity figures produced in 1975 by the Society of Motor Manufacturers and Traders, which show the U.K. motor manufacturers well to the bottom of an international 'league table' based on value added per man. Nor is the picture vastly different in the steel industry where, in terms of output per employee, British Steel lags far behind its major competitors in the U.S., Germany, and Japan.

One has only to refer to the Year Book of Labour Statistics (published by the International Labour Office in Geneva) for the last ten years to find that figures like those detailed above for car manufacture are not untypical.

Comparisons with Germany, Holland, Belgium, Norway, Switzerland and Sweden (even allowing in some cases for differences in population size) show that in the number of disputes, workers involved and (particularly) working days lost, our record is getting worse, not better. From 1,755,000 working days lost in 1963, within ten years we had reached a staggering 23,909,000 working days lost. For the same period, whilst in the U.K. only once did the total number of disputes drop below 2,000, Switzerland only once reached double figures (eleven in 1971); in four consecutive years they recorded only one dispute a year and in two years two disputes. The figures for Norway, Sweden and Germany were equally modest. Small wonder our industrial relations record is referred to on the continent as the 'English sickness'.

Disputes and working days lost would matter less if our productivity compensated for large strikes, as it does in the United States, but the I.L.O. statistics reveal it is not so. For the ten-year period 1963–73 we have been consistently bottom or next to bottom of the productivity league. Moreover, the problem has been compounded by the U.K.'s consistently high rate of inflation.

Unless these harsh realities are faced and accepted, intelligent discussion between management and unions and the government cannot begin. Part of the difficulty in analysing this dismal performance by a nation that once prided itself on being 'the workshop of the world' is lack of agreement on the causes. Reasons commonly given include lack of investment, bad management, militant shop stewards, lack of component manufacturing capacity, poor industrial relations, inadequate communications.

LACK OF INVESTMENT

Figures published by the O.E.C.D. certainly show a poor record of investment compared with our competitors. But this is not the whole story. There are examples of vast amounts of public money having been pumped into enterprises. Harland & Wolff has one of the most modernized shipyards in the world, but has been unable to show a profit. British Steel's return on its massive investment of £27 million in a new blast furnace at Llanwerm in South Wales was still nil over twelve months after completion of its construction as a result of union opposition.

Some of the investment in British industry has been curiously placed, reflecting, as we hope to indicate later, a bias in our educational system.

Sir Alan Cottrell, former scientific adviser to the government, at the 1975 meeting of the British Association, remarked that Britain spends more on research and development than it can currently exploit. Britain has consistently spent around 2·3 per cent of its gross national product on research and development, more than France, West Germany and Holland or even Japan. What it has failed to do is to invest in applying the results.

Half of Britain's investment in research goes into fields that account for only 5 per cent of industrial output, such as electronics and aircraft. In contrast, Japan spends less than Britain on research into aircraft and electronics but more in electrical and mechanical engineering, motor manufacture, chemicals, and, conspicuously, motor vehicles. In aircraft, our research and development has amounted to as much as one third of turnover, compared with mechanical engineering (only 2 per cent), yet aircraft production is actually falling. A similar story can be told of nuclear power. At one stage research and investment in nuclear power was absorbing 2·5 per cent of the gross national product but at the moment it is still only supplying 3 per cent of the country's energy.

In 1964 Harold Wilson was able to win an election with visions of a technological revolution. With the discovery of oil off the north-east coast at about the same time, the occasion was ripe for the fullest exploitation of a new technology, supplying the equipment to drill and bring the precious product ashore. Yet, as an article in *The Economist*[1] points out, Britain failed in almost every respect to take advantage of this opportunity.

Not one of the expensive pipelines now lying on the seabed has been supplied by Britain. Around £900 million will be spent on putting down pipelines by 1980 but most of that work will be dominated by five foreign companies.

Estimates show that the world will need up to 800 rigs by 1985 but there is still no British design. The only British yard building rigs is on the Clyde – and that is owned by the American-based Marathon company ... of the 246 rigs operating in the world at the start of 1974 only one was wholly owned by a British company.

When it comes to supply ships however the record is a disgrace for a maritime nation. It is forecast that the North Sea will see almost 400 such ships by 1977. Britain has less than ninety to offer and its share of the business is declining. Even tiny Norway has 150 already. The rest will be American, Dutch and German. North Sea contractors have been discouraged by the late delivery of most of the seventeen ordered in Britain over two years ago.

It is not as though British shipyards at the time were being overwhelmed with orders. Britain's response to the new North Sea technology and its reluctance to risk investment in new technology (whether at private or governmental level) has been in striking contrast to that of Norway. By 1976 Norway will be exporting over twice its own needs and, by 1980, oil revenues will be equivalent to 25 per cent of the Norwegian budget, but a Government White Paper in 1975 spelled out a broadly social democratic strategy for spending this wealth, priority being given to health, education, housing and the working environment as opposed to private consumption.

We have dwelt at some length on aspects of investment in technology because, as we suggested earlier, we believe it reflects a flaw in the British educational system and has a bearing on industrial relations.

MANAGERIAL EDUCATION AND THE BRITISH SYSTEM OF EDUCATION

If one of the causes of our low productivity is lack of investment, a contributory factor could be poor management. This in turn could stem from an inability to attract able and ambitious people. An examination of university applications over the last ten years reveals that almost as many students applied for a first degree in Welsh as in production engineering.

British managers, particularly in manufacturing industries, tend to be less well qualified than their European counterparts. A survey carried out by the journal *European Business* in 1971 showed that only half of the chief executives in Britain had a university degree, compared with France 83 per cent, West Germany 81 per cent, Belgium 85 per cent and Sweden 77 per cent. Able and ambitious youngsters are not attracted by the manufacturing industry. In 1974 out of 52,000 graduates only 15·7 per cent went into industry – equivalent to about one-third of students doing science-based subjects.

The Department of Industry carried out a survey of seven major manufacturing companies in Sweden, where it found that four-fifths of all directors and top executives were engineers by training. The report concluded that:

The tradition of most large Swedish companies is to recruit graduate engineers almost exclusively for future management positions. These potential managers are initially put into production which is generally thought to be the most important technical function. British higher educational institutions, unlike some Continental and North American ones, have failed to provide industry with able generalists with qualifications which are predominantly technical and commercial.[2]

It is sometimes argued that the reason for such low commitment to industry is the paltriness of its financial rewards. And it is true that in terms of both gross and net income (in Britain we are taxed directly more heavily), the salary a British manager is likely to receive compares badly with that of his continental counterparts.

But the problem is more complex than that: it reflects the way in which our universities and schools operate. For those who proceed from school to university there is an unbroken circle of educational experience. It goes like this. A student at university graduates in one or more disciplines. He then enters a school to teach at secondary level the same disciplines in which he himself was trained at university. The pupils trained by him are selected so that the most able will reproduce the disciplines in which the teacher himself was originally trained and so enter university. The iron band which encloses the circle is the nature of the university academic disciplines. (No wonder there is a demand for properly trained career masters!)

Whilst the system was appropriate for those who sought careers in state or church, it did not equip people for the tasks imposed by the Industrial Revolution. During the Victorian era, colleges of technology and art and education and commerce were established to equip people with the skills necessary in an industrial and urban society.

The Redbrick universities, many of which were originally founded as vocational schools in such activities as textiles or engineering, soon succumbed to the fundamental ethos of the ancient universities, that of providing a liberal education; so the dominance of the academic disciplines soon reasserted itself. Universities were there to provide their students with well-stocked minds, not to help them perform a task or fill a role. Telford, Brunel, Faraday, Stevenson (none of whom benefited from higher education) on the other hand dealt in technology – the understanding and creation of means to ends and the solution of defined immediate problems. In America too, as an emerging country, the thrust was towards solving problems. Their educational system reflected the need more appropriately than our own.

It might appear that the abolition of direct grant grammar schools and their replacement by comprehensive schools will lead to a different situation. Not so long, alas, as the fundamental assumptions of the people organizing the schools are the same, namely that the highest peaks of education are the universities with their emphasis on traditional academic disciplines. However, if the polytechnics can be accepted as equal in status with the universities, however practical and vocational their work may be, this will have a significance for schools. As a director of a polytechnic remarked:

> It may be that the imbalance in the educational system lies at the very heart of our present social and industrial crises. This country has established a system of education which gives priority and eminence to precisely those people least able or willing to contribute to its growth and efficiency. This may have been adequate in an age of leisure and cultivation, but neutrality is of no use as a permanent frame of mind.[3]

A Government minister remarked at about the same time: 'It simply will not do to allow universities and polytechnics to produce whatever people they fancy or to relate the number and kind of places they provide to the applicants that come forward.'[4]

We have spent some time on this matter of education since we see it to be an important, if not immediately apparent, strand in our industrial relations situation. The situation is something of a vicious circle. Salaries for production managers compared with landscape architects or chief information officers in local government are derisorily low. Working conditions are far from congenial. Noise and muck are common companions. Machines, raw materials and people must be brought together to produce the greatest possible number of any item in the shortest possible time. Compare this life with that of the civil servant who in addition enjoys greater job security and inflation-free pensions.

Trade unionists, with the record of unofficial strikes, may well ponder, as well as teachers, why it is that students have an antipathy towards industry. In 1974 Ford factories in Germany were strike free. In Belgium 417 man/days were lost through strikes. In Britain the figure was 482,000 man/days. Who would wish to enter such a profession?

We are concerned here with the element of efficiency and the appropriateness and objectives of our educational system. We have, earlier in the book, referred to the socially divisive aspects of our society which are also reflected in our educational system and serve only to reinforce the imbalance already described.

INDUSTRIAL RELATIONS AND POLITICS

While the educational system we have inherited has an effect on our pattern of industrial relations, and the structure and origins of the trade union movement present us with problems which other countries have managed to avoid, it is also time to say that business does not operate in a vacuum. No business enterprise can operate in any country outside the context of the economic, social and political policies pursued by that country.

In Germany and France, in spite of sharp political differences, there has been a broad consensus in government about the desirability of strong business development and the role of private business. Even Sweden, with its strongly Social Democratic government, recognizes a large and legitimate stake for private business.

In stark contrast, business in Great Britain has had to operate in a fluctuating environment. It has suffered from the erratic nature of government attitudes towards private business. There has been a perpetual debate about the purpose of business and the value of the free enterprise system. As governments change, so do economic policy and tax laws. Industries have been nationalized and denationalized. Such uncertainty makes long-term planning difficult.

When governments intervene, it is not always with great sensitivity. The Labour Government's rescue of British Leyland in 1975 is a case in point. Any company which from 1968 to 1974 averaged profits of only 2·3 per cent on sales and sold fewer units in 1974 than in 1968 and 1969 is a dubious entity commercially, yet on the basis of a report completed in little over six weeks, amounts of public money amounting to £1,400 million over eight years were to be invested in British Leyland. No consultancy firm with any vestige of reputation would have contemplated undertaking the work of the Ryder Committee in less than a year. Despite an immediate injection of £200 million, British Leyland announced its first ever loss in 1975 of over £100 million.

The inadequacy and ineffectiveness of much state intervention, inspired by quasi-political reasons rather than practical commercial considerations (as in such socialist countries as Norway and Sweden), is by no means a monopoly of Labour administrations. It is the product of the last thirty years and of a variety of governments of differing political opinions, all of which have failed to bring much commercial reality even to the major state enterprises under their direct control.

The situation has not been helped by the emotive language used, such as the refusal 'to come to the rescue of lame ducks'. The crucial question is whether workers whose *real* employment has disappeared owing to the industry's lack of competitive ability, as in the case of the motor-cycle industry, should be kept in *unreal* work, subsidized by the rest of the community. When a loss-making operation is kept alive with public funds, other sectors of the community are deprived of the resources used.

It is fruitless to portray advocates of modernization as though they are Victorian taskmasters, a collection of Mr Gradgrinds, who believe in something inhuman such as the 'market economy'. Unfortunately, that is the only kind of economy there is. People delude themselves if they imagine that exchange can ever take place

271

at less than full cost. Somebody always pays. Some still seem to believe, however, that there can be enterprise without entrepreneurs, savings without riches, higher output per man without fewer men, differential effort without differentials, the rights of women to equal earnings without fewer women to earn.

IMPROVING INDUSTRIAL RELATIONS

So much for the diagnosis. What are the possibilities for improvement? As individual citizens, managers or shop stewards, we cannot directly influence our complex and diverse system of industrial relations. We can exercise only a marginal influence on, for example, government policy or our educational system. Can we learn anything though from other countries, despite their different histories and traditions?

Surely the most remarkable country of all is Japan. When it was revealed that the equipment used in the White House for recording the Watergate tapes was made by Sony, it was plain for all to see that the most advanced, sales-conscious country in the Western world was relying on Japanese technology. Even the German *Wirtschaftwunder,* a recovery which left the rest of Europe gasping, lags far behind the achievements of Japan since her total defeat at the hands of the Western allies at the end of the war, when her economy was totally destroyed and her foreign trade non-existent. A country which before the war was best known for its shoddy imitative goods is now eminent for its top quality cameras, watches, television sets, cars and motor cycles.

Like Great Britain it is a country with practically no natural resources which needs to import almost all raw materials. In Japan a system of paternalism operates which is difficult for a Westerner to appreciate. Though wages are generally low by Western standards, employees of large firms enjoy free or cheap housing, shops, meals, transport and holidays. Workers appear accordingly to feel an extreme loyalty to the company, even to the extent in some cases of singing the company anthem each morning and wearing badges that proudly proclaim them as members of its staff, behaviour that would seem ludicrous to the British worker. A trade union leader bemoaned the fact that workers were worried when they went on strike lest their firm should fall behind its competitors. How has this economic miracle been achieved?

An economic study put forward seven main reasons for Japan's amazing recovery.

1. The high educational level of the people.
2. Liberal capital investment.
3. A dedicated labour force.
4. A flexible banking and credit system.
5. The presence of strong group loyalties.
6. Capable government.
7. Well organized planning.

In the U.K., only the banking system and educational attainment of the people could be said to match the Japanese.

Nearer home is Sweden, a country which has progressed from being one of Europe's poorest agricultural nations to a position of world leadership in business expertise and social welfare. Sweden is often seen as an exemplar of good industrial relations, but a number of conditions obtain there which do not apply in the U.K. Trade union membership (at nearly 90 per cent of the workforce, compared with the U.K. equivalent of nearly half) is very strong. In a very real sense the Swedish trade unions, in a near monopoly situation as regards the labour market, are part of the country's Establishment. The Social Democratic Party aided by the union vote has been in power since 1932, its legislation remarkable for producing the most advanced state of welfare in the world committed to the aim of creating an egalitarian society. The Secretary of L.O., the Swedish T.U.C., is a key figure on the country's economic and political stage. The L.O. is also seen as a ladder to political advancement in the Social Democratic Party. This produces a high degree of consensus in industry despite the fact that 95 per cent of Swedish industry remains in private hands. The harsh judgement of British capitalism, namely that Tory equals capital and Labour equals union, does not exist. So the Swedes show an absence of entrenched class attitudes which is also a product of their educational system, with its absence of public schools and élitism.

There is more agreement over what industry is aiming at, which is quite simply economic prosperity. With the general economic and social course of the country guided by a sympathetic government, there is less room for the kind of doubt that exists in the U.K. about the objectives of the trade union movement. What grounds are there for class war in a nation with one of the highest standards of living in the world? Profit is not a dirty word but a means by which a small country, with a small home market and therefore a paramount need to export, can maintain its place in world markets. In the U.K., by contrast, we cannot seem to agree about profit as a desirable goal.

The declared aim of the Swedish Government is full employment. In this it is aided by the work of the National Labour Market Board, a semi-autonomous body which is responsible for employment services and grants to individuals to increase mobility whilst re-training. It has powers for creating work, rehabilitating the disabled, providing grants to aid the unemployed. It can determine how companies may use their investment funds. If there is a downturn in business, funds can be used to place orders with firms who may have to lay off workers, even if it means stock-building. (Perhaps in the U.K. the recently established Manpower Services Commission may evolve a similar organization.)

This board – composed of representatives of industry and the unions, not politicians and civil servants – with some of the powers of the Departments of Trade, Industry, and Employment in the U.K., but with the independence of the T.U.C. and C.B.I., is a unique body and gives workers a sense of ownership and security. Obstructing the introduction of labour-saving machinery (so common in British industry) would not occur to the worker in Sweden. Again, the Swedish organization is far more centralized, based on voluntary agreements entered into by the L.O. and the Swedish Employers' Confederation (S.A.F.) who lay down an overall framework, into which various industry agreements fit.

Swedish experiments in job enrichment at Volvo, Kockum, and Saabs, the appointment of worker directors, the attempts at participation, must therefore be seen in the context of the social and political life of the country as a whole. What works in Sweden works because psychologically and culturally they have a different life style. Their culture is less individualistic; they are more respectful of the law, for instance.

So, too, for the German model, with its emphasis on Works Councils, Supervisory Boards and Worker Directors. They arose, as we have indicated earlier, out of a different history. Germany, after the war, was on its knees. Management and union found a common bond in working together to restore the country. The experience of going down to the scrap yard together to salvage the metal needed to rebuild a factory bred a comradeship, a commitment on both sides to the need for co-operation – a commitment which is not manifest in Great Britain. Works Councils have existed in Germany for a long time. In Britain, they are seen as largely irrelevant, though there have been a few outstanding exceptions – for example at Fred Olsen's Terminal at Millwall, at Glacier Metal, and at I.C.I. Fibres at Gloucester – with high workforce co-operation.

The direct application of the German or Swedish model to the U.K. would be more likely to result in a deterioration in industrial relations than an improvement. In Britain we view ourselves differently, our laws, our state. We must evolve our own methods. If the power lies at the plant level, it is there we must look for solutions.

MANAGING OUR OWN WAY

The individual manager (and the shop steward for that matter) is left in a dilemma. He can sit back and argue that the problems of industrial relations are all at a 'macro' level – societal, structural and governmental – and accept the arguments of writers such as John Child or Lane and Roberts, which are almost a recipe for doing nothing. Child argues that the most recent research in social science has indicated that 'the ability of managers to influence behaviour and to avoid the presence of conflict within their organizations may be severely limited by determinants over which they have little control'.[5] Lane and Roberts in their analysis of the Pilkington strike concluded 'no amount of managerial ingenuity can remove what is built into the system'.[6]

And yet the manager must observe, as Donovan pointed out, the new system of procedural substantive norms being developed at plant level in conflict with traditional institutions of job regulation by industry-wide bargaining. In this system, in the eyes of both management and employee, the shop steward is more important than the trade union official. The problem, as Allan Flanders recognized, is that 'the actual texture of relations in industry is being continually transformed along with their technological and economic background, yet they remain pressed uncomfortably into the world of institutions which, though outmoded, are resistant to reform'.[7] But the institutions of collective bargaining must eventually become more consistent with the structural location of effective bargaining power. Although one also has to acknowledge the further trend towards comprehensive state regulation of matters relating to the use of manpower and growth of incomes, it is the experience and belief of the authors that management and unions are not helpless in the grip of forces beyond their control.

The assumption that the business enterprise is not a unitary organization and that there is no natural harmony of interests between employers and employees because managers are dominated by the need to represent the interests of a consumer-oriented society (and thus are always looking for ways to raise productivity by reducing labour costs) overlooks a number of factors. One is that workers are consumers as well as producers. But more important are the lessons in co-operation learned by managers and unions in those long discussions entailed in the more progressive productivity deals during the 'sixties. It also leaves out of account the future prospect that the exciting possibility of extended worker participation holds out. This development could be bedevilled by an excessive concentration on procedures, or by union jockeying for position.

We would be the first to acknowledge, however, that the improved industrial relations necessary to take us as a nation forward will require more skill from both managers and shop stewards, particularly during a period when the meek no longer inherit the earth (if ever they did) and when there is a widespread belief that it is perfectly legitimate to advance a sectional interest at almost any cost to others.

The calls made by political parties for a more participative problem-solving role on the part of managers and shop stewards, however, represent an invitation into unfamiliar territory. A shop steward who advocates such an approach finds few supporters. Competitive behaviour is more stable than collaborative. New skills are required for these new roles, and they entail much more risk, and therefore much more anxiety.

But change is forcing people to examine new attitudes. There are, as we know, changing social expectations. Despite the continued existence of a class division, the spread of middle-class tastes and standards into working-class life presents new problems for the unions. In one sense, old-style unionism provided the same kind of stability as the church, a sense of security, boundaries and meaning. But society now is experiencing a sense of purposelessness and alienation.

The lesson seems to be that uncertain and ambiguous times

provide the opportunity for either innovation and social progress or for turning ploughshares into swords. The Chinese calligraphy has two ideograms for 'crisis', one meaning 'opportunity', the other 'danger'. Direct action is an appallingly successful-looking strategy for the dispossessed (those not at the right end of the wages differential), the more so when the dispossession has psychological and not merely physical aspects.

But if we are to survive as a nation, managers and unions must seek new ways of developing some acceptable interdependent relationship. Many managers feel they are being ground between the power of capital and the new power of labour. They need to demonstrate that they are acting in the public good, not in support of some ideology or party with which half the country do not agree, but in the continuous improvement of the economic resources under their control for the good of the community. They need to cultivate the capacity to accept upward influence, to become better listeners, to realize the need of workers for psychological as well as physical security. Collaboration is related to the degree of control it is possible to exercise over a situation. It depends critically on people as much as procedures.

Over a period of two years, some riggers on a large chemical site with which one of the authors was familiar had developed a degree of collaboration with managers. There had previously been a tradition of militancy. Their fear was lest managers should change and new ones appear with different ideas about how to run things. An idea they were exploring in terms of continued future collaboration which would safeguard their position, was that they should have some say in the appointment of future managers. Revolutionary? It is perhaps in gestures such as this that Britain can forge its own way towards improving the industrial relations scene, different from European models, but unique to our own situation.

Improvements are unlikely to take place unless planned, and hence industrial relations training must play a critical role. It is for that reason that we end by emphasizing its importance.

TRAINING IN INDUSTRIAL RELATIONS

What contribution can training make to the improvement of industrial relations? What do we mean by industrial relations training? What form ought it to take? How has it been interpreted and handled up till now? Whose responsibility is it?

In our introduction we defined industrial relations as that system of formal and informal procedures of negotiation, consultation, communication, conciliation and arbitration concerned with the regulation of relationships between employers and workpeople. So the first thing to be said is that training in the subject is something that *both* management and work people need.

Good relationships do not just happen. They have to be worked at. They call for an effort from both parties to understand and accept the legitimacy of the other's point of view and interests, and a readiness to undertake genuine and realistic consultation and negotiation. The willingness to listen involves the creation and fostering of suitable attitudes and the development and application of relevant knowledge and appropriate skills. Training and education, as in other fields, can contribute significantly to this process.

Because both parties have a mutual interest in the subject it does not follow that industrial relations training should only be undertaken jointly although, as we argue later, there are considerable benefits to be obtained when both sides can from time to time be brought together in a training context. Commonsense would suggest that there are areas of common training need but the differing traditions, responsibilities and institutions of the two sides of industry are such that separate training needs to be given to management and workers' representatives.

The history of industrial relations training has not been an inspiring one. The subject has not been systematically thought out in the way that craft apprentice or engineering training has. Both sides have attempted it, working from different bases, holding different assumptions and having different objectives. Efforts have been fragmentary, not aspects of a comprehensive whole.

If management, as they attempt to do in some firms, organize industrial relations training, the tendency is to present a programme whose philosophy, stripped of its inessentials, is one directed towards *attitude change*, 'if only you would see it my way'. Liberally supplied with tea and biscuits, shop stewards are plied with damaging comparisons between their own firm and that of their international competitors in such matters as profitability, manning, return on capital or restrictive practices. Some firms will even go to the considerable expense of flying mixed management/union teams to view plants in the United States, just to show that their stories are based on fact not fiction. Shop stewards invariably return from such trips, not determined to change their mode of operations at home, but with stories of the style of life of American trade unionists and some admiration for the American manager. What they tell you is that he starts work the same time as the men, that he eats sandwiches out of a tin, and that there appears to be less structure and formality.

Not unnaturally the main union thrust in industrial relations training, when the unions themselves assume responsibility for it, is to harness it to union activity. By and large the trade union movement's own facilities for training are inadequate. The National Council for Labour Colleges (N.C.L.C.), subsequently subsumed into the T.U.C., performed a useful role through, amongst other methods, well-developed correspondence courses. These courses concentrated on the main skills needed by the shop stewards. Basically the trade union effort has been designed to make sure that shop stewards know the union rules, and learn about representing a member and handling a grievance. Tony Corfield's admirable booklet, prepared when he was with the W.E.A., is concerned with shop stewards mastering a set of drills. If the drills seem elementary, it must be borne in mind that generally a shop steward's formal education ended at the age of fifteen; moreover it is an occupation with a high rate of turnover. So the mastery of a few basic skills is likely to take precedence over knowledge about the economic state of the country, or the complicated processes of marketing, investment, planning, and pricing policy that so preoccupy the minds of managers.

The trade union movement quite rightly claims it as its own responsibility to train its members. Because of lack of resources it frequently has to farm out its work to other institutions such as technical colleges, polytechnics, the W.E.A. or university extra-mural departments, and the Industrial Society.

One of the advantages of such agencies is that they enjoy a reputation for independence and are not seen as pushing any party line. Academics, however, would not be academics if they did not wish to educate any audience. So their programmes are likely to contain some sessions providing a scholarly analysis of industrial disputes in the car industry or 'international economics for the layman'. One would not wish in any way to disparage these attempts at broadening the education of shop stewards – and such courses if they are well organized (and the authors have been closely involved in many such programmes) will also contain practice in the skills of negotiation and communication – but one feels at times that there is still an element of 'them' and 'us'. Not 'them', the capitalists and managers, and 'us' the workers; but 'them', the establishment (albeit an academic and educated one), and 'us', the less well-educated. It is not a property gap but an educational one. Many of these courses could be criticized for aiming too high.

It is only since the B.E.C./T.U.C. joint declaration of 1963, urging employers to release shop stewards for training on a day-release basis, with the company paying wages and course fees as they do for apprentices, that there has been a serious attempt to cater for the enormous market of 175,000 shop stewards. Initially, and even now in some places, the unions regard the educational bodies as suspect, guilty of diluting the pure doctrine of trade unionism. Many trade unions like to make a clear distinction between mastering the union rules and procedures, and general education which is 'a good thing provided there is time for it'. So the T.U.C. devised a packaged course which they license colleges to conduct on their behalf. College-based courses, independently mounted, are successful to the extent that intensive consultation and involvement of local full-time officials and senior shop stewards has taken place. If they can be involved in the planning, so much the better. In this way they do not enter into a foreign environment but something they already partly own – and ownership is key to interest and commitment.

So we have some firms persuading unions to see their point of view, a kind of indoctrination; but not much attempt by unions to invite management to educational efforts mounted by them in order to explain the union point of view.

Some of the most successful attempts to tackle industrial relations were at Esher College, the E.E.T.P.U. Staff College, pioneered by Jock Haston, the Union's Education Officer. Here managers, supervisors and shop stewards from single companies came together to grapple with problems they were facing at work. Living closely together, in a *union* environment, encouraged an unusual frankness. To hear able national union officers analyse the economic situation as they saw it, urge their members to participate in the creation of larger profits (so that the unions could get a bigger cut), and chastise English managers for being inefficient – all this was educative for managers and shop stewards alike. Again the sense of owner-ship was an important factor. Management were guests on union premises.

In industrial relations education there is a complex of loyalties.

Education is influenced by the perceptions the differing parties have. The Company feel that an employee's first loyalty should be to the organization which provides him with work and pays him. Many trade unionists would argue that a man's prime loyalty is to his union. Jobs come and go but union membership and support persists through good times and bad. Given these assumptions, educational programmes will tend to reinforce existing structures.

There are a number of steps which might lead to some advances in industrial relations training. Something needs to be done at a national level. As Philip Nind, director of the Foundation for Management Education, put it in an address at the London Business School in April 1973:

> No social or corporate policies can be nationally effective without a constructive contribution from the unions. I believe that the harshest acerbities of our industrial relations on a national level will never disappear until the two-sided bargaining table is abolished and replaced by a round one. . . . Where on a national or regional scale are the vital industrial and social problems of the day being discussed conceptually, constructively, in a neutral environment, by the representatives of government, management and the unions? If union leaders will not go to business schools, understandably perhaps, for fear of being thought to be bought by the bosses in the mind of their members, one or more new institutions must be established where such activities can take place in unequivocally open and responsible surroundings.
>
> The perceptive among the union leaders are fully aware of the value of business-school-type programmes, not only for learning techniques and deeper understanding of industrial and national problems but also for the opportunity for the feelings and philosophies of the unions to be understood in an atmosphere conducive to constructive discussion. Whether or not the unions have their own training colleges is beside the point; it is the catalytic effect of all the elements in national and industrial life getting together for significantly long periods that is important. Is it not remarkable that national strike succeeds national strike, year after year, yet there is no co-ordinated scientific attempt to study each strike, its cause, more importantly the day-by-day and hour-by-hour progress which led up to the final breach? If a year or two after the end of a strike, when the temperature had cooled, some of the

principal parties could be brought together under academic chairmanship to study what went wrong and when and why, we could build up an instructive library of industrial relations lore.

It is wishful thinking to hope for the 'two-sided bargaining table' to be abolished. What one might reasonably expect is that it could be put aside, when negotiations have ended, and replaced by a round one at which problem-solving might take place. Perhaps some new independent institutions will need to be created. Such places are few, however. Esher College was a place where dialogue was possible, but Esher was unique. There was always some tension even within the E.E.T.U. as to the suitability and value of joint management/union courses, particularly if they competed for space with the more traditionally-based union courses. In 1973 the educational pioneer Jock Haston left, to take up a similar post with the General and Municipal Workers. Perhaps it is expecting too much to ask a union-financed residential establishment to undertake responsibility for joint management/union programmes, even if management covered the expenses of the particular courses they were involved in.

The problem of large overheads might have been eased had other unions collaborated in its running and maintenance, and shared in its usage. But trade union needs for separate identity are as fierce as those to be found in the private sector of industry. The words 'fraternal delegate' and 'brother' do not mean that unions, any more than firms, are not opposed to mergers and takeovers in their own world. Words like 'rationalization' of pension funds and other benefits, and 'better resource allocation' cannot lightly wipe out seventy or eighty years of trade union history.

Perhaps the T.U.C. could staff such an institution; this would remove the problems of inter-union rivalry. But men on the shop floor, who pay some of the lowest union dues in the world, would not lightly add to them a levy for the establishment of one or a number of staff colleges which could be used for management/union dialogue.

Separate institutions however could be established (or converted – one thinks of such places as Ruskin College or Fircroft). What is important is the need for considerable union investment and ownership in such places. Government subsidy would be necessary but must not be to the exclusion of union backing. A number of Training Boards, conspicuously the Food, Drink and Tobacco Industry

Training Board, have made quite considerable efforts to persuade managers to take a more active interest in the I.R. training programmes.

So much for the national level. But more needs to be undertaken at the local level, and educational institutions should seriously question how they tackle this. All features which remind the audience of a school atmosphere such as the disposition and type of furniture, teaching style of the lecturer, the academic content of the subject matter, will act as inhibitors to meaningful discussion.

Some of the most fruitful 'change programmes' which the authors have been involved in, have not been at the 'macro' level about the state of the nation's economic health, but in the shape of discussion in informal surroundings, planned jointly by managers and shop stewards, and concerned with how jobs might be done differently, matters on which they have knowledge and commitment. As suggested in Chapter 8, such dialogues are best held off the site, where shop stewards and managers can dress 'on equal terms'. It helps to have an independent chairman or facilitator, an academic perhaps, but one familiar with the work situation and skilled in group dynamics. This is very different from an academic, however well-intentioned, summoning people to his place, to partake of a meal of his devising.

The structure for such an event should be a light one. It helps if the shop steward, rather than the manager, explains the purpose of the day. A chairman can usefully check what members feel about being present (particularly if it is the first time they have so met), as feelings of mistrust, inadequacy, cynicism, boredom can importantly influence their contributions. The more openly they can admit to their feelings, the more understanding is likely to take place and the more fruitful the subsequent discussion.

We have referred earlier to the educational and social gap between managers and managed. Planning such events means trying to narrow that gap. Part of the problem of much management/union discussion is that it is influenced by stereotype thinking.

One successful experiment pioneered by the Teesside Industrial Mission was the series of conferences run at Sandsend. The membership of these conferences included managers, shop stewards, full-time union officials, clergymen, students, teachers, local councillors, nurses, local government officers. The main limitation on membership was that they should be drawn from Teesside, people concerned about its problems and redevelopment, compounded by its new county borough status amalgamating four local authorities. The content of the conference was twofold – to offer people help through the advice of others towards the solution of their problems, and to study inter-group behaviour. Although it was not the prime purpose of the conference, one of the effects was that managers and managed developed an enhanced respect for each other and a deeper insight into the nature of inter-group dynamics, and therefore the effect it could have on management/union relations. As a consequence of these conferences, shop stewards from one firm went away and together with their management set up a series of conferences for their own firm to explore more deeply some of the relationships fundamental to British industrial relations.

Such ventures would be considered too advanced for many firms and involve a certain amount of personal risk-taking for participants, both management and union, but until managers and shopfloor can talk more openly about some of the issues which characterize and exacerbate the industrial relations scene, rather than confine 'training' exclusively to skills and drills on the one hand or economic enlightenment on the other, improvement is likely to be slow.

A Systematic Approach

What we have described have been the various initiatives undertaken by management, unions and independent institutions.

What is required in each organization is a properly designed scheme of industrial relations training, identifying all the subjects and skills in which training is required and the levels for which it is required. Any organization which is serious about offering effective industrial relations training must formulate clear policies as it does in, for example, marketing or research. It should set out in writing (as nothing so clears the mind as putting thoughts to paper) its attitudes and objectives in industrial relations, and then define an institutional framework within which these objectives may be achieved. It should then become possible to describe the functions and responsibilities which each level of management is required to undertake and accordingly design an appropriate training programme for them.

Esso, for example, at the end of the fifties began issuing to managers attending their training programmes the following statement of the company's attitude to trade unions.

THE COMPANY AND TRADE UNIONISM

Trade Unionism is not a subject which is of interest only to the specialist. There may be some, in the Company, who think that it is merely the affair of the Employee Relations Department and that, at the most, on the Marketing side only a few District or Terminal Managers, or Bulk Plant Superintendents are involved, and, at the Refinery, Foremen and a few Senior Managers in Process and Mechanical Departments.

On the contrary, everyone is vitally affected by trade unionism. We may never knowingly see a trade unionist, meet a trade union official or hear the trade unions ever mentioned in connection with our work from one year's end to another, yet everything we do depends upon the healthy relationship between the Company, the trade unions with which it negotiates, and the employees for whom they negotiate.

Every forecast we make, consciously or unconsciously, assumes that, among other things, the Company and industry at large suffers no untoward upset in its industrial relations; for without stable relationships in this field, the most carefully laid plans will flounder.

Company Policy on Trade Unionism
Our association with trade unions goes back now over a number of years. At Fawley, we've negotiated with both the Craft Unions and the T. & G.W.U. since before the last war. On our Marketing side, we have had dealings with the T. & G.W.U. since 1940 when we became members of the Petroleum Board Conciliation Committee. These relationships have stood the test of time and there is no doubt that they have been successful up to the present and have played a major part in ensuring a good state of labour relations generally in the Company.

In recent years, i.e. since 1952, these relationships have been based on two main principles:

(a) that the Company believes it to be in the best interests of both Operatives and Management that all workers, whose wages are the subject of agreements with the Unions, should become members of their appropriate organizations.

285

(b) At the same time there shall be no discrimination, by either Union or Employer, against any worker by reason of his membership or non-memberhip of a trade union.

A company's attitude to the need for and the type of training to be offered to trade union representatives and other employees should be made explicit. Such training may take the form of secondment to the short full-time courses at the T.U.C. Training College in London or at such places as Woodstock College (the residential training college of the General and Municipal Workers); day-release at the local technical college; or joint in-company courses for shop stewards and supervisors. As has been mentioned earlier, the T.U.C. frown on joint industrial relations courses, believing them to be impaired by a confusion of training objectives. Individual unions do not necessarily share this view. Joint courses do, however, depend on a high level of co-operation between management and union at local level. In those companies which are successful at running them, they are not offered in place of more straightforward shop steward training but in addition, since they regard courses leading to more effective union representation at the place of work as an essential element in the conduct of industrial relations.

But all of these activities should flow from a carefully thought out industrial relations policy, not as an exercise in public relations or to obtain grants from a training board. One company formulated its industrial relations objectives very exactly, including such matters as: a common standard of employment (notice, permanency etc.); removal of the differentials between clerical and factory grades (clocking on, canteen facilities, holidays etc.); and a deliberate and sustained attempt to promote the dignity of the individual in every job.

It was recognized that this would be a long, hard task involving a radical change of attitude in many quarters. As the Board declared, 'having reached a unanimous and consistent attitude amongst ourselves, it should be stated, so that management, particularly those entrusted with the control of factory employees, should be aware of it and adopt it themselves'. Some years later, it added to its declared industrial relations policy by stating: 'In the future, industrial affairs will be conducted with a much greater participation by employees at all levels, and it would be sensible to accept the recommendation of the Donovan Report that the greatest possible use should be made of the trade union organization.'

Some of the consequences of this commitment were an increase in union membership to 100 per cent in one of its factories, improved trade union organization on the clerical side and the notion that union membership was not antagonistic to the commercial goals of the company.

It is much easier to design a training programme when such a declaration exists than where no policy has been stated. The company acknowledged that their new policy, and the attendant training, had not brought an era of industrial peace in its wake but it had produced a much greater readiness to bring points at issue to discussion, rather than confrontation, and to solve them by a process of trying to understand each other's view.

Although, as Donovan envisaged, the area of decision-making has moved from the national to the local level, plant bargaining still takes place within, and influences, the national context. So decisions made locally have implications and consequences which go far beyond the workplace, the company and even the industry. In such circumstances it is irresponsible to leave industrial relations training to chance.

Reference Notes

Chapter 1
1. Robertson, Andrew. *The Trade Unions* (Hamish Hamilton, London, 1965) p. 17
2. Phelps-Brown, E. H. *The Growth of British Industrial Relations* (Macmillan & Co., London, 1965) p. 116
3. Ibid. p. 117
4. Pelling, H. *A History of British Trade Unionism* (Penguin, Harmondsworth (2nd edition) 1971) p. 37
5. Ibid. p. 38
6. Flanders, Allan D. *Trade Unions* (Hutchinson, London (7th edition) 1968) p. 12
7. Ibid. footnote to p. 12
8. Cole, G. D. H. *A Short History of the British Working Class Movement 1789–1947* (Allen & Unwin, London, 1966) p. 169
9. Flanders, Allan D., op. cit., p. 13
10. (1867) L.R. 2 Q.B. 153
11. Cole, G. D. H., op. cit., p. 203
12. Ibid. pp. 203–204
13. Clapham, Sir John. *An Economic History of Modern Britain* (Cambridge University Press, 1967) p. 163
14. Clegg, H. G., Fox, A. and Thompson, A. F. *A History of British Trade Unions since 1899*, Vol. 1 (Oxford, The Clarendon Press, 1964) p. 101
15. Ibid. p. 111
16. *Amalgamated Society of Railway Servants* v *Osborn* (1910) A.C. 87
17. Quote from Henry Collins: 'The Marxism of the Social Democratic Federation' in Asa Briggs' *Essays in Labour History 1886–1923* (ed. Briggs, Asa and Saville, John) (London, Macmillan, 1971) p. 55
18. Flanders, Allan D., op. cit., p. 15
19. Thomas, G. Bowan. 'The Role of the State' from *Industrial Relations in Britain* (ed. McCarthy, W. E. J., (Lyon, Grant & Green, London, 1969) p. 87
20. Bell, J. D. M. 'Trade Unions' from *The System of Industrial Relations in Great Britain* (Flanders, A. D. and Clegg, H. G.) (Blackwell, Oxford, 1967) p. 139
21. Coker, E. E. 'Local Negotiations' from *Industrial Relations in Britain* (ed. McCarthy, W. E. J.) op. cit., p. 131
22. Welton, H. *The Trade Unions, the Employers and the State* (Pall Mall Press, London, 1960) p. 24
23. Ibid. p. 29
24. Clegg, H. G. *The System of Industrial Relations in Great Britain* (Blackwell, Oxford, 1972) p. 396

25. Royal Commission on Trade Unions and Employers' Associations 1965–1968 (The Donovan Report) (H.M.S.O.) para. 28
26. Ibid. para. 26
27. Wilson, David. *The Observer* 21 April 1974
28. The Donovan Report, op. cit., para. 77
29. Clegg, H. G. *The System of Industrial Relations in Great Britain* (1972) op. cit., p. 133
30. The Donovan Report, op. cit., para. 729
31. Ibid. para. 81
32. Fox, A. F. *A Sociology of Work in Industry* (Collier–Macmillan, 1971) pp. 107–134
33. Wilson, David. *The Observer* 5 May 1974
34. Fox, A. F. *A Sociology of Work in Industry* op. cit., p. 111

Chapter 2
1. Taylor, A. J. P. (ed.) *The Communist Manifesto – Marx and Engels* (Penguin, Harmondsworth, 1967) p. 85
2. Ibid. p. 82
3. Carter, E. H. and Mears, R. A. R. *A History of Great Britain from Early Times to the Present Day* (Clarendon Press, Oxford, 1937) p. 697
4. Ibid. p. 784
5. Wedderburn, K. W. *The Worker and the Law* (Penguin, Harmondsworth, 2nd edition, 1971) p. 313
6. Ibid. p. 304
7. Ibid. p. 317
8. Maslow, A. H. *Motivation and Personality* (Harper & Row, New York, 1954)
9. (1964) A.C. 1129
10. (1963) I.Q.B. 623
11. Grunfield, Cyril. *Modern Trade Union Law* (Sweet & Maxwell, London, 1966) p. 439
12. Clegg, H. G. *The System of Industrial Relations in Great Britain* (Blackwell, Oxford, 1972) p. 345
13. Ibid. p. 344
14. Wedderburn, K. W., op. cit., p. 15

Chapter 3
1. Written Evidence of the Ministry of Labour to the Donovan Commission (H.M.S.O., 1968) p. 19
2. Ibid. para. 58
3. Ibid. para. 149
4. 'Local Negotiations' from *Industrial Relations in Britain* (ed. McCarthy, W. E. J.) (Lyon, Grant & Green, 1969) p. 135
5. C.I.R. Report No. 35: *Industrial Relations at Shoop Floor Level* (H.M.S.O., 1973)
6. Goodman, J. F. B. and Whittingham, T. G. *Shop Stewards in British Industry* (McGraw-Hill, London, 1969) p. 25

7. Ibid. p. 23
8. Marsh, A. I. and Staples, J. W. 'Three Studies in Collective Bargaining – Check-off Agreements in Britain', Research Paper No. 8 for the Donovan Commission, 1968 (H.M.S.O., 1968)
9. McCarthy, W. E. J. *The Closed Shop in Britain* (Blackwell, Oxford, 1964)
10. Hoxie, R. F. 'The Economic Programme of Trade Unions' from *Trade Unions* (ed. McCarthy, W. E. J.) (Penguin, 1972) p. 43
11. The Donovan Report, op. cit. para. 594
12. Marsh, A. I. 'Disputes Procedure in British Industry', Research Paper No. 2 (Part 1) for the Donovan Commission (H.M.S.O., 1968) p. 18
13. Ibid. p. viii
14. McCarthy, W. E. J. and Parker, S. R. 'Shop Stewards and Workshop Relations', Research Paper No. 10 for the Donovan Commission (H.M.S.O., 1968) p. 83
15. Whittingham, T. G. 'The Effects of Productivity Bargaining on Shop Stewards' from *The New Bargainers – A Symposium on Productivity Bargaining* (ed. Towers, B. and Whittingham, T. G.) (Department of Adult Education, University of Nottingham) p. 75
16. C.I.R. Report No. 33 (H.M.S.O., 1972)
17. 'Shop Steward Education and Training', T.U.C. Education Committee Chairman's Opening Statement at a Meeting with the Parliamentary Under-Secretary of State, D.E.S., 14 May 1973
18. Ibid. p. 2
19. The Donovan Report, op. cit. para. 122
20. McCarthy, W. E. J. 'Productivity Bargaining and Restrictive Labour Practices', Research Papers No. 4 for the Donovan Commission (H.M.S.O., 1967)
21. Henderson, Joan. *The Case for Joint Consultation* (Industrial Society Publication, 1970) p. 2
22. Clegg, H. G. *The System of Industrial Relations in Great Britain* (Blackwell, Oxford, 1972) p. 2
23. Ibid. p. 191
24. Industrial Relations Code of Practice (H.M.S.O., 1972) para. 70
25. Argyle, Michael. *The Psychology of Interpersonal Behaviour* (Penguin, 1972) p. 133
26. Ibid. p. 133
27. McCarthy, W. E. J. and Parker, S. R. 'Shop Stewards and Workshop Relations' op. cit. p. 29
28. Ibid. p. 17
29. Goodman, J. F. B. and Whittingham, T. G. 'Shop Stewards and Workshop Relations' op. cit. p. 74
30. Ibid. p. 84
31. Seear, Nancy. 'Relationships at Factory Level' from *Industrial Relations* (ed. Roberts, B. C.) (University Paperbacks, Methuen & Co, Ltd, 1968) p. 163

32. Shop Stewards' Handbook (Transport and General Workers' Union, 1970) p. 9
33. See, for example, Brown, William. *Piecework Bargaining* (Heinemann, London, 1973) pp. 96–122
34. Ibid. p. 99
35. Wedderburn, K. W. *The Worker and the Law* (Pelican (2nd ed.), 1971) p. 98
36. Flanders, Allan D. *Management and Unions: The Theory and Reform of Industrial Relations* (Faber & Faber, 1970) p. 113
37. Written Evidence of the Ministry of Labour (to the Donovan Commission) op. cit. p. 38
38. The Donovan Report, op. cit. p. 100
39. From an article in *The Observer*, 25 February 1973
40. Ibid.
41. Allen, V. L. *Militant Trade Unionism* (The Merlin Press, London, 1972) pp. 94–117
42. Ibid. p. 111
43. *Good Industrial Relations – A Guide for Negotiators* (T.U.C., 1971) p. 6
44. Ibid. pp. 17–18
45. Cowan, L. D. *The Impact of Europe on Industrial Relations in the U.K.* (Personnel Management (an I.P.M. Journal), August 1973)
46. Banks, Anthony. 'International Trade Unionism – the Need for International Co-ordination of Trade Union Action' from *International Industrial Relations* (Industrial Society and the Young European Management Association, 1972)
47. Ibid. p. 13
48. Balfour, Campbell. *Industrial Relations in the Common Market* (Routledge & Kegan Paul, 1972)
49. Ibid. p. 11

Chapter 4

1. Lumley, Roger. *White-Collar Unionism in Great Britain* (Methuen, London, 1973) pp. 24–9
2. Bain, G. S., Coates, D., and Ellis, V. *Social Stratification and Trade Unionism* (Heinemann, London, 1973)
3. Bain, G. S. *The Growth of White-Collar Unionism* (Oxford University Press, 1970) p. 39
4. Clay, Henry. *The Problem of Industrial Relations* (Macmillan, London, 1929) p. 155
5. *The Growth of White-Collar Unionism* op. cit. pp. 144–5
6. Ibid. pp. 138–9
7. Ibid. p. 133 and *White-Collar Unionism in Great Britain* op. cit. p. 59
8. *The Growth of White-Collar Unionism* op. cit. p. 140
9. *White-Collar Unionism in Great Britain* op. cit. p. 92
10. Ibid. p. 68
11. 'Industrial Society', December 1973

Chapter 5
1. Cmnd. 7321, 1948
2. Clegg, Hugh. *How to Run an Incomes Policy and Why We Made Such a Mess of the Last One* (Heinemann Educational Books)
3. Trades Union Congress *Economic Policy and Collective Bargaining in 1973*
4. Cmnd. 6151 'The Attack on Inflation' (H.M.S.O., London)
5. Donaldson, Peter. *Economics of the Real World* (British Broadcasting Corporation and Penguin, 1973) p. 90
6. Commission on Industrial Relations 'Clothing Wages Councils' (C.I.R. Report No. 77)
7. Department of Employment Gazette, May 1975
8. Trades Union Congress, 1969 *Collective Bargaining and Trade Union Development in the Wages Council Sector*
9. Department of Employment Gazette, May 1975
10. Commission on Industrial Relations 'Clothing Wages Councils' (C.I.R. Report No. 77)
11. Low Pay Unit 'Survey of the low paid' March 1974–February 1975
12. The Ministry of Labour *Industrial Relations Handbook* (H.M.S.O. 1961) pp. 20–22
13. Ibid. p. 24
14. *The Royal Commission on Trade Unions and Employers' Associations 1965–68* (H.M.S.O. 1968) (The Donovan Report)
15. Ibid. para. 205
16. Ibid. p. 268
17. Cmnd. 3888 'In Place of Strife – A Policy for Industrial Relations'
18. Ibid. p. 13
19. Turner, H. A. *Is Britain Really Strike Prone?* (Cambridge University Press, 1969)
20. Heffer, E. *The Class Struggle in Parliament: a socialist view of industrial relations* (Gollancz, London, 1973)
21. Trades Union Congress, 1969 *Programme for Action*
22. Heffer, E. *The Class Struggle in Parliament: a socialist view of industrial relations* (Gollancz, London, 1973)
23. Speech by Victor Feather, 12 November 1970, reprinted in 'Background Notes on Industrial Relations' (W.E.A.)
24. S. 121 (1)
25. General Council Report to Trades Union Congress, September 1971
26. Trades Union Congress 'Reason' The Case against the Government's proposals
27. Incomes Data Services; Brief 21, September 1973, p. 2
28. Macbeath, Innis *The Times Guide to the Industrial Relations Act* (Times Newspapers Ltd, London, 1972) p. 11
29. Lloyd, John. 'Last Act', from the Journal of the Industrial Society, June 1974, p. 10
30. Elliott, John. 'Case for voluntary labour relations', from the *Financial Times*, 2 October 1972

31. Trades Union Congress 'The Development of the Social Contract'
32. Department of Employment Gazette, March 1975

Chapter 6
1. The Donovan Report (H.M.S.O.) para. 24
2. Stewart, Rosemary. *The Reality of Management* (Heinemann, London, 1963 and Pan Books Ltd, London, 1970) pp. 15–29
3. Taylor, F. W. *Scientific Management* (Harper and Row, New York, 1974)
4. Drucker, Peter. *The Practice of Management* (Heinemann, London, 1955 and Pan Books Ltd, London, 1971) pp. 338 and 340
5. Mayo, Elton. *The Social Problems of an Industrial Civilization* (Routledge & Kegan Paul, 1949)
6. Maslow, A. H. *Motivation and Personality* (Harper and Row, New York, 1954)
7. Herzberg, F., Mausner, B., and Snyderman, B. *The Motivation to Work* (Wiley, New York (2nd edition) 1959)
8. Argyris, C. *Interpersonal Competence and Organizational Effectiveness* (Tavistock, London, 1962)
9. McGregor, Douglas. *The Human Side of Enterprise* (McGraw-Hill, New York, 1960)
10. Likert, R. *New Patterns in Management* (McGraw-Hill, New York, 1967)
11. Burns, T., and Stalker, G. M. *The Management of Innovation* (Tavistock, London, 1961)
12. Dale, E. and Michelon, L. C. *Modern Management Methods* (Penguin, Harmondsworth, 1969) p. 61
13. Drucker, Peter. *The Practice of Management* (Heinemann, London, 1955 and Pan Books, London, 1971) pp. 331–2
14. The Donovan Report, para. 95
15. Code of Practice (H.M.S.O., London, 1972) para. 3
16. C.I.R. Report No. 34 (H.M.S.O., London, 1973)
17. Ibid. para. 66
18. Ibid. para. 77

Additional Reading
Pollard, Sidney. *The Genesis of Modern Management* (Edward Arnold, London, 1965)
Smiles, Samuel. *Self-Help* (John Murray, London, 1858)

Chapter 7
1. Schmidt, Warren H. and Tannenbaum, Robert. 'The Management of Differences' (Harvard Business Review, November–December 1960)
2. Blake, R. R. and Mouton, J. S. *The Managerial Grid* (Gulf, Houston, 1964)

3. Blake, R. R. and Mouton, J. S. *Corporate Excellence Through Grid Organization and Development* (Gulf, Houston, 1968)
4. Fox, Alan. *Beyond Contract: Work, Power and Trust Relations* (Faber & Faber, London, 1974)
5. Blake, R. R. and Mouton, J. S. *Managing Intergroup Conflict in Industry* (Gulf, Houston, 1964)
   Sherif, Muzafer. 'Experiments in Group Conflict' from *Scientific American* (1956), San Francisco
6. *The Managerial Grid* op. cit.
7. Clegg, H. G. *Industrial Democracy and Nationalization* (Blackwell, Oxford, 1951) p. 22

Chapter 8
1. McClelland, D. *The Achieving Society* (Van Nostrand, New Jersey, 1961)
2. McGregor, D. *The Human Side of Enterprise* (McGraw-Hill, New York, 1960)
3. Revans, R. W. 'Participation in What?' private paper circulated by A. L. P. International, 1974
4. 'Industrial Democracy' An Interim Report by the T.U.C. General Council (Trades Union Congress, 1974)
5. 'The Responsibilities of the British Public Company' Final Report of the Company Affairs Committee (C.B.I., September 1973)
   B.I.M. Study Group on Company Affairs – Final Report B.I.M., March 1974
6. 'The Community and the Company – Reform of Company Law' Green Paper; Report of a Working Group of the Labour Party Industrial Policy Sub-Committee (Labour Party, London)

Additional Reading
Jenkins, David. *Job Power* (Heinemann, London, 1974)
Jaques, Eliot. *The Changing Culture of a Factory* (Routledge, Kegan & Paul, London, 1951)
Fogarty, Michael P. *Company Responsibility and Participation: A New Agenda* (Research Publications, London, 1975)
Macbeath, Innis. *Power Sharing in Industry* (Gower Press, Epping, 1975)
Worker Participation in Britain, Social Policy Research (Financial Times, London, 1974)
Stephen, Frank H. *Workers' Participation* Northern Ireland Committee of the Irish Congress of Trade Unions
C.I.R. Study No. 4, 'Worker Participation and Collective Bargaining in Europe (H.M.S.O.)
International Institute for Labour Studies, Bulletin 6, 'Workers' Participation in Management' (June, 1969)
International Labour Office, 'Workers' Management in Yugoslavia' (Geneva, 1962)
Clegg, H. G. *A New Approach to Industrial Democracy* (Blackwell, Oxford, 1960)

Reference Notes

Blumberg, P. *Industrial Democracy: The Sociology and Participation* (Constable, London, 1968)

Pateman, C. *Participation and Democratic Theory* (Cambridge University Press, 1970)

Lewis, J. S. *Partnership for All* (Kerr-Cross, London, 1948)

Cassidy, B. *Workers on the Board* (Conservative Political Centre, London, 1973)

Flanders, A. *Management and Unions* (Faber, London, 1970)

Poole, M. *Workers' Participation in Industry* (Routledge & Kegan Paul, London, 1975)

Woodward, J. *Industrial Organization, Theory and Practice* (Oxford University Press, London, 1965)

Fox, A. *A Sociology of Work in Industry* (Collier–Macmillan, London, 1971)

Cotgrove, S. F., Dunham, I. and Vamplow, C. *The Nylon Spinners* (Allen & Unwin, London, 1971)

Flanders, A., Pomeranz, R. and Woodward, J. *Experiment in Industrial Democracy* (Faber, London, 1968)

Clegg, H. G. *The System of Industrial Relations in Great Britain* (Blackwell, Oxford, 1972)

McCarthy, W. E. J. 'The Role of Shop Stewards in British Industrial Relations, Research Paper 1', Royal Commission on Trade Unions and Employers Associations (H.M.S.O., London, 1967)

Research Paper 10, Shop Stewards and Workshop Relations

Flanders, A. *The Fawley Productivity Agreements* (Faber, London, 1964)

Dahrendorf, R. *Class and Class Conflict in Industrial Society* (Routledge & Kegan Paul, London, 1954)

Hyman, R. *Strikes* (Collins, London, 1972)

Chapter 9

1. National Board for Prices and Incomes Report No. 36 (Productivity Agreements Cmnd. 3311) (H.M.S.O., London)

2. Walton, Richard E. and McKersie, Robert B. *A Behavioural Theory of Labour Negotiations* (McGraw-Hill, New York, 1965)

3. McGregor, Douglas. *The Professional Manager* (McGraw-Hill, New York, 1967) p. 98

4. Gay, G. F. 'Labour Costs and International Competitiveness' *National Institute Economic Review*, August 1972, Number 61

5. Smith, Adam. *An Inquiry into the Nature and Causes of the Wealth of Nations* (J. F. Dove, London, 1826) p. 15

6. Taylor, F. W. (1911) *The Principles of Scientific Management* Reprinted in *Scientific Management* (Harper, New York, 1947)

7. Royal Commission on Trade Unions and Employers' Associations, Productivity Bargaining Research Paper No. 4 (H.M.S.O., London, 1967)

8. Flanders, A. *The Fawley Productivity Agreement* (Faber, London, 1966)

9. Ibid.
10. Ibid.
11. Reader, W. J. *Imperial Chemical Industries, A History* (Oxford University Press, London, 1970)
12. Some of the most popular works were:
    Likert, R. *New Patterns of Management* (McGraw-Hill, New York, 1961)
    Argyris, C. *Personality and Organization* (Harper & Row, New York, 1957)
    Argyris, C. *Integrating the Individual and the Organization* (John Wiley, New York, 1964)
    Herzberg, F. *The Motivation to Work* (John Wiley, New York, 1959)
    McGregor, D. *The Human Side of Enterprise* (McGraw-Hill, New York, 1960)
    An interesting account of the influence of the behavioural sciences can be found in *Bargaining for Change* (edited by Towers, B., Whittingham, T. G. and Gottschalk, A. W. (Allen & Unwin, London, 1972)
13. For a detailed account read:
    Cotgrove, S., Dunham, J. and Vamplow, C. *The Nylon Spinners – A Case Study in Productivity Bargaining and Job Enlargement* (Allen & Unwin, London, 1971)

Chapter 10
1. Figures quoted from *Militant Trade Unionism* by Allen, V. L. (Merlin Press, London, 1966)
   A.S.S.E.T. is now part of A.S.T.M.S.; D.A.T.A. is now part of T.A.S.S. (Technical and Supervisory Section of Amalgamated Union of Engineering Workers); C.A.W.U. is now part of A.P.E.X. See Chapter 4
2. Ibid.
3. Ibid.
4. Ibid.
5. Ibid.
6. Ibid.
7. Revans, R. W. 'Participation in What?', a private paper distributed by A.L.P. International, 1974

Chapter 11
1. *The Economist*, 26 July 1975
2. Crowther-Hunt, Lord. 'Why Britain Can't Manage' *The Observer*, 30 November 1975
3. Nuttgens, Dr P. J. 'Dead Hand of Learning Should be Turned to Useful Skills' *Times Higher Educational Supplement*, 21 November 1975
4. Crowther-Hunt, Lord. 'Why Britain Can't Manage' *The Observer* 30 November 1975

Reference Notes

5. Child, John. *British Management Thought* (George Allen & Unwin, London, 1969) p. 169
6. Lane, Tony and Roberts, Kenneth. *Strike at Pilkingtons* (Collins/ Fontana, London, 1971) p. 242
7. Flanders, Allan. *Management and Unions: The Theory and Reform of Industrial Relations* (Faber & Faber, London, 1970) p. 84

Index